# *Rediscovering* PASSOVER

## Joseph Stallings

Resource Publications, Inc.
160 E. Virginia St., #290
San Jose, CA 95112

Editorial director: Kenneth Guentert
Production editor: Elizabeth J. Asborno
Cover design: George Collopy
Cover production: Ron Niewald

**Library of Congress Cataloging-in-Publication Data**

Stallings, Joseph, 1928-
  Rediscovering Passover.

    Bibliiography: p.
    1. Passover—Biblical teaching. 2. Last Supper. 3. Bible—Criticism,
Interpretation, etc. I. Title.
    BS680.P33S7   1988    296.4'37    87-62531
    ISBN 0-89390-106-7 (pbk.)

54321

*Grateful acknowledgment is made for permission to reprint excerpts from the
following copyrighted material:*

JOSEPHUS: THE JEWISH WARS by Gaalya Cornfeld. Copyright © 1982 by
Massada Ltd. Publishers, Givatayim & Gaalya Cornfeld, Tel Aviv. Used by
permission of Zondervan Publishing House.
Scripture texts used in this work are taken from **The New American Bible with
Revised New Testament** Copyright © 1986 Confraternity of Christian Doctrine.
All Rights Reserved. No part of **The New American Bible with Revised New
Testament** may be reproduced in any form without permission in writing from the
copyright owner.

# CONTENTS

# INTRODUCTION

Back in the late 1940s, when I was still in my teens, I wanted to know what blessings Jesus said at the Last Supper (i.e., Lk 22:17,19). In fact, I seemed to have an urgent need to know what they were. The only information I could find was that the Last Supper was a Passover supper.

I was born a Southern Baptist and went to Sunday school in the big, white Baptist church on the corner of Tamarind and Myrrh streets in Comptom, CA, until I was twelve years old. I had wonderful teachers who instilled in me a lifelong love of and commitment to the Bible. It was also they who bestowed upon me my great curiosity to learn more about the Bible. But they couldn't answer all of my questions. My quest led me to the Catholic Church, which has a grasp of ancient tradition and history. But even the Church could not answer all of my questions about the Last Supper, except that it is the origin of the Eucharist. That was enough for me, and my newfound love for the Eucharist led me to become a Catholic right after my eighteenth birthday.

By the time I was twenty, I was a postulant (student) Franciscan Brother at the Old Mission in Santa Barbara. There I learned that there was such a thing as a Haggadah, a book containing the blessings, prayers, and ritual of the Passover sup-

1

per, and I was allowed to acquire a copy for study. That first Haggadah was important because it contained copious footnotes. But how much of the first century ritual was contained in a twentieth century Haggadah? None of the priests, teachers, or clerics at Santa Barbara had an answer for me.

I did not take solemn vows, but instead joined the U.S. Marine Corps. I needed the Korean G.I. Bill to go to college, and I took with me my quest to learn as much as possible about the Last Supper. That quest took me to a Passover seder aboard the navy ship I was assigned to at Bikini Atoll in the 1950s. At that time, I was a U.S. Marine Security Guard attached to the Atomic Energy Commission during Operation Castle when five hydrogen devices were tested at Bikini. In spite of the strictest security, kosher supplies were sent to our ship so that the navy, marine, and civilian Jews could celebrate an authentic Passover seder.

Much later, as a civilian, I was working for Kaiser-Macco Aggregates in Israel. There I was privileged to be invited to the home of a friend for a Sephardic Jewish seder. My friend and his family were from Morocco. By that time, I was familiar with the present-day ritual and was able to appreciate the colorful diversity possible in the celebration of Passover among Jews living in widely disparate cultures.

By this time, I was convinced that Passover was the legitimate inheritance of Christians as well as of Jews because the Last Supper was the Passover. I began to celebrate a Passover seder every year myself, first among close friends and then, when I was married, Passover became a firm, family tradition.

In the late 60s, I enrolled in the School of Applied Theology (SAT) at the Graduate Theological Union, Berkeley, CA. Although no one there could answer all my questions about the details of the Last Supper, instructors pointed out lines of research that I might pursue in my quest for answers. I learned that the current Haggadah looks back on the celebration of Passover at the time of the Second Temple as the definitive Golden Age. As a consequence, most of the blessings and readings are substantially the same today as two thousand years ago. At SAT I learned about the New Covenant and how it was based upon the Sinai Covenant (Jn 13:34,35 NAB). I also learned about the longlost concept of the Eucharist as the anamnesis (reactualization) of the Last Supper.

After graduation, I was assigned to a parish, in charge of adult religious education. I soon found out that the adult students in my classes were just as hungry as I to know more about the Last Supper. At that time, my wife introduced me to a Jewish co-worker at San Jose Hospital who was curious about my interest in Judaism. Milt Shuch (rhymes with "luck") was especially interested in my intention to write a Christian Haggadah for use in my adult education classes, and he volunteered to help. He combed the libraries of the Santa Clara valley and brought me books to read that were a goldmine of important information. Milt could read Hebrew, and that gave me another hunger: to learn to read and speak Hebrew.

It was soon apparent that the ritual of Passover had changed very little in two millennia. But in all the books supplied by Milt, I found no definitive description of a first-century Passover to use to reconstruct the actual ritual of the Last Supper. Then, by chance, I happened upon a volume of the Talmud, tractate Pesachim. Gradually, as this volume of the Talmud opened up to me, it began to answer my questions; the Passover seder of the first century began to come into focus.

What I finally learned was that the Passover seder of the Last Supper was something quite different from what most Christians picture. Jesus was not alone with only twelve disciples but had with him more than 120 male disciples, their wives and young children. The women, some of whom are named in the Gospels, were an indispensable part of the observance and celebration of Passover. The children's presence was obligatory as well. The ritual of the seder of the Last Supper was lengthy, lasting at least from sunset until one or two in the morning. It was also an elaborate and elegant banquet, rich in meaning and tradition. The menu was established by Divine Law and many centuries of custom.

This book contains the fruit of my quest, the answers to all of my questions. Now that I've gotten my answers, it is only right that I share them with all the others who are just as curious as I am about what the Last Supper was really like.

I will always remain in debt to Milt Shuch for his research and for helping launch me on further research. I am indebted to Phyllis Shuch for her editing of my original work, "Passover Seder and Memorial Agape," which I used to conduct Passover seders at various churches in the South Bay area. The original is not suitable for publication at this time for a number of reasons, but it gave birth to this book. *Rediscovering Passover* could not have been written without the help of Milt and Phyllis and the suggestions of Blessie and Ernie La Scola, Rock Palladino, Dorothy Hughes, and Fran and Jim Bermudes. They all read the original manuscript and returned it with their comments and requests. Blessie and Ernie La Scola conduct the yearly Passover seder at our parish church. Fran and Jim do the same for the 6th graders in our religious school. Rock formerly worked for the local newspaper, and Dorothy was our parish librarian and ran the bookstore. They are keenly aware of what people want to know.

I am very deeply and sincerely grateful to Rabbi Joseph Gitin, Rabbi Emeritus of Temple Emanu-El in San Jose, and Rabbi David Robins, former senior rabbi of Temple Emanu-El. For years they have opened Temple Emanu-El to the Christian community of the South Bay and made it our temple as well. The community of Temple Emanu-El has gone out of its way to enlighten us on the meaning and observance of Judaism.

Once a year they have an open service for all Christians, after which we can go to the hall and see displays about every Jewish Holy Day. We are encouraged to sample the foods typical of each Feast Day. For all of their important help in my education, I would like to dedicate this book. The dedication must not be construed as an endorsement by the rabbis or the community of everything in the book. The dedication is only intended to be an expression of my gratitude and love for them in helping me find my own "Jewishness." Barukh HaShem!

I have used the New American Bible as my primary source of biblical quotations. All of these translations are marked "(NAB)." There were times, however, when I made the translation myself. In those cases you will find no notations of a biblical source except the Bible itself.

Joseph M. Stallings

# ONE

# History's Oldest, Continuous Feast

Leonardo da Vinci's great masterpiece, "The Last Supper," holds a great fascination for all of us. We not only stand in awe of its beauty, but we are subtly seduced by it. Because the image is so familiar, it has become *the* image of the Last Supper, and we are tempted to assume that da Vinci is depicting the event as it was.

Nothing could be further from the truth. Da Vinci's work is great art but bad history. All of the details in the painting are historically and scripturally inaccurate. The painting depicts daylight outside the window, whereas the actual Last Supper took place at night (Mk 14:17). The figures are seated about the table on benches, whereas Jesus and his disciples reclined on couches at the actual supper (Jn 13:12; *anapeson palin*, "reclining again"). Da Vinci portrays the meal as consisting of fish and ordinary leavened bread whereas, if the Last Supper was a Passover meal, it had to consist of unleavened bread (*mat-*

*zah*), roast lamb (*pesach*), and bitter herb (*maror*) (Ex 12:8, BT
Pesachim, 116a-b). In da Vinci's painting, Jesus is alone with
the Twelve Apostles, whereas the Synoptic Gospels record that
the disciples prepared the Supper during the day, and that it was
evening when Jesus arrived with the Twelve Apostles (Mt
26:17-20; Lk 22:7-14; Mk 14:12-17). Women are omitted from
the painting, yet the Passover had to be eaten by whole families,
including women (Ex 12:3,4 & 13:8). Children are also omitted
from the painting, yet the laws of Passover require children to
ask questions so that they can learn the meaning of the Passover
Supper from their parents (Ex 3:8 & BT Pesachim 116a).

Da Vinci's masterpiece is a symbolic depiction of the event;
literally, however, it is a picture of thirteen Renaissance Italian
males, in some supposed oriental costume, sharing a mid-after-
noon collation in an elegant room of a sixteenth-century Floren-
tine palazzo.

This was hardly unusual.[1] Until recently, artists depicted
events as if they had taken place in the artist's own locale. In
the Vatican, miles of murals and great art by all of the masters
of the Renaissance render the entire history of the Bible as
though it had taken place entirely in Italy and involved individuals who represent biblical people but who are obviously
Italians.

It is time to put away misconceptions about the Last Supper
and to rediscover how Passover was observed at the time Jesus
celebrated the Passover of the Last Supper. The Last Supper
was not a simple collation or light meal shared by Jesus and his
friends, but a complex and elaborate banquet that included a
great amount of food, very ancient traditions, and a cherished
ritual that revealed the soul of the Jewish people.

Without a clear understanding of all that Passover means,
Christians cannot appreciate what they mean when they
proclaim that Jesus is the Lamb of God (Jn 1:29) or what Paul
meant when he proclaimed that Jesus was our Passover

sacrifice (1 Cor 5:7,8). With a renewed appreciation of Passover's symbolism and essence, Christians can better appreciate their Eucharist, their holy communion, and their celebration of the Lord's Supper, which is a reactualization of the Last Supper (1 Cor 11:23-25).

## Chag Ha-Pesach: The Pilgrimage Feast of Passover

Passover was the most important and the most popular feast of the year for first-century Jews.. It remained so throughout the centuries and is still important and popular today. While the Temple was still standing, Jerusalem, a city that ranged in population between 30,000 and 80,000,[2] would balloon in size as hundreds of thousands of pilgrims arrived from all over the known world. Even though Jerusalem was not the political capital of Judea in the first century — Caesarea Maritima was the administrative capital for Samaria and Galilee as well as Judea — the Roman procurator and Jewish king moved into Fortress Antonia and Herod's palace for the eight days of Passover. Jerusalem was the religious center of the Jewish people and the Jewish world. The Holy City existed in service to the Holy Temple. She was there to care for and wait upon all of those who came there to worship in the Temple.

Passover was already an ancient feast by the first century. No one knows for sure how far back it dates. Passover is a memorial of the Exodus from Egypt (Ex 12:14), but it contains recollections from throughout Jewish history. There are memories from the days of the patriarchs, the judges, the kings, the Exile, and the rule by the Greeks. Today's Passover contains memories of the hard and disastrous rule of the Romans. And, if you know where to look, you can find important components of Christianity.

Many Jewish historians trace the roots of Passover back to a prehistoric shepherds' festival. The patriarchs, who were herdsmen and nomads,[3] may have celebrated such a festival in early spring when it was time to move from winter to summer pastures. The families picked out the choicest lambs for sacrifice. This was to insure the safety and well-being of the family and its herds. A life was to be given so as to protect the life and health of the flocks. The blood of these lambs was smeared onto the tent posts of the family dwelling to ward off any evil or threat to the health of the family. The lambs were roasted over an open fire and shared in a banquet that celebrated the unity of the family and its oneness with the tribe. From very ancient times, banquets such as those have been a symbol of fellowship, well-being, and family unity.[4]

When the Israelites came in contact with the farmers of Cana'an, they were introduced to the Festival of New Leaven. This also took place in early spring, at the time of the barley harvest.[5] Barley and spring have always been associated. The Hebrew word for spring, *aviv,* is derived from the word for a budding ear of barley, *avav.* "This day of your departure is in the month of Abib (spring)" (Ex 13:4 NAB).[6]

How bread became leavened was a great mystery to ancient people. All they knew was that if they took a light dough and kept it in a warm place, something would happen to it and it would ferment. If they put some of this fermented dough into another batch of dough, the new batch would rise. This miracle could be duplicated from spring until fall, but during the winter chill it was difficult to start a new batch. The leaven already on hand had to be guarded and nurtured until warmer weather returned. The mass of leavening was known as a "starter" or "mother." Care was taken to add just the right things to it and protect it, or it would sour and become useless. New batches could be started, but it took several days. Ancient people had no idea that wild, airborne yeast was responsible. That fact was not discovered until the nineteenth century. The whole process remained mysterious and sacred for them. From that mystery arose the farmers' Festival of Unleavened Bread. Each spring, the old leaven from the last year was thrown out. A new mass of dough was set aside in a warm and sacred place for the magic to happen once again. From it, all of the bread of the coming year would be made. But while they waited, they would prepare and eat only the simple hearth-cakes, flat sheets of dough baked on the hot rocks arranged around the hearth-fire. Those flat, round cakes represented a new beginning and a New Year.

The children of Israel may well have taken those two primitive festivals with them when they settled in the land of Egypt (Gn 47:1-5). Moses may have been referring to the Feast of the Shepherds when he asked Pharaoh to let the Israelites go into the desert to offer sacrifice to God (Ex 8:21-23). They would at least have been familiar with the idea of offering up the life of a lamb to preserve the life of others, and of eating bread made without leaven at the beginning of a new year and a new life. Those symbols came together with the Exodus from Egypt.

## Seder Mitzrayyim: The Order of Passover in Egypt

And the LORD (YHWH) said to Moses and Aaron in the land of Egypt, "This month shall be for you the foremost of the months. It shall be for you the first of the months of the year. Speak to the whole community of Israel, saying, on the tenth of this month they shall take for themselves, each person, one of the animals from the flock for a family; an animal of the flock for each house. If the house is too small for an animal from the flock, it shall take in its next-door neighbor according to the number of persons. They shall count the number of animals according to what each one can eat. The lamb must be a perfect, year-old male animal from the flock. It may be from the sheep or from the goats that they take it. And you shall keep it until the fourteenth day of this month. The whole assembly of the community of Israel shall kill it between the two evenings. They shall take from the blood and put it on the two door posts (*mazuzot*) and on the lintel of the houses in which they eat it. *On this night they shall eat the flesh, roasted with fire, and they shall eat it with unleavened bread and bitter herbs.* They shall not eat it raw nor boiled with water but roasted with fire, with its head, with its legs, and with its innards. They shall not leave any of it until morning. They shall burn with fire what has been left until morning. This is the way you shall eat it, with your loins girded for flight, your sandals on your feet and your staff in your hand. You shall eat it in haste! *It is the Passover of the LORD (YHWH)!* This night I will pass through the land of Egypt and I will smite every firstborn in the land of Egypt from the people unto the livestock. I will execute judgments on all of the gods of Egypt! I AM the LORD (YHWH)! The blood shall be as a signal for you upon the houses where you are. I will see the blood and I will pass over you. The plague shall not be upon you to destroy you when I smite the land of Egypt. This day shall be a memorial (*zikkaron*) for you. *You shall celebrate it as a pilgrimage feast to the LORD (YHWH) throughout your generations! You shall celebrate it as a law forever!"* (Ex 12:1-14, translation and emphasis mine).[7]

What a terrible, long night it must have been in that long ago spring in the land of Egypt. That first Passover was anything but joyous. Families were huddled about the small tables in their shacks made of dried mud. They could feel the intense quiet outside where they heard only an occasional sound of someone running in panic. On the table had been placed a large, wooden platter that held a whole roasted lamb surrounded by sheets of unleavened bread, or hearth-cakes, and bitter herbs. Everyone grabbed bits and pieces of the food and gulped them down. It was not a banquet to be enjoyed, but merely sustenance to give them energy for the long journey ahead. They were all ready to flee as soon as the signal was given.

Toward morning, their Egyptian neighbors began pounding on their blood-marked doors and insisted on pushing gold and jewelry into their hands. The Egyptian people were frantically and tearfully begging them to leave—leave before all of the people in the land of Egypt should die. Great cries and shrieks swelled out of the houses and palaces of all of the people, from those of the poorest and from those of the noblest. Every family bewailed the sudden loss of their loved ones. Such a curse had befallen the land of Pharaoh that even their gods were smitten and helpless, and they too were in danger of dying. All of Egypt had lost, and bitterly, to the God of Israel. The strange Israelites, then, had to be pressured into leaving Egypt as quickly as possible.

In the morning, just as the sun rose over the eastern desert, Aaron and his family blew their signals on rams' horns, and, in the greatest haste possible, the children of Israel left Egypt. They left carrying their meager possessions and the great wealth that the Egyptians had forced upon them. They fled into the desert as far as the Sea of Reeds (Yam Suf, Ex 13:18), but there they found themselves in a trap. The stubborn Pharaoh had changed his mind once again and went out with the army and its chariots to round up the Israelites and return them to slavery (Ex 14:5-9). Before their very eyes, however, God brought about one of his most wonderful acts: the sea parted to let them pass through on dry land (Ex 14:13-22). When the chariots of Pharaoh pursued them onto the sea bed, the waters flowed back together and the sea swallowed them up — horses and drivers (Ex 14:23-28). The fright and panic of the Israelites was turned, suddenly, into wonder, then relief, and then into ecstatic joy! (Ex 15:19-21). They danced and sang, clapped and shouted as the great miracle of God began to sink in. The events of the whole Exodus experience now occupied their thoughts and conversations, from the plagues to the parting of the sea. The Exodus became deeply etched into the minds and consciousness of the whole people. They would never forget it. And, as the Lord God had commanded them, neither would their children, nor the children of their children, forever (Ex 12:17, 26-27; 13:8).

## HaB'riyt: The Covenant

Just three months after they left Egypt, the children of Israel witnessed an even greater wonder and miracle (Ex 19:1,2). God, Himself, came down upon the mountain of Sinai as a cloud of fire and entered into a covenant relationship with them that was to govern their whole lives from then on. The escaped slaves of Pharaoh became the people of God, a holy nation, a royal priesthood: The Nation of Israel (Ex 19:6). The receiving of the Covenant from God was to be a memorial for them (Dt 6:1-3), just as was Passover. The Exodus and the Covenant were to mark them forever as a unique and special people. Through the observance of God's laws, they were to remain separate and distinct from all other people on earth. If the Exodus alone had occurred, then we might never have learned much about them, but the Sinai Covenant fashioned them into the chosen people. They were always to bear the heavy burden of being the "firstborn of God" (Ex 4:22).

The second Passover was celebrated the very next year (Nm 9:1-5). And that second Passover was a celebration indeed. The children that were too young to remember the events of the Exodus were told of them over and over again. Passover not only celebrated their escape from Egypt, but also their birth as a nation. Those who could not join them in the observance, for one reason or other, had to be given a dispensation to celebrate the feast one month later (Nm 9:6-12). Passover became so essential to their identity that anyone who did not observe the feast was expelled from the nation (Nm 9:13).

The second Passover is not described in detail in the Book of Numbers, but we have a good idea of what it must have been like because the Samaritans in Israel still observe a more primitive celebration each year on Mount Gerizim. They still pitch their tents in the area of the mountain where the Samaritan temple once stood. The men dig a number of fire pits according to the quantity of lambs to be cooked and burn fires in them until they are very hot. Everyone bathes to become ritually clean and most of the men dress in long, white robes. After the lambs are ritually slain in sacrifice, the men prepare them for roasting by scalding the hides with boiling water and plucking out all of the hair. They place the lambs, with skin on, in the fire pits and cover them up in a manner very similar to the Hawaiian luau. The women prepare the rest of the food. There are lengthy recitals of prayers by the men and the singing of Psalms. When the cooking is completed, the men uncover the pits and lift out the lambs. The whole roasted carcass is placed on trays around which the families will gather for the feast. Any food that is left over after midnight is thrown into the fire pits and burned up.

The Samaritan way of preparing Passover may have been very much like the way the Israelites prepared the feast before the Exile in Babylon. The Samaritans are the descendants of those left behind on the land when the upper classes of the northern kingdom were carried off into exile by the Assyrians and, suspected of being halfbreeds and heretics, were not allowed to join the people of the southern kingdom when they returned from Babylon. The more primitive observance of Passover would have been all that they knew.

In those early days, the entire ritual was conducted by memory as most of the people could not read. Although Moses had set down the commandments and laws of the Covenant in writing, all of those writings were kept in the safekeeping of the priests. During the preparations for the feast, the priests could read all the laws of Passover to the people, but it was up to the people to remember the laws and to implement them. Fortunately, the Hebrew language is perfect for use by the storyteller. It has a cadence and emphasis that makes the telling of a story forceful, colorful, and vivid. Out of the need to remember everything arose a class of people who were the official storytellers and keepers of the history and traditions of

the nation. Events that occurred during the Exodus from Egypt
and during the time in the wilderness became sagas and epic
poems in the hands of those storytellers. These sagas and epics
were retold at the celebration of every feast and at every clan
and family gathering. Storytelling followed strict rules. Events
could be embellished and elaborated so as to excite the hearer's
imagination, but the record of the events had to be retold in
their entirety as a sacred obligation. No important event or
detail could be skipped or forgotten. Listeners were as familiar
with the story as the storytellers, who would be quickly cor-
rected if a mistake were made, a detail omitted, or an attempt
made to falsify the account. By the time the Israelites settled in
the land of Cana'an, the epic poems and sagas of Passover, Pentecost, and Tabernacles were firmly established and very well
known by all of the people. Among Semitic peoples, storytelling and history recalling is still a finely polished and exact art.

The first Passover in the land of Cana'an was celebrated at
Gilgal. But there is a strange incident recorded: "On this occasion, the LORD (YHWH) said to Joshua, 'Make flint knives
and circumcize the Israelite nation for the second time'" (Jos
5:2 NAB). The scribe who arranged the book in its final form
may have added the information that those males born on the
desert journey through the wilderness had not been circumcised. This has biblical historians perplexed. It doesn't seem
possible that an important covenant such as circumcision
(*b'riyt milah*) would have lapsed among those who had followed Moses and Joshua. Some historians now surmise that
the followers of Joshua were met by others who were also descendants of Abraham and who wanted to join them in the conquest. But they were not allowed to do so until they too were
circumcised. Some historians believe that not all of the Israelites left Egypt with Moses. A great number of people related to them might have left Egypt for Cana'an earlier when
the Hyksos were deposed. They would have already made a

meager beginning in the conquest of Cana'an. But they were only squatters and opportunists who had no clear purpose or vision until they met those who had followed Moses and Joshua. Before the "squatters of Cana'an" could join the others, they had to be circumcized in the covenant at Gibeat Ha-Aralot (Height of the Foreskins). Then they could participate in Passover and relive the birth of the nation. Passover, then, took on added meaning. Previously, it was the way parents introduced their children to the Exodus experience. At Gilgal, Passover was used to introduce others to this experience. By participating in the ritual, they became full members of the nation of Israel.

The Book of Joshua presents historians with a number of problems. It does not always fit with the evidence of archaeology.[8] The main problem is with the chronology of events, but this is a concept that is more important to modern people than to ancient people. We are prisoners of time. We have clocks everywhere that dictate to us the precise time we are to make every move we make. We have phrases like, "At this moment in time" that punctuate our conversations. We are able to find out the exact time of any spot on the globe. However, for the writers and editors of the Book of Joshua, the concept of time was exactly the opposite. Time was fluid and pliant. Their "clock" was a sun dial, which registers shorter hours in the morning and late afternoon than at midday and shorter hours in the winter than in the summer. Ancient calendars were even more fluid. The biblical months began with the sighting of the new moon. The beginning of the month, therefore, depended on the weather and varied from place to place. And it could be manipulated by political and religious authorities. Time was fluid, not precise. The only constant that the ancient Israelites could count on was the Sabbath. Every seventh day was Shabbat, rain or shine. No wonder, then, that storytellers concentrated more on what happened and why it happened than on when it happened.

Archaeologists have evidence that the events recorded in the Book of Joshua could not have happened in the lifetime of one man. This seems especially perplexing to some Christians, but a rabbi taught me to ask who really performed these wonderful deeds, Joshua or the Lord? In Hebrew, Joshua is Y'hoshu'a, which means "YHWH is Salvation" or "The Lord Saves." For the biblical writers, it was the Lord who won all the victories over the Cana'anites through Joshua. Joshua was His commanding general. In the minds of the storytellers, others were subordinate to the commanding general and he was subordinate to God. Y'hoshu'a did it. "YHWH Is Salvation" led the people of Israel to victory over the Cana'anites. "The Lord Saves" parted the waters of the Jordan river and led the people into the Promised Land.

The Aramaic form of Y'hoshu'a is "Y'shu'a" or "Jesus" (Mt 1:21). That is one reason Jesus asked to be baptized by John in the river Jordan. Just as Y'hoshu'a had led the people of God into the Promised Land through the waters of the Jordan, so does Y'shu'a lead the family of God into the kingdom of God through the waters of the Jordan.

## The Promised Land

The entrance into the Promised Land was reminiscent of the Israelite departure from Egypt. When the Levites had carried the Ark of the Covenant into the waters of the Jordan river, which was in a springtime flood state, the river stopped flowing. The Israelites were able to cross over on dry land as they had done through the Sea of Reeds. After they had all crossed over, the river flowed again (Jos 3:15-17). That made an indelible impression upon the people. From that time on, the waters of the river Jordan became identified with the waters of the sea that had parted for them as they escaped from Egypt. The Jordan became holy to them. More than a thousand years later, when John the Baptist wanted to lead the people to repentance, he did not lead them across the desert to the Sea of Reeds, which was believed to be an extension of the Red Sea. He led them to the River Jordan. The waters were the same.

After crossing the Jordan, the Israelites moved away from the fortified cities into the hill country. By subjugating the highland areas first, they avoided a full-scale frontal attack against the Cana'anites until they were stronger. When the hill country was under control, the Ark of the Covenant was brought to Shechem where it would be enshrined permanently. Joshua had a great altar built on Mount Ebal in sight of Shechem. He offered a burnt offering and peace offerings to the Lord there. Then Joshua had half of the Israelites face Mount Gerizim, the mountain representing God's blessings, and the other half face Mount Ebal, the mountain representing God's curses. The Law of Moses was then read to all of the people, who renewed their commitment of the Covenant (Jos 8:30-35).

After the death of Joshua, the confederation of the twelve tribes seemed to fall apart. The Cana'anite city states were in a state of decline and collapse at that time, but they remained a formidable enemy to the divided tribes. The changes that had occurred from the time of Joshua to the time of the Judges are described in Judges,

> An angel of the LORD (YHWH) went up from Gilgal to Bochim and said, "It was I who brought you up from Egypt and led you into the land which I promised on oath to your fathers. I said that I would never break my covenant with you, but that you were not to make a pact with the inhabitants of this land, and you were to pull down their altars. Yet you have not obeyed me. What did you mean by this? For now I tell you, I will not clear them out of your way; they shall oppose you and their gods shall become a snare for you."

When the angel of the LORD (YHWH) had made these threats
to all the Israelites, the people wept aloud; and so that place came
to be called Bochim. They offered sacrificed there to the LORD
(YHWH) (Jgs 2:1-5 NAB).

The religion of the Cana'anites was concerned with the fertility of the lands, crops and livestock, and prosperity. This was
the religion of all the western Semites and it was spread over
the region of what we now call Israel, Jordan, Lebanon, Iraq,
Syria, and parts of Arabia. This was the religion of the ancient
Phoenicians, who were closely related to the Israelites in both
language and blood. They spread the religion throughout their
colonies, especially to Carthage in North Africa. It was seductive religion because it was so openly sexual. Its worshipers
believed that the sky-father, El or Ba'al (Master, Lord), had to
have intercourse with the earth-mother, Ashtarte (Ishtar), in
order to insure the fertility of their lands, flocks, and families.
People believed that they could ensure fertility if they had an
orgy in the wooded groves around the temples of Ashtarte.
Seeing them, the father-god would be aroused to do his duty.

But this religion was not all fun and games. They had to pay
for the blessings they received. Their firstborn sons belonged
to the goddess, Ashtarte, and had to be given to her through the
horrendous god, Molekh. His name probably meant "king"
(*melekh*), but the Israelites replaced its vowels with "o" and
"e" from the Hebrew word, *boshet*, which means "shame."
Molekh, the idol, had a very large and wide open mouth.
Projecting up and out from that big mouth were outstretched
arms. A fire burned in the belly of the god when he was worshiped. The firstborn, and any other children consecrated to the
goddess, were rolled down the arms and through the mouth of
Molekh to be incinerated in his belly. From Dr. Francis Kelsey's
excavations of the Tophet, or sacred precincts of the goddess
Tanit (Ashtarte) at Carthage in 1925, we know that the cremated
remains of the children were buried in special urns in grounds

sacred to the earth-mother goddess.[9] Seduced by Ashtarte and Ba'al, many Israelites were drawn into this abominable practice.

> They immolated their sons and daughters by fire (2 Kgs 17:17 NAB).

> "The people of Judah have done what is evil in my eyes," says the LORD (YHWH). "They have defiled the house which bears my name by setting up in it their abominable idols. In the valley of the Ben-hinnom they have built the high place of Topheth to immolate in fire their sons and daughters, such a thing as I never commanded or had in mind" (Jer 7:30,31 NAB).

Tophet is the biblical name for the precincts and cemeteries sacred to Ashtarte. The Tophet referred to in Jeremiah was located in the valley just south of Jerusalem. That place became so disgusting to the Jews that after they finally wiped out the worship of Ashtarte, they used the valley for a dump where the smoke from the constant fires could always be seen. In Hebrew, the name of this place is Gey Ben-hinnom. In Aramaic, it is Gehenna, a place synonymous with hell.

During this dark period, Passover suffered. Families that still observed Passover did so soberly and sometimes fearfully. But it was still one way the faithful could hold on to God and remember his salvation. As a family feast, it could be observed in secret. In communities where the majority remained faithful to God and his Covenant, Passover was celebrated as it had always been. But in villages where some families were just remnants of the faith, Passover was a time for the family to renew its commitment to God. They remained steadfast and God would not abandon them. When the Hebrews were overwhelmed by catastrophe because they had deserted the true faith, they repented and God sent champions to rescue them and bring them back to the Covenant. We call those champions the Judges.

## The Monarchy

At long last, under the direction of the prophet Samuel, a new day dawned. The Twelve Tribes were brought together again, but this time under a king. The first king, Saul, was a disappointment. But King David lived up to his name, "Beloved." The people loved him and God loved him. David became the model of the perfect king. Through the prophet, Nathan, God promised David that his descendants would rule forever. Israel had entered its golden age.

> I will raise up your heir after you, sprung from your loins, and I will make his kingdom firm. It is he who shall build a house for my name. And I will make his royal throne firm forever. I will be a father to him and he will be a son to me.

> Your house and your kingdom shall endure forever before me; your throne shall stand firm forever (2 Sm 7:12-14, 16 NAB).

That was the message that Nathan delivered to David. God had promised that the reign of David would last forever, and God keeps his promises. Yet after the death of king Solomon, the nation split in half. Then when Babylon conquered the kingdom of Judah, the royal dynasty of David ended completely. The failure of the Davidic line gave rise to the belief in a Messiah who would restore the line forever. Christians see the fulfillment of the prophecy of Nathan in the person of Jesus Christ whose Hebrew/Aramaic name, Y'shu'a Ha-Meshiach, which means "Joshuah the Messiah." Jews, however, cannot accept this because their Messiah is supposed to establish a worldwide kingdom of peace, forgiveness, and healing. Perhaps the reason they cannot accept Jesus as the Messiah is that

Christians have failed to keep covenant with Jesus and establish this kingdom of agape-love themselves.

Yet, all of the Gospels proclaim that Jesus is the Messiah. The Gospel of Matthew, written by a Jew for other Christian Jews, makes it very explicit that Jesus is the Messiah in a uniquely Jewish way. He adapts the genealogy of Jesus to form three groups of fourteen generations. He does that to emphasize that Jesus is the Son of David who is the rightful one to restore the House of David. Fourteen is the numerical value of David's name. The letter *dalet* equals four, the letter *vav*[10] equals six, and dalet another four. Since vowels are not counted, the sum of the three Hebrew letters that form David's name is fourteen. The technique of giving a numerical value to every name and word in Hebrew is called *gematriya*. Every letter of the Hebrew alphabet is also a number. Vowels do not count because none of the letters are vowels (vowels originally were added by the reader and later indicated with small marks). Since every letter is also a number, it follows that every word has its numerical value as well. Consequently, numbers were not abstractions, but symbols that had a direct bearing on faith.

But we're getting ahead of ourselves. Momentous changes took place during the reign of David and Solomon that affect the way Passover is celebrated today. As David united the twelve tribes and established his kingdom, he conquered Jerusalem and made it his capital. Jerusalem was in a strategic location because it was centrally located and, more important, had not been part of any one tribe's territory. It was neutral. When David brought the Ark of the Covenant to Jerusalem, the city began its role as the central shrine of Judaism. The tribes maintained their own major shrines and holy places, but Jerusalem became preeminent over all of them.

When David built his palace in Jerusalem and established his royal court there, he hired scribes to keep the royal records. At that time, every court had scribes who kept written records of every transaction that took place at court. With the scribes, Israel entered the world of written history.

Until the reign of King David, only the priests kept any written accounts. But they were only interested in the laws of the Covenant and the sacred rituals. They preserved family genealogies of each of the twelve tribes, but they were not interested in activities outside the various shrines and holy places. The priests had preserved only a skeleton of the history and traditions of the people. There now arose a need to flesh out those dry bones by setting down the sagas and epic poems of the people.

A scribe under either David or Solomon began the collection and recording of the sagas and poems. He was a master storyteller himself and a maestro in the use of Hebrew. We have no record of who he was or what his name was, but he left us his legacy in a writing style that is easy to recognize. Scholars call him the "Yahwist" because he consistently refers to God as "YHWH," even when he is recording events that took place long before the Divine Name was revealed to Moses (Ex 3:11-14). The stories of Adam and Eve, the Flood, and the Tower of Babel belong to the Yahwist. This is called the "J" source, oddly enough, because the Germans who discovered the source referred to him as the "Jahvest."

The reign of King David brought the conquest of Cana'an to an end. The defeated Cana'anites were now gradually absorbed into the Israelite tribes and become the Jewish people. In the established kingdom, the majority of the people began giving up the semi-nomadic life of herdsmen and farmers and settled into villages, towns, and cities. With the growth of Jewish communities, the influence of the storytellers was bound to weaken. It was of vital importance that all of the history, recollections, and traditions of the people be set down in writing. The Yahwist, and those who followed his example, began our Bible. In the beginning, the Bible was not a single book, but a collection of scrolls preserved in the Temple archives and in the royal library. While other kings collected the records of conquests and victories in battle, as well as the tributes paid them by the conquered, the Jewish scribes were obsessed with God, the true king, and his relationship with his people, Israel. Central to his rule was the record of his victory over Pharaoh and the gods of Egypt and his Covenant with his people at Mount Sinai. The epic events of the Exodus were now put down in writing and the Passover saga could be read from a scroll.

The Yahwist was not alone in his monumental work. Others, such as the Elohist in the north, followed him. The Elohist got his name the same way the Yahwist did, by consistently calling God by the same term, "Elohim" in his case. Where the Yahwist was primarily interested in the traditions of the south, the Elohist recorded the northern traditions. He is now called the "E" source and best preserved the sagas of Abraham, Isaac, and Jacob. The priests began to collect their own material and that is called the "P" source. Most of it is very technical and less interesting to the lay reader, but they also wrote the first chapter of Genesis, which is one of the greatest masterpieces of Hebrew literature. Much later, another school called the Deuteronomists, or the "D" source, came along. The Deuteronomists were influenced by the prophets, and while the earliest traditions were very legalistic in their understanding of Israel's relationship to God, the Deuteronomists introduced the concept of *chesed w'emet* (eternal love) into that relationship. God was not only the king who established his kingdom at Sinai, he was also a husband who married his beloved bride, Israel, at Sinai. The Deuteronomists had great influence on the religious reforms of King Josiah, and, of course, the Book of Deuteronomy is their work and masterpiece.[11]

The four original sources of our written Bible are like the four sources of the river Jordan. The Nahr Leddan, the major summer source, flows from the springs at 'Ain Leddan on the slopes of Mount Hermon in Israel. It is joined at Huliot by the Nahr Banias, which rises on the southern base of Mount Hermon in Syria. Nahr Hasbani, the chief winter source, rises on the western slope of Mount Hermon in Lebanon and joins the Banias and Leddan at S'deh Nehemia in Israel to become the Jordan river. They are joined by the Nahr Bareighit, which flows from the western-most slopes of Mount Hermon at the springs in Merj 'Iyun and then flows over a sixty-foot falls at et-Tannur before joining the others in the Jordan.[12]

Another process had also begun. As Jerusalem established itself as the capital of the nation and the site of the Temple, it became the major shrine and outshone all of the others. The scattered and various religious traditions of the people were now gathered there. The numerous and divergent recollections of the events of the Exodus were brought together in one holy place. The traditions of Passover, instead of being dissipated at various other shrines, were now centered on Jerusalem.

## Eliyahu Ha-Navi: Elijah the Prophet

A mighty stream joins the river. A stream that changes the nature of that river forever. And that was the prophet Elijah whose Hebrew name, Eliyahu, means "My God, He is Yah (YHWH)." Many weak and evil kings ruled over Israel and Judah after the death of David and Solomon. Some, like King Ahab and his evil queen, Jezebel, allowed and even fostered the worship of the old Cana'anite gods. But Elijah challenged the king and the people at Mount Carmel to prove who was really God, YHWH or the Ba'alim. The altar put up by the prophets of Ba'al remained undisturbed while the altar arranged by Elijah was consumed by fire from heaven. The people realized the Lord was truly God and they killed the prophets of Ba'al (1 Kgs 18:16-40). Elijah performed many other miracles, but is especially remembered because he saved the faith of Israel from the pits and snares of the old Cana'anite gods. Elijah did not die. He was carried up to heaven in a fiery chariot (2 Kgs 2:1-11). The people understood this to mean that he would return to them one day, and so he became associated with the coming of the Messiah. Elijah would prepare the way for him and announce his coming.

> Lo, I will send you
>     Elijah, the prophet,
> Before the day of the LORD (YHWH) comes,
>     the great and terrible day.
> To turn the hearts of the fathers to their children,
>     and the hearts of the children to their fathers,
> Lest I come and strike
>     the land with doom (Mal 3:23,24 NAB).

As Passover evolved over the centuries, it began to look more and more to the future and the coming of the Messiah. As that happened, Elijah became more and more a presence at each Passover celebration. He was expected to arrive at Passover and prepare the parents and their children for the Messiah's coming. Many centuries later, a special cup of wine would be set on the Passover table exclusively for the prophet Elijah. As the wine would evaporate during the ritual, the little children would notice that there was less wine in the cup and exclaim that Elijah had slipped in unnoticed and sipped from his cup. They still sing,

> Elijah, the Prophet.
> Elijah, the Tishbite.
> Elijah, the Gileadite.
> Come, speedily in our day,
> With the Messiah, the Son of David!
>     (Haggadah shel Pesach)

With the inclusion of the presence of Elijah in the celebration of Passover, it became a feast of the past, present, and future. Each observance looked forward, with great expectation, to the coming of the Messiah.

## Passover and the Prophets

North of the Sea of Galilee, where the river Jordan enters the Great Rift Valley of the Jordan, there used to be a great number of swamps. Recently, the Israelis have drained them and turned the area into fertile farmland and fish ponds. Until modern times, however, the valley was a malarial wasteland. I like to think of the waters of the Jordan flowing through there as the pure, running waters of Judaism and Passover and the swamps as the religion of the Cana'anites, threatening to change the nature of the Jordan. The river reacts to preserve its purity.

Judaism reacted in various ways to the seductions of Ashtarte, Ba'al, and Molekh. One reaction concerned an abhorrent dish offered to the earth-mother goddess. To symbolize their willingness to offer their children to the goddess, worshipers prepared a dish wherein a young kid (goat) was cooked in its own mother's milk. "You shall not boil a kid in its mother's milk," is written in Exodus 23:19 and again in 34:26 and Deuteronomy 14:21 (NAB). This was a "heavy" commandment, and it led to *kashruth*, the dietary law that states that meat could not be eaten at the same meal with dairy products.

Judaism reacted to the Cana'anite religion in its practice of Passover as well. I have found no history of the dish called *charoset* before it is mentioned in the Talmud (BT Pesachim 114a). It was a regular feature of the meal by the first century, but the rabbis disputed whether it was a religious obligation or not. As a mixture of fresh fruit, it is reminiscent of a popular Cana'anite offering called a "raisin cake." Its popularity could have proved a temptation to the Israelites. To counter that temptation, some enterprising Jewish cooks may have created charoset, with its raisin base, as a worthy offering to the Lord God of Israel. Originally, charoset might have represented the fruitfulness of the earth—it still has some of that connotation today. But as part of the Passover ritual, it had to take on more meaning than representing the fruitfulness of the land. So, it was called charoset, which is from the Hebrew word for "clay,"[13] to remind everyone of the bricks they were forced to make for Pharaoh (Ex 1:11-14).

During the rainy season, fresh water rushes down the wadis in the hills on either side of the river valley and refreshes the river Jordan just as the prophets were sent by God to refresh and strengthen Judaism. The prophets had an impact upon the Passover as well. Passover had always been the feast that relived the Exodus events, but the prophets reminded the people that without the Covenant, the Exodus experience would have been little more than a footnote in history. Through the influence of the prophets, the Covenant became the Torah, an all-encompassing word that describes a total way of life in relationship to God.

The prophets gradually forced the people to look upon the Covenant in a whole new way as well. Originally, the Covenant was seen as the Law, those edicts and rules that they had received through Moses that defined the reign of God over them. At first, the Covenant was like those ancient Suzerainty Treaties, whereby kings established their rule over conquered peoples.[14] God had established his rule over them and they had become his subjects. Because they had received justice from the Lord, they had to exhibit justice and honesty toward members of their covenant community. But the prophets understood that there was much more to it than that. They began to lead the people from the concept that they were vassals of an all-powerful king to the realization that they were actually the children of an all-concerned father. Later, under the influence of Amos and Hosea, the people began to understand that they were the beloved of an all-loving father and Lord.

The Hebrew word "chesed," which describes God's covenant relationship with Israel, has shown the evolution of those ideas. At first, "chesed" was defined as "mercy," then as "kindness," then as "loving-kindness." Finally, the prophets impressed on the people that chesed was the love between the bridegroom and his beloved and that God had married the people on Mount Sinai. That was why the prophets condemned apostate Jews as adulterers rather than idolaters. They had left the "bridegroom" and gone off whoring with the false Ba'alim of the Cana'anites. Significantly, *ba'al* means "husband" as well as "Master" and "Lord."[15]

Chesed is important to an understanding of the New Testament. In the Hebrew Scriptures, chesed describes God's covenant relationship with his people and the people's correct relationship with each other within the Covenant. When translated into the Koine Greek of the New Testament, "chesed" required two words: *charis* describes God's loving relationship with us while *agape* describes our love relationship with each other within the New Covenant of Christ.

Another important point: "Chesed" is usually combined with *emet* as in *chesed w'emet*. "Emet" means "truth," but it also means "everlasting." When it is combined with "chesed," it is usually translated as "everlasting" or "enduring." "Emet" is written with the three letters, *alef, mem,* and *tov,* that is, with the first, middle, and last letter of the Hebrew alphabet. That means that emet is the same in the past, present, and in the future, and therefore, "always" and "everlasting" as well as "enduring." Does that sound familiar? In Revelation 1:8, Jesus announces to John that he is "the Alpha and the Omega," that is "the First and the Last." This is clearly a translation into Greek of the concept of "emet" meaning "the first, the last, and the always". When Jesus announced at the Last Supper that he was the Truth (Jn 14:6), he meant that he was Everlasting Truth.

## The Reforms of King Josiah

Abruptly, the river Jordan flows into the fertile and beautiful Sea of Galilee, called Yam Kenneret in Hebrew. This freshwater lake is surrounded by fruitful valleys, population centers, and mountains. The mountains to the east rise suddenly to the height of 2,700 feet to the plateau of Hauron. On the west, the greener hills and mountains rise more gradually. Steep passes in the western mountains have been the site of famous battles over the centuries. Numerous caves in the mountains have hidden refugees and revolutionaries.

The surface of the Sea of Galilee lies 696 feet below sea level and the surrounding valley and plains have an almost tropical climate. The fertile soil makes the area ideal for agriculture and the production of fruit. The lake is some 13 miles long and eight miles wide and has a religious aura about it. Jews, Christians, and Arabs claim it as their own. Great quantities of fish are harvested daily from the lake. A popular fish is called "Moses fish" by Jews and "Peter fish" by Christians. When Jerusalem was lost to the Romans at the conclusion of the second Jewish revolt under Bar Kokhba in 135 C.E., the area around the Sea of Galilee became the site of several rabbinical schools where major work was done on the Jerusalem Talmud.

To me, this beautiful lake represents the sudden and glorious reign of King Josiah (640-609 B.C.E). His name in Hebrew is Y'oshiyah and means "May Yah (YHWH) give." He had a major and permanent impact upon Judaism and Passover. After years of kings who had allowed paganism to flourish and the Temple to be neglected, Josiah set about establishing the religious reforms the prophets had called out for. He had the altars of the Cana'anite gods destroyed and their shrines and high places abolished. He even removed the numerous altars to YHWH because rituals at those places had been influenced by surrounding pagan cults. He centered worship in Jerusalem and the Holy Temple. But even the Temple itself had to be cleaned out and restored. Over the years, altars to other gods had been set up in the outer courts. The worst offense was a statue of an Assyrian god, with an altar, placed there in hopes that the Assyrians might not destroy the southern kingdom as they had destroyed the northern kingdom. The act worked politically, but it was a religious disaster. Prophets referred to it as the "abomination and desolation" of Israel: abomination because an idol was placed in the Temple of the one God, and desolation because the Shekhinah, the cloud of fire that was the visible presence of God in the Holy of Holies, disappeared. The nation, like its holiest place, was dark and desolate.

King Josiah supplied funds to workmen to repair the Temple. During the restoration, the high priest Hilkiyah discovered a book of the Law that had been hidden in the rubbish. He brought it to the king, who had it proclaimed to the whole people, who then renewed their commitment to the Covenant (2 Kgs 23:1-3; 2 Chr 34:29-33). That book of the Law is believed to have been the fifth book of the Pentateuch, Deuteronomy, which means "the Copy of the Law" in the Septuagint Greek. Deuteronomy records the final words of Moses to the Israelites and recounts the laws of the Covenant and the people's relation to it. Against the legalism of Exodus and Leviticus, Deuteronomy seems gentler and gives more expression to God's love for his people. Deuteronomy contains the magnificent Sh'ma, the great profession of faith of Judaism (Dt 6:4-9).

By making the Temple the only shrine in the nation and Jerusalem the only place pilgrims could come to celebrate the three mandatory feasts (Ex 23:14-17), King Josiah changed the observance of Passover forever. Previously, it had been observed either at home or at one of the local shrines. Under Josiah, it became a pilgrimage feast or *chag* to Jerusalem and a sacrifice in which the paschal lambs were sacrificed — and at first eaten — in the courts of the Temple.

For a long time, there had been two separate Passover sacrifices. The more familiar universal observance is detailed in Exodus, especially in chapter twelve. There was another equally important Passover sacrifice of the priests and Levites.

> On the fourteenth day of the first month falls the Passover of the LORD (YHWH), and the fifteenth day of this month is the pilgrimage feast [chag]. For seven days unleavened bread is to be eaten. On the first of these days, you shall hold a sacred assembly and do no sort of work. As an oblation you shall offer a holocaust to the LORD (YHWH), which shall consist of two bullocks, one ram, and seven yearling lambs that you are sure are unblemished, with their cereal offerings of fine flour mixed with oil, offering three tenths of an ephah for each bullock, two tenths for the ram, and one tenth for each of the seven lambs; and offer one goat as a sin offering in atonement for yourselves. These offerings you shall make in addition to the established morning holocaust; you shall make exactly the *same offerings each day for seven days* as food offerings, in addition to the established holocaust, with its libation, for a sweet-smelling oblation to the LORD (YHWH). On the seventh day, you shall hold a sacred assembly and do no sort of work (Nm 28:16-25 NAB, emphasis mine).

This second Passover sacrifice had been the exclusive obligation of the priests and Levites. They had kept the obligation at various shrines and holy places throughout the land, but especially at the central shrine, first at Shechem (Jos 8:30-35), and now at Jerusalem (2 Sm 6:1-19). Although it was known as Pesach or perhaps Ha-Pesach Ha-Kohenim (Passover of the Priests), it had been observed separately from the sacrifice of the paschal lambs. Even though this second Passover sacrifice is described as a holocaust, other biblical references say that only selected parts of the animal were consumed in the fire while the remaining parts were boiled (2 Chr 35:13). In contrast, the paschal lambs had to be roasted.

To celebrate his victorious triumph over the Ashtartes, Ba'alim, and Molekhs, Josiah sponsored a magnificent Passover celebration in the Temple such as there never had been before. *He combined the two Passover sacrifices into one splendid observance.* The entire celebration, including the suppers, took place within the Temple courts. Josiah encouraged the whole nation to make the Passover pilgrimage to Jerusalem. Not everyone came. In spite of Josiah's success in tearing down the pagan altars, he had not divorced all of the people from their Ba'alim. But those who had remained faithful to the God of Israel came and participated in Josiah's remarkable, "new" Pesachim.

> Josiah contributed to the common people a flock of lambs and kids, thirty thousand in number, each to serve as a Passover victim [*l'pesachim*] for any who were present, and also three thousand oxen; these were from the king's property. His princes also gave a free-will gift to the people, the priests and the Levites. Hilkiah, Zechariah, and Jehiel, prefects of the house of God, gave to the priests two thousand six hundred Passover victims together with three hundred oxen. Conaniah and his brothers Shemaiah, Nethanel, Hashabiah, Jehiel and Jozabad, the rulers of the Levites, contributed to the Levites five thousand Passover victims, together with five hundred oxen.

> When the service had been arranged, the priests took their places, as did the Levites in their classes according to the king's command. The Passover sacrifice [*ha-pesach*] was slaughtered, whereupon the priests sprinkled some of the blood and the Levites proceeded to the skinning. They separated what was destined for the holocaust and gave it to various groups of the ancestral houses of the common people to offer to the LORD (YHWH), as is prescribed in the book of Moses. They did the same with the oxen. They cooked the Passover on the fire as prescribed, and also cooked the sacred meals in pots, cauldrons and pans, then brought them quickly to all the common people. Afterward they

prepared the Passover for themselves and for the priests. Indeed the priests, the sons of Aaron, were busy offering holocausts and the fatty portions until night; therefore the Levites prepared for themselves and for the priests, the sons of Aaron. The singers, the sons of Asaph, were at their posts as prescribed by David: Asaph, Heman and Jeduthun, the king's seer. The gatekeepers were at every gate; there was no need for them to leave their stations, for their brethren, the Levites, prepared for them. Thus the entire service of the Lord was arranged that day so that the Passover could be celebrated and the holocausts offered on the altar of the Lord, as King Josiah had commanded. The Israelites who were present on the occasion kept the Passover and the feast [*chag*] of the Unleavened Bread for seven days. No such Passover had been observed in Israel since the time of the prophet Samuel, nor had any king of Israel kept a Passover like that of Josiah, the priests and Levites, all of Judah and Israel that were present, and the inhabitants of Jerusalem. It was in the eighteenth year of Josiah's reign that this Passover was observed (2 Chr 35:7-19 NAB).

King Josiah had created a entirely different Passover. From his time on, the only complete observance of the feast could occur in Jerusalem. Passover became the Passover sacrifice. The paschal lambs, moreover, could only be sacrificed in the Temple courts along with the oxen and bulls of the priests' and Levites' Passover Sacrifice, as well as the goats offered for the atonement of sins. The combining of the two sacrifices into a single observance is reflected in Deuteronomy, "You shall offer the Passover sacrifice [pesach] from your flock [*tzon*] or your herd [*baqar*]..." (Dt 16:2 NAB). The two Hebrew words make a clearer distinction between "tzon," which means "sheep, goat, flock," for the people's Passover sacrifice, and "baqar," which means "cattle, cows, herd, kine, oxen,"[16] for the priest's Passover sacrifice.

The two Passover sacrifices (Pesachim) remained combined until late into the first century B.C.E. By that time, the number of pilgrims so overwhelmed the facilities of the Temple and the Holy City that drastic adjustments had to be made. One of those adjustments was separating, once more, the two Passover sacrifices. That returned the second offering to the near exclusive use of the priests and Levites. The second sacrifice retained its name of Passover, or "Pesach" in the Hebrew/Aramaic and "Pascha" in Biblical Greek, but when the Temple was destroyed in 70 C.E., both sacrifices ceased and the priestly Passover was forgotten. The only recollections of it may be in the stipulation that boiled meat could be served at the *shulchan orekh* (Passover meal) to replace the roasted lamb that was no longer obtainable without the Temple.

When King Josiah placed Passover under the control of the priests and Levites, it became a "communion sacrifice" and a "peace offering" (*zebach sh'lamim*) as well as a "thanksgiving offering" (*ha-todah*). However, there was one important difference. In all of the other sacrifices, parts of the animal were divided up between the priests, the people, and God. Priests received the forequarters (Lv 7:28-34; 10:14,15), God received the blood and the fat, especially the kidneys (Lv 3:9-11,14-17; 7:22,23), and the people received the hindquarters.[17] For the Passover sacrifice, the blood and the fat still belonged to God, but there could be no such thing as a priestly portion. The Lord had commanded that each family must eat the entire paschal lamb including, "its head and shanks and inner organs" (Ex 12:8,9 NAB). Israel was a "kingdom of priests" (Ex 19:6), and at Passover every man, woman, and child shared in the priestly role. In sharing the paschal lambs, every priest and Levite became just another supplicant and communicant.

Philo alludes to this phenomenon in his description of Passover:

"After the New Moon comes the fourth feast, called the Crossing-feast which the Hebrews in their native tongue call Pascha. In this festival, many myriads of victims from noon till eventide are offered by the whole people, old and young alike, *raised for that particular day to the dignity of the priesthood*. For at other times the priests according to the ordinance of the law carry out both the public sacrifices and those offered by private individuals. *But on this occasion the whole nation performs the sacred rites and acts as priests with pure hands and complete immunity.*"[18]

Passover was to become a feast of equality as well as a celebration of unity. Everyone shared equally in the celebration and supper as *amo yisrael* (his people, Israel). With the priests, Levites, and people sharing equally in the Passover supper, the fat and blood portions offered to God took on added meaning as well. They were God's portion of the feast as well as of the sacrificial offering. God now had his place at the head of every Passover table.

Because everyone shared the role of the priest at the Passover sacrifice and supper, they had to conform to stricter rules of sanctity. Everyone had to be in a levitical state of purity. Every dwelling had to be cleaned and scrubbed in preparation for the feast. Even the dust had to be removed lest some leavening agent remain lurking within (Ex 12:15). Then all the people had to immerse themselves in the purifying waters of the *mikveh* (ritual bath) (Lv 7:19,20; BT Pesachim 109a). Finally, men, women, and children had to wear priestly garb, white linen tunics, as an expression of their participation in the sacrifice (Ex 39:27; BT Pesachim 109a).

The reign of king Josiah broke into the dismal history of weak and evil kings the way the sun breaks through the clouds. His reign was cut short, but his memory lasted long after his death (2 Chr 35:23-25).

## The Babylonian Captivity

A great cataclysm destroyed the nation of Judah in 586 B.C.E. Against the advice of the prophet Jeremiah, the new king of Judah joined in an alliance against Babylon. That was a mistake. Babylon crushed the tiny nation. Nebuchadnezzar carried the king, the royal family, the nobles and warriors, artisans and landowners into exile in Babylon. Just the middle and upper classes were taken. With all hope of rebellion removed, the farmers were left to cultivate the land. But Jerusalem was left in ruins, and worst of all, Solomon's glorious Temple was destroyed. The sacred vessels of the Temple became trophies of war and were carted off to Babylon.

A hundred years before, when the Assyrians destroyed the northern kingdom of Israel, a huge number of northern refugees fled south to Judah. The refugees who fled to the south took with them many of their sacred scrolls from their shrines (1 Kgs 12:26-31) and holy places. Included among them were the writings of the Elohist (Brown et al., *Jerome Biblical Commentary* 1:15). The priests of Jerusalem accepted the northern scrolls and placed them in the archives and library of the Temple. When Judah went into exile in Babylon, they took the scrolls with them. Unlike the Assyrians, the Babylonians allowed their captives relative freedom once they were deported. That allowed the priests to begin a monumental work. The scrolls were many and unwieldy, and the priests were afraid that many would be lost in some future crisis. As a result, the priests began to combine the numerous smaller scrolls into larger scrolls that were easier to protect. They combined them into three sections: the Torah, the Prophets, and the Writings.

The Torah, or "The Five Books of Moses," is the most sacred of the Hebrew Scriptures and was at that time closed to any further additions. The Torah included all of the writings of the Yahwist and the Elohist, the sagas and epic poems, and the works from the schools of the priests and the Deuteronomists. Although Moses was the impetus behind Torah, many others added to his writings.[19] The Hebrew throughout the Torah displays many writing styles and an evolution of idioms and vocabulary that spans many hundreds of years. That fact does not diminish the sacredness and veracity of the Torah, however, for the priests respected everything that they had received and did not alter anything, even those passages that they no longer understood. What we have received from their hands is very much the Five Books *of* Moses and not just the Five Books *by* Moses.

The canon of the Prophets was not yet closed. God was still speaking to his people through prophets such as Ezekiel. The same was true of the third part of Hebrew Scriptures, the Writings, which included the books of history, the Psalms, and such other books as Ecclesiastes and Ruth. The core history and traditions of the people were still being established.

The assembling of the Five Books of Moses into a single scroll[20] called Torah made the work accessible to all the exiled people. They began to gather into Torah study groups. They reasoned that their ignorance of the Law had left them vulnerable to the alien cults and that this had brought the Lord's wrath down upon them. They wanted to study, listen, and learn from the priests, Levites, and prophets and to return to God's Covenant and to the observance of all of its commandments, laws, and ordinances. The study groups evolved into the synagogues, which were houses of study as much as places of worship and prayer. The synagogues were a new concept. Before the Exile, religion had been the primary responsibility of the priests and Levites and had consisted mainly in sacrifices at the temples, shrines, and holy places. The ordinary people participated during great feasts and regional festivals, but for the rest of the year they depended upon their own devices. This easily led to superstition. But during the Exile, the people realized that the observance of their religion was the responsibility of each and every individual. Everyone now believed they had to learn God's law in order to submit to it.

It soon became evident that learning required reading. The study groups quickly became schools. Every male felt the need to learn how to read for himself. That need soon became a requirement and then a law. Every male, by the time he was thirteen years of age, had to demonstrate before the community his ability to read and his willingness to take upon himself all the obligations of divine law. He became a "son of the commandment" or *bar mitzvah*. At thirty years of age, he could retire from the family business and devote all of his time to the study of Torah. That zeal for study has been a characteristic of the Jewish people ever since.

The Exile was a busy time. The Israelites had lived apart from the main stream of history. Now they were thrust into the midst of one of the world's great civilizations. Many of them were already traders and merchants, but they were now confronted by "world markets." Their native Hebrew could not cope with those new conditions. They had to adopt a new language, Aramaic, to compete in those new markets. Fortunately, Aramaic is also a semitic language closely related to Hebrew. They found it easy to learn because many of the Aramaic words were similar to the related words in Hebrew. For example, the word for son is *ben* in Aramaic and *bar* in Hebrew. The sentence structure of the new language and most of its idioms were the same as those they already knew. Aramaic was the lingua franca of the whole Middle East and was understood even in Egypt. By learning it, they became citizens and participants in a whole new and much greater world. Some of the exiles became very rich very soon. They had one clear advantage over every other group: they had the highest literacy rate in the ancient world!

Aramaic also gave the Jews access to the latest in science and technology. The Babylonian civilization was the most advanced in mathematics, astrology, water management, record keeping, and many other areas. For this studious and curious people, there were now whole new horizons to explore. So they adopted Aramaic as their everyday language and retained Hebrew for religious use.

Still, the exiles faced an enormous crisis of faith. The Babylonians, who were the most advanced in astrology and technology, were the most advanced in mythology as well. In fact, they had ingeniously combined the three. Astrology was presented as both a science and a religion, and as such, was powerfully seductive. The Jewish intellectuals, who already used a numerological system, were drawn to the Babylonian system. Astrology became the passion of many. Some even entered the schools of astrologers, who were called magi. But the manipulation of numbers and star charts came embedded in a mythology, and this was becoming as attractive to these Jewish intellectuals as the Cana'anite religion had been to the Jewish peasants.

At the very center of this new challenge to Judaism was the Babylonian creation myth, called *enuma elish* or "when on high." Since it was so bound up with astrology, it was almost impossible to embrace the one without embracing the other. This creation story presented a war between the good gods of light and the evil gods of darkness and matter. The Babylonian religion was based upon acceptance of two equal but opposing divine principles ruled over by the gods of light and the gods of darkness, who are always in a contest for mastery. In that primal war, the gods of light were victorious and decided to create the world out of their spoils of victory. They first separated light from darkness and balanced the two forces. Then they entered the waters of the abyss and separated the water above from the water below by building the firmament of the sky. They arranged to have gates in the firmament so that they could be opened to allow the water above to flow through as rain. Then they separated the water below into the seas and the dry land. The land was created by chopping up the evil Tiamat, the monstrous serpent of the deep waters, and molding her remains into the earth. After they had finished the three separations of light from darkness, the waters above from the waters below, and the dry land from the seas, they set about furnishing the three areas. They furnished the light with the sun, and the darkness with the moon and stars. The waters above were furnished with birds and the waters below with fish and sea monsters. Then the lands were furnished with the plants and animals. The human being was then created and put on the land for the sole purpose of worshiping the gods and nourishing them with adoration. When they finished, the gods of light celebrated.

The Jewish priests met the threat of the Babylonian creation myth head on. They had never thought of the world as having a beginning before, and they thought that they had no other revelation about how the world began except for the very few details given in the origins of the human race (Gn 2:4-7). They searched their Scriptures to see if God had revealed to them more about creation, something that they could use to counter the Babylonian myth. After careful study, they found it in their reading of Torah, in Exodus 3:14. God had revealed his name to Moses as "YHWH asher YHWH," which they had always read as "I AM who I AM." But that same passage could be read just as well in the "hif'il" or causative form of the Hebrew verb, and, by doing so, the divine name would be read just as well as "He-Who-Causes that which Comes-Into-Existence."[21] That was a tremendous and exciting revelation to the priests. They had read in the Torah that God alone is the creator of all that has been created, that everything that God had created was good. From that revelation they launched their very successful counterattack. They accepted the mechanics of the Babylonian myth — that is, the three separations and the three furnishings — but they added what God had revealed to them: God alone is creator, all that God created is good, and God put humanity on earth to prosper and to freely enter into a covenant relationship with Him. The mechanics of the six events, plus the celebration, fit neatly into the theology of Judaism. The three separations and three furnishings were redefined as six days, the six working days of the week, and the celebration of the victorious gods was redefined as the Sabbath of the Lord. While they were still in Exile or shortly afterwards, the priests added to the beginning of Genesis some of the most impressive and exciting Hebrew in the Bible, and yet a Hebrew that reflected Babylonian Aramaic (Gn 1:1-31 to 2:4).[22] Judaism was saved from a vulnerable parochialism that had threatened to undermine it, and it was now able to flourish in a worldwide environment of new science and new technology.

Naturally, the Exile changed the way Passover was celebrated. The emphasis was once more on liberation and salvation. The people longed to go back home again and see Holy Zion, and they pleaded with God to rescue them again and remove them from another house of bondage. They prayed that he would restore their nation to them and rebuild his Temple where they could again celebrate the complete Passover sacrifice. There were no paschal lambs for them to eat in Babylon. Their priests had no authority to gather animals for sacrifice, and they were not allowed to sacrifice to their God in that pagan land. They no longer had their own Temple and the sacred altar of sacrifice. But Passover was also the Feast of Unleavened Bread or Chag Ha-matzot. Therefore, they were able to apply all of the symbolism of the paschal lambs to the Unleavened Bread or matzot. It already represented "sincerity," "purity," and "a new beginning," and to that was now added the character of "poverty" and "affliction." In Deuteronomy, the Passover matzah is called "the bread of affliction" or *lechem 'oni*. The concept helped them express the pain of being exiled in a strange land. Out of their pain, they added a new prayer to the Passover seder: "The Invitation to Passover," which is still said in Aramaic as a memorial of the Exile. The first line in Aramaic is *ha lachmah anya,* which can be translated as "Behold, the bread of poverty" (or affliction, poor, or wretched).

> Behold this, the bread of poverty,
> which our ancestors ate in the land of Egypt.
> All who are hungry, come and eat.
> All who are needy, come share Passover with us.
> Now we are here, next year may we be in the land of Israel.
> Now we are slaves, next year may we all be a free people.

The people mourned the loss of the nation, the City, and the Temple where they could freely worship their God.

> By the streams of Babylon,
> we sat and wept
> when we remembered Zion
> (Ps 137.1 NAB).

However, the people drew great strength from the ritual of the Passover supper. Had there been no Exile, Passover would have continued as King Josiah had reformed it and might have become a completely institutional feast. But with no Temple, Passover once again became centered in the home. And even when the Passover sacrifice was restored in the rebuilt Temple, the feast would retain its family character.

In the cosmopolitan world of Babylon, however, the Passover supper began to take on some of the trappings of the surrounding civilizations. The Babylonians were among the first people on record to enjoy salads. They were not the tossed salads we know but lettuce and other raw vegetables dipped into vinegar, salt water, or mixtures of oil and herbs. Soon lettuce and raw vegetables began appearing on Passover tables. Lettuce was used to wrap around portions of food in the same way as the unleavened bread was. Dipping food into various condiments and bowls of salt water became a regular feature of the supper. Passover was now taking on airs of sophistication, and it would continue to do so down through the centuries. The people adopted the custom of reclining on dining-couches from the Persians, Greeks, and Romans. Reclining on couches was a symbol of freedom and demonstrated their confidence that God would eventually liberate them.

## Persian Conquest and the Return

From the Achaemenid line in Persia came the king of Anshan, Cyrus II, who conquered the Medes in 553 B.C.E. and Croesus in Asia Minor in 546. He became a threat to Babylon, which had become weakened by a succession of feeble kings, and finally defeated the Babylonian army at the river Tigris in 539 B.C.E., taking over the whole kingdom of Babylon intact. The seventy-year-long prayer of the Jews was answered in 538 when "Cyrus the Great" issued the decree that permitted them to return to Judah and Israel.

The sudden release from captivity was a dream come true for those exiles who dreamed of returning to Zion. But it caused confusion among others. Some of the Jews had become rich and influential in Babylon, now Persia. Their scholarship, literacy, and fluency in Aramaic made them important in the court of the great king and throughout his new empire. They did not want to give up their wealth and prestige to go on a long journey into an uncertain future. They felt that they could be of more use to those who did return by supporting them with their newfound wealth and influence. Those who did not return became the first Jews of the Diaspora. However, those Jews remained powerful and influential. Among them was the great queen, Esther, and her influential uncle, Mordachai. Learned rabbis arose among them, and some, like Rabbi Hillel, became noted authorities on the teaching of the Torah.

The prince of Judah, Sheshbazzar, lead the returning exiles home. They carried with them the sacred scrolls of the Torah, the Prophets, and the Writings. They also carried the sacred vessels of the Temple, which the Babylonians had removed but which Cyrus had given back to them. Eventually, they would rebuild the Holy Temple and restore the daily and festival sacrifices. Without realizing it, however, they were returning with three distinct religious institutions that operated independently: the family with its distinct celebrations, the synagogue with its study and worship under the guidance of the rabbis, and the Temple with its sacrifices and rituals conducted by the priests and Levites. At first, the priests and Levites exercised the greatest influence over the people, but the rabbis' influence grew as time went on. There would be only one Temple, but there were synagogues everywhere. The families never forgot, however, that it was in the home that Judaism survived in that alien land. It was in individual homes where the study groups began what became the synagogues.

The priests and Levites rebuilt the altar of sacrifices before the ruins of Solomon's Temple and restored the daily sacrifices. They began work on rebuilding the Temple, but they found that there were not enough artisans among them and the work came to a halt. However, the prophet Zerubbabel encouraged them to continue and try to complete the work. Under the high priest Joshua, the Second Temple was finished in 515 B.C.E. But the rebuilt Temple was a great disappointment. It was not as grand and glorious as the First Temple that Solomon had built.

The Jewish courtier Nehemiah, at the Persian Court in Susa, heard of the sad situation in Jerusalem. He was the cup bearer to King Artaxerxes I, and he used his influence with the king to become the governor of the restored province of Judah. Nehemiah went to Jerusalem and led the people in the rebuilding of its walls. The northerners in Samaria, who had survived the Assyrian conquest, tried to join the returned Jews in the rebuilding of the Temple and the Holy City. But Nehemiah and the priests thought of them as halfbreeds who practiced a corrupt offshoot of Judaism. After all, it was in the northern kingdom where the worst apostasies had taken place before the Exile. So Nehemiah and the priests refused the Samaritan offers of assistance. That rebuke angered the governor of Samaria, Sanballat. Joining with Tobiah, the governor of Amman and Geshem, and the governor of the Arabian province, he tried to interfere with the work going on in Jerusalem. His anger spread to the people of Samaria, who from then on became bitter foes of the Jews. Their hate was returned by the Jews, who now refused to have anything to do with Samaritans. They became "untouchables" who were cut off and forbidden any contact with the Jews in the south.

Rebuffed and rejected, the Samaritans were not influenced by any of the changes that had taken place among the exiles. Their religion remained a sort of pre-exile Judaism. They eventually built their own temple on Mount Gerizim, near Shechem. Their longing for the Messiah was more open than that of the Jews. Foremost in their hearts was a yearning for respectability and an eventual acceptance into the house of Israel. The Messiah could heal the bitter wounds that separated the two peoples.

## Judah, the Captive of Empires

With the restoration of Jerusalem, the river Jordan flowed once again through the lands of Judea and Samaria. From the Sea of Galilee, the river twists and turns through the Great Rift Valley called the Ghor. In its meandering, the river drops gently from 675 feet to 1300 feet below sea level. The valley of the Ghor is about twenty miles wide in the north and south, and much narrower in the middle. The mountains rise more than a thousand feet on either side of the Ghor. The climate of the valley goes from tropical in the north to arid desert in the south.

The Jordan, which is from 60 to 80 feet wide, has cut a deep bed in the valley floor, called the Zor. The Zor is about a mile wide and 150 feet deep. It is a thicket of shrubs and stunted trees. In ancient times it was the lair of wild animals and some lions. The water of the Jordan is brackish in this area, and not suitable for irrigation. But there are other sources of water and springs in the hillsides, such as at 'Eyin Ghedi, that allow extensive cultivation. Vegetables and fruits, including bananas, abound in the north, and date palms and melons flourish in the south. Although the Jordan is sacred to both Christians and Jews, it is disappointing when a person first sees it. It just does not live up to its promise.

The return from Exile did not live up to its promise, either. Never again were the people free from foreign domination. Empire after empire ruled over them until the Romans destroyed the nation in 70 C.E. and again in 135 C.E.

During the period of Persian rule, the people struggled to restore the province of Judah. They received help from relatives who remained behind in Mesopotamia, but the restoration took a long time and the Jews often became discouraged. About 400 B.C.E., the Egyptians threw off the yoke of Persian rule, which destabilized the situation in Israel. The prophet, Ezra, traveled to Israel to encourage and organize the people. He was a member of a priestly family and was called a "Scribe of the Law of God." He was certain that the only hope for the people was the faithful observance of the Law. In dramatic moves, he assembled the people in the Temple courts and had the entire Torah read to them. The Levites explained the difficult points of the Law to the people. Every man, woman, and child swore their allegiance to the Covenant. They assumed the title of "The People of the Book" (Neh 8:1-18).

As soon as the Temple was rebuilt, the Jews began to celebrate Passover as they had done during the reign of King Josiah. The people sacrificed the paschal lambs in the Temple courts and skinned them there. The Levites sacrificed the oxen and rams of the priestly Passover sacrifice in the Temple courts as well and skinned them there. The people roasted the paschal lambs over open pits of fire while the Levites boiled the meat of the bulls in great kettles. Then priests, Levites, and people shared the Passover supper in family groups arranged about the Temple in the surrounding courts. The population of Judea remained small enough to fit within the Temple courts for quite a number of years until they could convince their relatives in Persia to join them for the pilgrimage feasts of Passover, Pentecost, and Tabernacles. Only then did they outgrow the Temple courts and have to move the site of the suppers to the surrounding city.

In spite of their faith in God and their obedience to his Covenant, the Jews felt under seige. The empires of this world were a constant threat to them. The age of the prophets seemed to come to a close with the deaths of Ezra and Nehemiah. Actually, prophecy had just changed to a new style that we now call "apocalyptic." Strange visions abounded and a cryptic language was used that foreigners could not understand. Apocalyptic literature typically described worldwide events that would shake to the foundations every empire that would rule over the people of Israel. God had control over all of the cataclysmic events and he would always save those who remained faithful to him. The people felt that their faith in the new style of prophecy was confirmed by the fall of the Persian empire to the armies of Alexander, the Macedonian.

## The Empire of the Greeks

Alexander, the son of Philip the Macedonian, defeated the vast Persian Empire. He then went on to conquer the whole known world and spread Greek culture throughout that world. After his death in 323 B.C.E., his vast empire was divided up among his generals. Ptolemy, who ruled Egypt from Alexandria, also controlled Judea. The Holy Land now came under the powerful influence of the Greeks. Eventually, people divided into two camps. The upper classes became Hellenists, who adopted Greek language and life style, while the lower classes religiously held onto their ancestral languages and customs. They retreated into their homes and synagogues and repudiated the Greek refinements as ungodly and as much a threat to their national well-being as the Ashtartes and Ba'alim had been before the Exile. They became even more observant of the Law. Some began to call themselves the Chasidim, from the word "chesed," which describes God's relationship with his people in the Covenant. A Chasid was an observant one who remained in the covenant relationship with the Lord God of Israel. The Chasidim evolved into the Pharisees.

The Greek culture had a powerful influence over all of the people, even over the Chasidim, who began to curl their forelocks. Greek men thought that curling their hair made them more handsome. Judea became more cosmopolitan and open to the great cultures of Europe, just as it had been open to the culture of Mesopotamia in earlier times.

The Greeks, and the Hellenists who copied them, were sophisticated diners. Their meals followed a definite set of courses. They served hors d'oeuvres before the meal, then the entree, which was followed by a dessert, then more drinking of wine and the popular symposium or philosophical repartee and discussion. The Passover supper soon conformed to the Greek manner of dining. Jews began serving the roasted giblets of the paschal lambs on beds of lettuce leaves as the hors d'oeuvres of the Passover supper. The Babylonian custom of dipping greens into salt water and herbal vinegar remained, but now the giblets wrapped in lettuce were dipped into those dishes. The hors d'oeuvres were followed by the meal itself, which officially began with the Kiddush, the blessing of the wine, and the

HaMotzi, which was the blessing and then sharing of bread, which in this case was unleavened bread or matzah. The dessert or the *afikoman* was simply a small piece — "the size of an olive" — of the Passover lamb that had been set aside and then served to everyone at the conclusion of the supper.[23] No eating was permitted after the afikoman nor any drinking of wine after the fourth cup. However, the evening continued well into the night with further discussions on the deeper significance of Passover and Passover games and songs to involve the children. However, the riotousness of the Greek symposium was expressly forbidden because it would demean the purpose of the supper (BT Pesachim 119b). Even so, the very word "afikoman" was a Hebrew/Aramaic adaptation of the Greek word, *epichomon* (BT Pesachim 119b).

The Greeks introduced advanced methods into the production of wine. Jews had always been producers and enjoyers of wine. They were probably familiar with the beverage in the patriarchal period even before they were pressed into making wine and beer for their Egyptian overlords. The Feast of Tabernacles (Booths), called Sukkot, one of the three major pilgrimage feasts (Ex 23:14-16), was originally a harvest festival celebrating the grape harvest and pressing. Wine was such an ancient tradition that it is recorded as going back to the time of Noah (Gn 9:20). Every sabbath and feast-day meal began with the blessing said over "the fruit of the vine."

Ancient people did not realize that airborne wild yeast produced both the leavening of their bread and the fermentation of their wine. Perhaps this is not surprising. Bread required a starter or "mother" that took several days to prepare, whereas grape juice began fermenting almost immediately without the addition of a starter. They did not know that the grey "dust" on grape skins was actually wild yeast. When grapes were pressed, the yeast mixed with the fruit sugars and began fermentation. From then on it was merely a matter of storage and caretaking.

Red wine was fermented with the skins for about two weeks. White wine was fermented without the skins and stems. The initial fermentation took place in cistern-like vats that had been carved into solid rock or were pits lined with watertight plaster. When that was complete, the new wine was drawn from those vats and placed into containers to mature and age. Great care was taken during the weeks and months of maturing, or what was intended to become good wine became vinegar instead. The traditional containers for the storage of wines had been made from the skins of animals such as cattle, sheep, and goats. The fur of the skin was coated with pitch or tar to seal and waterproof it, then the hide was turned inside out and sewn up to hold the liquid. One leg was left open and corked or plugged with a wooden spike. As the wine aged in the wineskin, it frequently took on the taste of the hide and pitch.

The Greeks created a much superior vessel for the production of wines: the amphora. The amphora was a two-handled, narrow-necked vessel made of high-fired, brick-like clay. It had a wide body that narrowed at its base for storage in wooden frames. They were used by the Greeks for the storage, aging, and shipping of wines and oils. The wine amphorae had a strategically placed hole where a stopper could be placed to allow or prohibit the entry of air. The Greeks had learned that wine, which is actually alive, has periods when it must "breathe" to survive and times when it must be cut off from airborne agents that could turn it into vinegar. Upper-class Jews adopted this superior method of wine production. Others modified their wineskins so that the necessary breathing and sealing could take place. But the skins were still not as good as the amphorae, which were glazed and kept the wine free of any taint of hide, pitch, or tar. And they could be used over and over.

But the improved methods of wine production increased the opportunity for drunkenness and debauchery. The Greeks added water to their wine, but their intention was to delay intoxication, as debauchery was an after-dinner feature of some of their celebrations. This scandalized the religious Jews. They began to add water, not just to smooth the taste, but to forestall drunkenness altogether. They made adding water to wine mandatory. This made the wine kosher, and only then could it be drunk. The Psalmist said, "Wine causes the heart of men to rejoice" (Ps 104:15), but drunkenness causes their hearts to become debased and their minds to become oblivious to their sacred obligations.

From the Greek period, at least, wine has been an obligation and an important part of the celebration of Passover.[24] Everyone is required to drink at least four cups or glasses (BT Pesachim 99b, 108b). Even those too poor to afford wine are obligated, and the community must take up a collection so that the poorest among them can drink at least the required four cups (BT Pesachim 99b). There must be joy in even the humblest dwelling at Passover. But that wine must be made kosher.

Under the Ptolemys, ruling from Alexandria in Egypt, there was a period of prosperity. Greek fashions and lifestyles were becoming very pronounced, even in Jerusalem. The wealthy, the nobility, and the hereditary classes felt the Chasidim's resistance to those influences was merely an example of lower-class ignorance. Many of the priestly families openly advocated Hellenistic practices, and this brought about a schism. The Chasidim began to divorce themselves from the authority and influence of the priests and Levites. Although they remained devoted to the Temple and the Temple sacrifices, they looked more and more to the rabbis as the true authorities in religious matters and to the synagogues as their primary place of prayer, study, and worship.

During that period, the number of Jews living in the Diaspora grew at a phenomenal rate. Besides those in Mesopotamia, there were Jewish communities everywhere. There was an especially large and influential community of Jews at

Alexandria in Egypt. It was becoming evident that more Jews spoke Greek than spoke Aramaic and understood Hebrew. Hebrew Scriptures were becoming unfamiliar to the majority of Jews. Under the paternal sponsorship of Ptolemy II, king of Egypt from 309 to 247 B.C.E, the Jews of Alexandria translated the Hebrew Bible into Greek. Tradition has it that this was done by seventy-two rabbis, and as a consequence, that Greek Bible is known as the Septuagint, from the Latin word *septuaginta* for "seventy." The name is commonly abbreviated by the Roman numerals, LXX. The Septuagint eventually contained seven more books than the Hebrew Bible. These extra books, such as 1 and 2 Maccabbees, were originally written in Greek, and the rabbis in Jerusalem felt no need to translate them into Hebrew. This accounts for the two different canons of the Old Testament accepted today. The first part of the Catholic Bible was translated into Latin from the Septuagint and became the Vulgate, whereas Protestants accept only the older Hebrew Scriptures for their Bible.

## The Hasmoneans

Events took another turn in 200 B.C.E. Antiochus III, the Seleucid king of Syria, defeated Ptolemy V of Egypt and annexed Israel to his area of the Greek empire. At first, this meant merely switching allegiance from Alexandria in the south to Antioch in the north. But after the death of Antiochus III, a storm swept over Israel that could have destroyed it. Antiochus IV became king — and he was crazy. He believed he was the manifestation of Zeus and so called himself Epiphanes (manifestation of the god), but his people twisted this to Epimanes (madman). He insisted that only the Greek religion be practiced throughout his territory, and that all of his subjects worship him as the incarnation of Zeus. The situation was perilous for Israel. Onias II was high priest at that time, but his brother Jason, a Hellenist, connived to buy the office of high priest from Antiochus IV. The king later replaced Jason with Menelaus, who then pushed for the complete Hellenization of Israel and Jerusalem. Finally, Antiochus decreed that Judaism was to be abolished and replaced by the Greek religion. Hellenists dedicated the Temple to Zeus. They replaced the altar of sacrifice with the classic Greek altar and installed a nude statue of Antiochus, to be worshiped as the official idol of Zeus. They made pigs the mandatory sacrificial animal because they were an abomination to the Jews. Collaborators gave in on the assumption that Antiochus IV Epiphanes could not live forever. But the Chasidim had enough and rose in revolt. The priest Mattathias of the Hashmon family stabbed to death one of the Hellenist priests as he ascended the altar of Zeus and rebellion broke out. Mattathias died soon after, and his sons took over the leadership of the war against Antiochus. His son, Judas, was so successful in his lightning guerilla attacks against the Seleucid army that he became known as the "Hammerer." The Hebrew word for hammer is *maqqevet,* which is reflected in the Greek word *makkabaios,* from which we derive Judas' nickname of Judas Maccabee. The nickname was extended to his brothers, who are all called the Maccabees. Their descendants, however, kept the family name of Hashmon and were known as the Hasmoneans.

The war was a horrible one. Antiochus tortured his enemies in terrible and fiendish ways. The two books of Maccabees record the heroic and grisly deaths of thousands of Jews. (The courageous martyrdom of those religious Jews so inspired the later Christians suffering a similar fate during their persecutions under the Romans that they canonized the Maccabees as saints. Their feast is on the first of August.) The Maccabees kept hammering at the Syrians until the war became too costly for the Seleucid kings. When Antiochus died, the Syrians stopped the war. The Maccabees had won, but they did not win complete independence from the Seleucids. They won religious freedom, but they were still part of the Greek empire. The Temple in Jerusalem was purified, restored, and finally rededicated in an eight-day ceremony and celebration. Chanukkah, which means "dedication," is an eight-day celebration of the re-dedication. Chanukah is known as the Feast of Lights, but it really should be celebrated as a feast of religious freedom.

Antiochus IV Epiphanes is remembered obliquely in the Passover ritual. After the Four Questions and the discussion of the Four Sons, there is a section of midrash. It begins with, "Go, learn what Laban the Aramean (Syrian) intended to do to our Father Jacob. Pharaoh's decree was only against the males, but Laban intended to destroy Jacob and his whole family. As it says in the Bible, 'The Aramean (Syrian) wanted to destroy my Father!'" That last line, a quote from Deuteronomy 26:5, is a rereading of the Hebrew, *arami oved avi,* which originally meant "My father was a wandering Aramean," to *arami ibed avi.* By supplying a different set of vowels, the sages changed the second word from an adjective meaning "wandering" to a verb meaning "annihilate (Alcalay, *Hebrew-English Dictionary,* col. 5)."

But victory did not prove to be sweet. The people became even more divided. The Chasidim felt that the Hellenists had betrayed them by collaborating with the Seleucids and had prostituted the office of high priest by putting it up for sale. The victorious Maccabees were of no help either. While they were noble in war, they were ignoble in triumph. They assumed for themselves both the throne and the high priesthood. The Hashmon family was a priestly family, but whether they were direct descendants of the high priest Zadok is doubtful. Nonetheless, they claimed the privilege. On the other hand, the Hashmons belonged to the tribe of Aaron but not the tribe of Judah. All those who were looking for an anointed king from the family of David believed that they had no right to the throne. In their

Hasmonean grab for total authority, the lawful high priest and his family were driven into exile. To legitimize their supremacy, the priestly families began to call themselves the "Sons of Zadok" or "Zadokim." The transliteration of Zadokim into Greek was "Saddoukaion," which became "Sadducees" in English. Curiously, the Sadducees remained avid Hellenists in spite of their fight against the Seleucids.

In reaction, the Chasidim began to repudiate the Sadducees as heretics and to radically separate themselves from them. The Sadducees, on their part, branded the Chasidim as "separatists," which is *p'rushim* in Hebrew, *p'rishayya* in Aramaic, *pharisaion* in Greek, and "Pharisees" in English.

One of the Hasmonean kings, John Hyrcanus I, began an important campaign of conquest. He subdued Samaria and destroyed the Samaritan temple on Mount Gerizim. He wanted the Temple in Jerusalem unopposed. His sons, Aristobulus I and Alexander Janneus, completed the conquest of what we know today as Israel, the Holy Land. They conquered lower and upper Galilee and converted the people to Judaism. The conversion of the Samaritans was not successful, however, and the Samaritans remained outcasts and a thorn in the side of Judah.

The crowning achievement of the Hasmoneans was to return to Jerusalem the glory she had known before the Exile. The Holy City was once more an important city. Long before all roads were to lead to Rome, pathways, caravan trails, and seaways led to Jerusalem. Pilgrims from everywhere came every year to the mountain of the Lord to worship in his Temple. The Temple had been repaired and restored to much of the glory it had displayed in the days of Solomon. From the paucity of pilgrims in the days of Ezra and Nehemiah, the population of Jews in the Holy Land and Diaspora had grown so much that the city and Temple had to make extra effort to accomodate the crush of pilgrims. The Passover of King Josiah had to be modified. The two Passover sacrifices, that of the paschal lambs and that of the priests, could still be offered up inside the Temple; but there was no way that the Temple courts could hold everyone for the Passover supper. Jerusalem had to be declared officially adjacent to and an adjunct to the Temple so that the Passover supper could be lawfully eaten anywhere inside the city. The two Passover sacrifices were still combined, but there may have been a move among the Pharisees to reject sharing in the boiled meat prepared from the priestly sacrifice as food tainted by the heretic Sadducees.

One of the conquests of John Hyrcanus was Idumaea, south of Judea. The Edomites ("Idumea" is Greek for "Edom") occupied the south of Judah after the fall of Jerusalem in 586 B.C.E. John Hyrcanus restored the area to Judea and the Idumaeans were forced to accept Judaism. An important Idumaean who converted to Judaism was Antipater, an associate of Hyrcanus II, and the father of Herod the Great. Herod won great favor with the Romans and they appointed him king of Judea. But there was already a king and it took three years for Herod to defeat him and install himself as king in 37 B.C.E. He then tried to win acceptance of the aristocratic Hasmonean family by divorcing his Idumaean wife, Doris, and marrying the granddaughter of Hyrcanus II, Mariamme. The Hasmonean, Mariamme, gave him some degree of legitimacy as king. He loved Mariamme, but his fears of conspiracy prompted him to kill both his wife and their two sons, Alexander and Aristobulus. That act moved the Roman emperor to joke that he would rather be Herod's pet pig than his son. Herod the Jew did not eat pork.

Mariamme was the last Hasmonean to sit upon the throne of Judea. By a series of assassinations and executions, Herod brought the Hasmonean claim to the throne to an end. Herod not only murdered all those who plotted against him, but all those who might have plotted against him some time in the future.

## Roman Rule

The Greek Empire fell to the might of Rome. When Pompey walked into the Holy Temple as a conquereror, he encountered a very strange god. The Holy of Holies was empty and dark. The God of the Jews had no physical form and had no idol to knock over. Just the same, when he walked into the Temple sanctuary in 63 B.C.E., Pompey demonstrated that Israel was now under the heel of Rome. Roman rule would be strict and increasingly oppressive. The dream of a coming Messiah became a national passion. Passover became the focal point of this aspiration because people believed that the Messiah would make his appearance during the feast. The Romans refurbished Fortress Antonia, built by King Herod, so that that they could oversee what was happening in the Temple courts. When a disturbance broke out, Roman soldiers entered the courts and mercilessly suppressed it. Many pious Jews would die by Roman spears and swords during Passover. The Romans would quickly execute anyone claiming to be the Messiah, the "anointed king" of the Jews, because that claim in itself was an act of rebellion against Rome.

The Roman genius was in establishing law and order, and this had an interesting impact upon Judaism. The rabbis reacted to the iron rule with the firm conviction that only the strict observance of the law of God would bring the Messiah. They developed a new idea called "building a wall around Torah." This meant that walls of new laws would be built around every one of the original 613 commandments of Torah. If a law had to be broken, the rabbis wanted it to be one of the new laws and not one of the great commandments of Torah. Influential schools arose around outstanding and famous rabbis. They were the recognized authorities on the oral law, which they believed had been handed down to them from Moses through the prophets. They were the foremost interpreters of that law. The oral law and the elucidations of it by the masters were all learned by rote. The students of the rabbis were expected to memorize everything. Those who were adept at memorization were called the *tana'im* or repeaters. The tana'im, in turn, were the authorities on the teachings of their masters.

This was the culture that Christianity was born into. The Twelve were the original tana'im of Jesus, responsible for memorizing his every word and then repeating them to others who were, in their turn, to memorize them also. The Twelve were not the only disciples that Jesus had, as is clear from the Gospels, but they were the keepers of his *mishnah* or the *kerygma*, the "body of repetition."[25]

The two most famous schools in the first century were those of Rabbi Shammai and Rabbi Hillel. The school of Shammai was the much stricter of the two. It tended to greater and greater legalisms. Rabbi Hillel, on the other hand, was a great humanist and was much more lenient in his interpretation of the Law. Hillel came from Babylon to teach in Jerusalem and had a great influence on Judaism. He introduced the Babylonian version of the Torah to the schools in Israel and saw it accepted as the official version. He also introduced the square Aramaic script and saw it accepted as the official Hebrew script, completely replacing the older form that had been used up until that time. As a rabbi and a Pharisee, Jesus favored the school of Hillel over that of the Rabbi Shammai. Jesus rebuked the multiplication of laws by the school of Shammai because legalism led to hypocrisy and to insensitivity to human needs (Mt 23:23).

## The Golden Age

In spite of the oppressive presence of the Roman occupation, Jewish culture and religion flowered during and after the reign of Herod the Great. Herod had a passion for pleasing the three great forces loose in the land at that time. They were the rule of Rome, classic Greek culture, and the faith of Israel. Herod built a magnificent capital city for the Romans on the shore of the Mediterranean and named it after for the Emperor: Caesaria Maritima. Then he bestowed upon Jerusalem a splendor far surpassing anything that it had known before, even at the time of David and Solomon. His Jerusalem was a jewel, displayed in a magnificent setting of classic architecture and culture. To please the people, he rebuilt and greatly enlarged the Holy Temple.

Jerusalem had been growing at a phenomenal rate ever since it became part of the Greek Empire. Its growth paralleled the growth of the population in the Holy Land and an even more impressive growth in the population of the Jews living in the Diaspora. In fact, the growth of Jerusalem was a direct consequence of the growth of the worldwide Jewish population. Jerusalem was much more than the capitol of Jewish kings. The city's primary function was to be of service to the Temple. At least three times every year, Jerusalem hosted the pilgrims who came to worship in the Temple on the feasts of Passover, Pentecost, and Tabernacles (Ex 23:14-17). As the number of pilgrims grew to the millions,[26] Jerusalem had to adjust. Fortunately, the escalation was gradual enough for the necessary changes to take place gracefully.

During much of the Persian period, the Passover celebration remained much as it had been under the reforms of King Josiah. But when it was no longer possible to accomodate everyone in the Temple courts for the Passover supper, the authorities separated the supper from the two Passover sacrifices.

In the Roman period, the worldwide Jewish population swelled to six million and Jerusalem was no longer able to even house all the pilgrims. First, the villages within two miles of the city were annexed to house the pilgrims. Later, people were allowed to put their tents up in nearby open fields and hillsides.

Even those adjustments were not enough. By the time of Jesus, the crowds were so enormous that the priests and Levites could not keep up with the work load. So the two Passover sacrifices were separated; the Passover sacrifice of the people was done in three shifts on the 14th of Nisan, and the second sacrifice of the priests was done on the following day and on each succeeding day (Jn 18:28). Since the number of pilgrims sharing in the Passover supper far outstripped the number of rooms available in Jerusalem, authorities granted special permission to use as "dining rooms" the various rooftops and courtyards of all of the buildings, and the open areas of the market places and bazaars "up to the threshold of the gates" of the city (BT Pesachim 85a).

The mammoth number of Passover pilgrims in the first century created other problems as well. Individuals and individual families could not just arrive and expect to find housing or be able to make arrangements for a place to share their supper. Every available room, courtyard, and rooftop was allocated months or even a year in advance of the feast. Everyone had to belong to and arrive with some Passover association. That company could be a village delegation, such as from Nazareth (Lk 3:41-44); a community of pilgrims from the Diaspora (Mk 15:21); members of a *chavurah* or Passover association to which whole families belonged; or as a rabbinical school whose members registered as a unit with their families and were led by their rabbi. Jesus made his pilgrimage to Jerusalem for the feast as the head of a rabbinical school (Jn 13:13: "You call me 'teacher' and 'master,' and rightly so, for indeed I am.") that was also a Passover chavurah (Mt 27:55; Mk 15:41; Lk 22:15

& 23:49). The Passover chavurah at that time was characterized by a close "sacramental fellowship" and would constitute an extended family unit or *bayt* ("household" or "family").[27] The rabbinical school was also recognized as a legal, extended family unit. "School" is also "bayt" in Hebrew, and the School of Jesus was called the Beyt Y'shu'a or House of Jesus.

Another major problem that had to be solved: Those entering the Holy Temple and those participating in the Passover supper had to bathe in a ritual bath before doing so. Jerusalem is built upon a mountain near the edge of a desert, so water is scarce. Monumental aqueducts built by Herod and Pilate provided for the city's ordinary needs, but the water used in the ritual baths had to be rainwater or water from a running spring. Gihon was the only spring in Jerusalem, and it could not possibly supply all the water needed. Consequently, all of the buildings in Jerusalem were constructed with flat roofs to collect the rain that should fall upon the city. Cisterns and water channels were cut into the bedrock underneath every building to collect the water that fell from the roofs, streets, and squares.[28] Houses and public buildings that could afford them had at least one private mikveh. Many more public mikva'ot have been uncovered near and around the Temple Mount.

The flat roofs of the buildings had two more practical uses. During the hot summer months, the rooftops became the living rooms of the people. Awnings were put up for shade and removable lattice screens were placed around the walls for privacy. With the arrangement of rugs, cushions, and furniture, those extra upper rooms became quite comfortable and even luxurious. In the spring, when the pilgrims arrived for Passover, the rooftop upper rooms were let out to groups who had made arrangements with the householder to eat their Passover supper there. The usual access to the rooftop rooms was an outside stairway from the courtyard of the building, and that secured privacy for both the household and the pilgrims.

When the eyes of those worshipers finally fell upon Jerusalem, they fell upon one of the most beautiful cities of the ancient world. King Herod had been successful in his desire for classic magnificence. The best artisans were brought in to work with the finest stone and erect the most marvelous buildings possible. As a city in the classic world of Greece and Rome, Jerusalem had its public Roman baths, Greek gymnasiums, Roman Hippodrome, and Greek theater. There were splendid palaces that housed Herod and his court, and the Hasmonean palace where Pilate and his entourage would stay during the Jewish festivals. There was the palace of the high priest, as well as the numerous mansions of the aristocratic families and the conspicuously wealthy. Most of those were on the western hill, which was the stronghold of the Sadducees. But these buildings gave the whole city an aura of graciousness and beauty. Most of the humbler dwellings were in the lower city, below the palaces and mansions of the rich. But even the stones of those buildings, a local stone of beige color, seemed golden.

King Herod's crowning achievement was rebuilding the Temple. The people marveled at the wonderful things he had done, but they never liked him and would not give him credit for the monumental work. They never called it the Third Temple, which is what it was, but insisted on calling it the Second Temple. It was finished in the whitest stone and the brightest gold. When the sun struck the great structure at just the right angle, onlookers were blinded by a light that was almost like peering into the sun itself. The Temple courts had become too small to accommodate all the sacrifices, so Herod enlarged the Court of the Gentiles. To do so, he extended the Temple Mount to the south and north, which required great supporting arches on the south. Within the Court of the Gentiles, he built an elaborate royal porch with a large basilica that became the meeting place of the priestly Sanhedrin or Beyt Din Ha-gadol (The Great Law Court).

During this period, people began calling the city "Jerusalem the Golden." People said God had bestowed ten portions of beauty on the earth but that he gave nine of them to Jerusalem, and the rest of the earth had to make do with the single one. They said that anyone who had not seen Jerusalem had not seen a magnificent city. They measured the imposing cities of Greece and Rome against Jerusalem and found all of the others wanting.

If this was the golden age of the city and the Temple, it was the golden age of Passover as well. Jesus celebrated his last Passover at a time when the ritual was as rich and meaningful as it would ever be. From the year 70 on, everyone would look back on that time as the pinnacle from which all traditions would flow.

Three famous rabbis had great influence on the final form of the Passover supper: Rabbi Shammai, Rabbi Hillel, and Rabbi Gamaliel the Elder. They codified the laws governing Passover and gave the supper a definite order and a set ritual. To this day, people refer to the Passover supper as the *seder*, which means "order" in Hebrew. The oral laws governing Passover were eventually set down in writing in the Talmud after the destruction of the Temple and were collected in the tractate Pesachim. These laws include Gamaliel's injunction that a person has not fulfilled his obligation if he has not explained the meaning of pesach (the paschal lamb), matzah (unleavened bread), and maror (the bitter herb) (BT Pesachim 116a, 116b). The rulings of both Rabbi Shammai and Rabbi Hillel are included as to how far the celebrants are to recite the first part of the Hallel (BT Pesachim 117a). And included therein is the famous anecdote of how the great Rabbi Hillel used to eat the Passover lamb by wrapping the meat in a sandwich of unleavened bread and bitter herb (BT Pesachim 115a). The making and eating of the "Hillel Sandwich" at the seder today commemorates the eating of the Passover at the time of the Second Temple.[29]

## The Dead Sea

In the end, the river Jordan flows into the Dead Sea, which lies at the lowest spot on earth. It lies at 1,302 feet below the surface of the Mediterranean sea; it is the lowest body of water in the world. The Dead Sea rests in a stark and arid valley of the Jordan that is bounded in the north by deltic salt marshes and on the south by soft mudflats that gradually rise toward the central ridge of Ha' arava. Beyond the valley is nothing but barren, empty desert all the way to Eilat and Aqaba on the shore of the Red Sea. To the east of the Dead Sea lies the fault escarpment of the flat Moab plateau. The mountains of Moab rise sharply 4,000 feet above the valley, but only 3,000 feet above sea level. To the west are the barren sides of the Judean mountains and south of them rise the Northern Negev highlands. Peaks there rise to 2,300 feet above sea level.

The Dead Sea is 51 miles long and about 11 miles wide. The average depth is 1,080 feet. The water is deepest in the north end, and shallow to very shallow at the southern end where it becomes muddy saltpools and salty mudbanks. The water is intensely salty, with a solids content of 25 percent, which includes magnesium chloride, sodium chloride, calcium chloride, potassium chloride, magnesium bromide and calcium sulfate. The high degree of salinity makes the water very buoyant and all swimmers stay continuously afloat. But the water irritates the skin, and bathers must shower in fresh water immediately after leaving the lake. Fish cannot live in its waters.

The Dead Sea exists in bold contrast to the Sea of Galilee. Where the Sea of Galilee abounds in life, nothing seems to live in the salty Dead Sea. While the surrounding valley, hills, and mountains of the Galilee are green and fruitful, the area surrounding the Dead Sea is an arid, seemingly infertile, desert. It is hot and insect infested. It is barren and almost devoid of life except for desert scrub, small rodents, and snakes. It is a spartan and inhospitable world.

## The Jewish War: The River Flows into Death

The Golden Age came to a bitter end. Jesus had warned, "When you see the desolating abomination standing where he should not (let the reader understand), then those in Judea must flee to the mountains" (Mk 13:14 NAB). It was not too many years before that prophecy was fulfilled. The Emperor Tiberius died on March 16 in 37 C.E. and was succeeded by the insane Gaius Caligula, who reigned as emperor from 37 to 41 C.E. Unlike Tiberius, Caligula insisted that his subjects worship him as a god. He wanted images of himself installed in all the shrines and temples throughout the empire. That included the Temple in Jerusalem and all the Jewish synagogues. King Herod Agrippa I (37-44 C.E.) urged the legate of Syria, to which Judea now belonged, not to press the emperor worship on the Jews. The legate, P. Petronius, delayed as long as possible. But some pagans residing in the coastal town of Yamnia erected a crude altar and image of Caligula and the local Jews tore it down. The incident was reported to the emperor, and Caligula retaliated by ordering a colossal image of himself to be set up in the Temple in Jerusalem. Petronius delayed implementing this order while trying to convince the Sanhedrin that it would be in their best interest to comply with the emperor's command. A great number of Jews went to Ptolemais to beg Petronius not to obey the emperor. At their insistence, Petronius wrote to Caligula, but this brought the insane wrath of the emperor down upon the legate's head. Then King Herod Agrippa went to Rome to try to dissuade the emperor from forcing a crisis in Judea, where the people had revolted over just such an issue once before. Caligula went into a rage, denounced everyone who resisted his will in the matter, including the king, and ordered that Petronius commit suicide.

That crisis passed suddenly when the emperor's own guard assassinated him on January 24 in 41 C.E. But the affair was not forgotten by the Jewish people. The memory of Antiochus

IV Epiphanes was still fresh, and now they knew that a Roman emperor could be just as mad and just as great a threat to them. The next emperor, Claudius (41-54 C.E.), was fairly benign and issued an edict of toleration for the Jews. But the people were not to be lulled into complacency. The situation was dangerous. Israel needed to unite to fight the enemy. King Agrippa supported them and gave his backing to the persecution of the infant Christian church because they were deviating too dramatically from the recognized norms of Judaism. It was during that time that James, the son of Zebedee, was martyred. He was beheaded about 44 C.E., the same year that Herod Agrippa I died suddenly at Caesarea while attending the Vicennalia games, which honored the Roman emperor.

Under his son and successor, Marcus Julius Agrippa II, the situation deteriorated. The people did not like Agrippa II at all. His incestuous relationship with his sister disgusted them, and he was in constant conflict with the high priest. As a consequence, he installed and deposed high priests at will. The successor to Pontius Pilatus was the notorious procurator, Marcus Antonius Felix (52-60 C.E.). He married the sister of Agrippa II, Drusilla, which made him a member of the Herodian family. The activities of the Zealots, who opposed the Roman occupation, became more intense at that time. Felix tried to rid the country of them by crucifying great numbers of them. But the Zealots only changed tactics. They began quietly assassinating political opponents during public functions by stabbing them with a small dagger called a *sicae;* the assassinations occurred almost daily. One of the victims was the high priest, Jonathan. The situation became critical when an Egyptian Jew claimed he was the Messiah and aroused the people to a wild enthusiasm against Rome and the Roman occupation. He led a crowd of Jews to the Mount of Olives, promising them that the walls of Jerusalem would fall before him and they would enter triumphantly and remove all vestiges of foreign domination

(Acts 21:38). Felix met them with heavily armed infantry instead, killing or capturing most of the Egyptian's followers, the Egyptain himself escaping.

The last and worst of the Roman procurators was Gessius Florus, who governed from 64 until the breakout of the Jewish Revolt in 66 C.E. He openly plundered the land and robbed the people. He took bribes, even from the Zealots. Under his procuratorship, the final insult to the Jewish people came. Nero was now emperor in Rome, and he granted superior civic rights to the Gentiles living in the Roman capital in Judea, Caesarea Maritima. The Gentiles proceeded to exercise those rights in closing the main synagogue there by building shops that blocked the entrance. A plea to Gessius Florus did nothing; he was not interested. Instead, he took for his own use 17 talents of silver from the sacred treasury of the Holy Temple. The people of Jerusalem responded by taking up a collection for the "indigent" procurator, who responded to the insult by turning part of the city over to his soldiers for plunder. The people did not resist, and Florus considered that a sign of groveling weakness. He let loose a malicious and bloody slaughter upon the city. The people withdrew into the Temple courts for protection, and they blocked off the connection between the Temple and the Fortress Antonia. Florus did not have sufficient forces to put down the uprising and fled to Caesarea instead. But the Jewish War of Liberation had begun.

At first, the Jews were successful. They drove Florus and his troops out of the country and even repulsed the troops of the Syrian Legate, C. Cestius Gallus. The people felt that they were fighting the victorious war of the Maccabees all over again. They rallied under the leadership of the two sons of the founder of the Zealots, John of Galilee. His sons were Eleazar and Menachem Ben-Yochanan. The emperor Nero responded by sending the field commander, Vespasian, and his son, Titus, to take charge. Vespasian attacked the Galilee in the winter of 66-

67 C.E. and had the Galilee again under Roman control within a year's time. Vespasian moved toward Jerusalem in the spring of 68 C.E. by way of the Jordan Valley. He was stopped, however, by the suicide of Emperor Nero on June 9th, 68 C.E. He waited to see what would happen in Rome. He waited a year, as it turned out, for 69 was the year of four emperors. Galba succeeded Nero but he was murdered in January 69. Otho became emperor for a few months, but he was replaced by Vitellius, who resigned in December of 69 C.E. The troops under Vespasian proclaimed him "imperator" on the first of July in 69, and he returned to Rome as the new emperor. After the resignation of Vitellius, his son, Titus, took over his command.

During this pause in their war with Rome, the Jews were not able to strengthen themselves. In fact, they became bogged down in a civil war. John of Gischala had been in command of the Jewish forces in Jerusalem, but he had acted like a ruthless tyrant. Simon Bar-Giora had been successful in staging small guerrilla attacks and plundering raids against the Romans, and when he finally entered Jerusalem, the people greeted him as a liberator and mustered about him. John of Gischala withdrew to the Temple with his loyalists and left Simon in charge of the city. John was rescued later by some Idumean soldiers and he forcefully took charge of the city once again. But the schism within Jerusalem continued and fractured into even more factions as time went on.

Just before Passover in 70 C.E., Jerusalem was again filling with pilgrims from all over the known world. But this time, the pilgrims came to join in the fight for liberation. Jerusalem was overflowing with its residents, the refugees from the north and pilgrims from all over the world, when the Roman siege began. Titus threw up a circumvallation around the city and cut it off completely from the outside world. The circumvallation consisted of a continuous, pit-like moat behind which there was an earthen wall. Titus crucified all Jews who tried to escape the city, and the crosses rose on hillsides in plain view of the defenders. Hunger, thirst, and the constant civil war so weakened the defenders that the Romans were able to retake the Antonia in July and to destroy it. From there, the commander had clear access to the Temple. He promised to spare the Temple if its defenders would surrender, but they refused. On the 8th of Av, the Romans set fire to the gates. They entered the Temple courts on the 9th and fought continuous hand-to-hand combat with the defenders all that day and throughout most of the next. On the 10th, someone set the Temple itself on fire. Titus tried to put it out but others continued to set more fires. Before the Temple was consumed, Roman soldiers entered and saved the seven-branch *menorah*, the altars of shewbread and incense, and some of the silver trumpets of the priests. Titus took those, as well as John of Gischala and Simon Bar-Giora, back to Rome with him to display in his victory march.

By September of 70 C.E., the last pocket of resistance had broken. The Holy City was plundered thoroughly by the victorious Romans and the ruins razed by a fire that quickly became a holocaust that consumed the dead and some of the living. When the slaughter ended, those pitiful few who survived were shackled and led off to slavery. The walls of Jerusalem were torn down and the Temple dismantled, leaving not one stone on top of another on the Temple Mount.

As strange as it may seem, the Jewish people were not overcome with complete despair. Most of them believed that they were living through a repeat of history. The first Temple had been destroyed by the Babylonians and the nation was left in ruins at that time as well. But seventy years later, they were able to begin to rebuild both the Temple and the nation. The rebuilt Temple and the restored nation even outshone the former in grandeur and glory. The tombs of that period right after the

Roman victory show that both Christians and Jews returned to Jerusalem to live there in the prayerful hope of seeing it arise again in splendor. They prayed that they would see the Lord rebuild his Holy Temple.[30]

## Yam Ha-Melach: The Sea of Salt

The Europeans named it the Dead Sea. Israel did not think of it as a dead sea at all. It's Biblical and Hebrew name is Yam HaMelach or "Sea of Salt," and salt is important to life. Actually, there are freshwater springs in some of the valleys cutting through the hills on either side, such as at 'Ein Ghedi. These springs allow for intensive farming. There are, as well, numerous hot mineral springs throughout the valley that have been developed into health spas by the modern Israelis. Even the saline waters of the sea are not completely devoid of life. Modern plants extract many minerals from the water that has been gathered into evaporation pools at the southern end of the lake.[31] One important mineral extracted from the lake is potash, which is turned into vital fertilizer and sold worldwide.

Almost dividing the sea in two is a peninsula that stretches out from the eastern shore. It is low, flat, and almost barren, but winter vegetables are sometimes grown on its northern shore. The waters to the north of the peninsula are deep, reaching a depth of 1,430 feet. The waters to the south are shallow ranging from three to 30 feet. At the southern end, where the dikes and evaporation pools were built, the depth ranges from 6 to 12 feet. Significantly, the name of the peninsula is Al Lisan or "The Tongue."[32]

# The Tana'im

Until the destruction of the Temple, all of the students of the rabbis memorized all of the teachings of their masters. Oral law was oral law, meant to be memorized, not written down. A student was a tana (one who repeats).[33] But the same crisis had to be faced by Judaism and by Christianity. Memorization of the Torah and repetition of the teachings of the masters was in jeopardy. (There was no longer a nation to support the tana tradition; the schools were destroyed.) There was a need to write the teachings down. The Church responded by writing the Gospels, and Judaism by writing the Mishnah, the oldest section of the Talmud.

During the early stages of the siege of Jerusalem, Rabbi Yochanan Ben Zakkai saw clearly that the war was going to end in national disaster. He saw, just as clearly, that the real "homeland" of every Jew was the Torah, their covenant relationship with God, and the Bible, the constitution of that Covenant. If the Romans were going to lay waste to the land of Israel, then it was imperative that the true homeland be saved. Rabbi Yochanan had his disciples carry him out of the Holy City and through the Roman army in a coffin. He believed that the soldiers would not stop a funeral procession, and fortunately he was right. Once free, he obtained permission from the Roman authorities to set up a school.

There was a village ten miles south of Jaffa called Yavneh Yam or Yavneh-on-the-sea. It is now called, variously, Jabneh, Jabneel, and Jamnia. The area is a fertile coastal plain famous for its orange groves and for the Jaffa Orange, which is known as the Tapuz-Yaffo or "beautiful orange." The beauty of the region is caught up in the name of its most important city, Jaffa, which means "Beautiful." There Rabbi Yochanan Ben Zakkai reestablished his school, which became known as the Yavneh Rabbinical College or Kerem D'Yavneh.

Rabbi Yochanan gathered around him many notable rabbis, together with their disciples, and collectively they set about creating a monumental work. Notable tana'im recited the oral law, the teachings of the important rabbis and their schools, while others set their "repetitions" down in writing. The word for "repetition" is "mishnah," and what they were doing was the beginning work of the Talmud. They were joined at Yavneh by the Sanhedrin of the Pharisees, or Beyt Din, which established its control over Judaism by making legal rulings, establishing an official list of authorized prayers, and excommunicating heretics. The chief rabbi who headed the rabbinical Sanhedrin was known as the Nasi, or Prince, and he became the supreme authority of Judaism.

Other famous Rabbis took up the work begun by Rabbi Yochanan. In the next century, Rabbi Akiva headed an important school at B'nai B'rak, near what is now modern Tel Aviv. His school continued, along with the rabbis at Yavneh, to record in writing the extensive volume of material collectively remembered by the tana'im. Rabbi Akiva introduced a systematic method of collecting and codifying the monumental work being done. His disciple, Rabbi Meir, continued and greatly expanded his work. Regretfully, Rabbi Akiva was outspoken in his support of Bar Kochba, who led the Second Jewish Revolt in 132-135 C.E. For his efforts, he was captured and martyred by the Romans. They roasted him alive on a grate, but instead of pleading for mercy or wailing in his agony, Rabbi Akiva continuously recited the Sh'ma until death released him.

After the failure of the Second Jewish Revolt, the rabbinical colleges were forced to move from the coast. They settled instead at Sepphoris, Tiberius, Caesarea, and Usha in the Galilee. There, at the end of the second century, Rav Yehuda Ha-Nasi or Rabbi Judah The Prince, in line with the work of Rabbis Yochanan, Akiva, and Meir, completed the first part of the official codification in writing of the previous centuries of oral law, now known as the Mishnah. The Mishnah is second only to the Torah as the primary object of rabbinical study.[34]

Before the final tragedy of the Second Jewish Revolt, the rabbis at B'nai B'rak put the final touches on the Passover ritual and formulated what we now call the Haggadah. Leaders in this work were Rabbis Akiva and Tarfon. Their work was twofold. They set down in writing all of the decisions of the previous rabbis and codified all of the laws governing Passover. They also had to face and adjust to a fundamental problem. There was no longer a Temple; consequently, there was no longer a place to sacrifice the paschal lambs or offer the burnt offerings and sin offerings of the priestly Passover sacrifices. The code of laws regulating the observance of Passover had to be reconciled to that reality. The regulations had to allow the celebration of Passover to continue uninterrupted, but without the paschal lambs.[35] They accomplished this in two simple ways. First, utilizing the ruling of Gamaliel the Elder, they transferred the symbolism of the paschal lamb to the matzah as had been done during the Exile (BT Pesachim 116b). Then, they made the shulchan orekh (the Passover meal) a specific and separate part of the ritual. At the time of the Temple and when the Last Supper was celebrated, the shulchan orekh was simply the designation of the meal from the Kiddush to the afikoman. But now it was inserted after the motzi-matzah and korekh as a separate entity altogether and became the actual meal of the new seder. The tasting of the matzah and maror was added to that of the karpas as the hors d'oeuvres of Passover. At the revised shulchan orekh, no lamb can be eaten and the meat should be boiled to contrast it to the obligatory roasted paschal lambs of the days of the Passover sacrifice. The new code was collected in the tractate Pesachim of the Talmud. Pesachim (Passovers) is in the plural to remind us that there were two Passover sacrifices.

The rabbis of B'nai B'rak are remembered in the Haggadah by a story that is told about them. The story is a little window into their world and gives us an indication of the years of discussion that went into their work,

> It is recorded about Rabbi Eliezer, Rabbi Y'hoshu'a, Rabbi El'azar Ben 'Azaryah, Rabbi Akiva, and Rabbi Tarfon, as they were reclining during the Seder at B'nai B'rak, that they spent the whole night discussing the Exodus from Egypt; until their disciples interrupted them by saying, "Rabbis, it is time for us to recite the Sh'ma of the Morning Prayers!"

> Rabbi El'azar Ben 'Azaryah said, "Observe! I am nearly seventy years of age, and yet I have not understood why the Exodus from Egypt is recited at night, until Ben Zom'a explained that, 'It is said (in the Bible), "...so that you remember the day you came out of the Land of Egypt all the days of your life" (Dt 16:3, translation mine); "the days of your life" would mean the days only, but "all the days" means the nights as well.'"

> The learned rabbis also explained, "The days of your life" means in this world only, but "all the days of your life" means as well, in the coming age of the Messiah! (Haggadah shel Pesach).

## The Passover Seder Today

The rabbis at Yavneh, B'nai B'rak, Sepphoris, Tiberias, Caesarea, and Usha built a dam that stopped the spiritual, life-giving waters of Judaism from being lost and dissipated in death. They diverted the water of Judaism into new channels that irrigated new fields in new lands throughout the whole world!

When we sit together about our Passover table, we are not only fulfilling the commandment to bring all of the events of the Exodus into the present.

Each person, in each generation, era, and place, must regard herself and himself as personally and actually to have come forth from Egypt in the Exodus:

Because that is what it means when we read in the bible, "And you shall tell your son on that day, 'This is because of what the LORD (YHWH) did for *me* when I came out of Egypt'" (Ex 13:8)(BT Pesachim 116b, my paraphrase for emphasis of *b'khol dor v'dor*).

We become, once again, participants in all of those great events of the Exodus. But reverberating in our voices are the numerous echoes of our ancient biblical past. Looking at our seder table we can see those faint images of the past materialized in the symbolic objects and foods enshrined in the celebration.

The **seder plate** recalls those great platters that brought the whole roasted paschal lambs to the tables during the time of the Holy Temple and at the Last Supper.

The **z'roa**, or roasted shank bone, remembers the time of Abraham, Isaac, and Jacob when the Shepherds' Feast was celebrated to insure the health of their flocks.

The **matzah** recalls the entry of the children of Israel into the Promised Land flowing with milk and honey where they celebrated the Festival of the New Leaven and a New Beginning. It recalls Kings David and Solomon and the Temple where the Altar of Shew Bread held twelve sheets of matzot to represent the Twelve Tribes of Israel.

The **charoset** recollects the age of the prophets who taught us that God married Israel at Mount Sinai and that his covenant relationship with us is that of chesed-love.

The **chazeret** recalls the Exile in Babylon where the addition of greenstuff was included in the observance of Passover as salad to be dipped into salt water and vinegar.

The **karpas,** or green vegetable, retains the memory of the Greek domination of the nation and the Hellenization of the seder by introducing an hors d'oeuvres to the supper.

The **baytzah,** or roasted egg, recognizes that the Temple was destroyed by the Romans in the summer of 70 C.E. The egg is a symbol of mourning and it mourns the loss of the sacrifice of the paschal lambs as well as the burnt offerings and sin offerings of the priestly paschal sacrifice.

The **maror,** or bitter herb, reminds us that throughout history evil men have sought to destroy or exterminate the people of God. There was Laban and Pharaoh, Antiochus and Nero, Vespasian, Titus, and Torquemada,[36] Hadrian and Hitler.

> His unfailing promise has sustained our ancestors and us. Not just one enemy (Pharaoh) has sought to destroy us, but men rise up to destroy us in every generation. But the Holy One, blessed is He, delivers us from out of their hands (Haggadah shel Pesach).

Besides the seder plate, the **matzah cover** is a reminder of the **afikoman.** The seder leader will break the middle matzah and then wrap one half in a cloth and hide it. It will be redeemed later for the dessert of the seder meal. Jews recall in these symbolic actions the destruction of the nation of Israel in 70 and again in 135 C.E., but there was the final restoration of the nation of Israel in 1948. Christians will reenact the breaking and death of Jesus Christ, his burial, and his resurrection through the hiding and recovering of the afikoman.

The **cup of Elijah** is a symbol of the coming Messianic Age. Elijah will come in the future, bringing the Messiah and his kingdom of universal fellowship. Christians see in the chalice, as well, the representation of the New Covenant of agape-love.

The **fruit of the vine** is the traditional, sweet kosher wine of Passover. The wine is a testimony to centuries of Christian persecution of the Jews. Not only did they falsely accuse the Jews of "killing Christ," they falsely accused them of murdering

Christian children and using their blood to make the bread and wine for use at Passover! In "retaliation," laws were passed that outlawed the sale of wine to Jews during the Easter season and Passover. Jewish wives and mothers carefully horded raisins and made raisin wine throughout those many centuries. The sweet raisin wine became such a feature of Passover that when wine was again permitted, it was purposely sweetened to adjust to the acquired taste.

The two lit candles recall that of all the sects, denominations, and factions of Judaism at the time of the Holy Temple, only two survived to bring light to this dark world. Those two are Rabbinical Judaism of the Torah and Talmud and Messianic Judaism of the Torah and the Gospels.

## NOTES

1. What was unusual is that da Vinci may have been angry about something. Until then, the Last Supper had been portrayed at the moment that Christ changed the bread and wine into his body and blood. No doubt that was what the monks expected to see on the walls of their refectory. But what Leonardo painted for all of the world to see was the moment when Jesus said, "Amen, I say to you, one of you will betray me, one who is eating with me" (Mk 14:18 NAB).

2. Scholars are not in complete agreement. Estimates go from 20,000 to 80,000. Jerusalem was destroyed so thoroughly by the Romans and rebuilt so many times thereafter that we can only guess.

3. The Central Conference of American Rabbis, *Union Haggadah*, 123ff.

4. Ibid., 125,127.

5. Ibid., 127,129.

6. Alcalay, *The Complete Hebrew-English Dictionary*, 4, 9.

7. Wherever the Hebrew text reads, "YHWH," I have written it as "LORD (YHWH)." This is my way of conforming with the tradition of substituting "Adonai" or "LORD" for "YHWH" when it occurs. This is in keeping with the commandment (Ex 20:7). As explained in its introduction, the *New American Bible* renders YWHW as LORD.

8. Yigael Yadin, "Is the Biblical Account of the Israelite Conquest of Canaan Historically Reliable?" *Biblical Archeology Review* 10, no. 1 (January/February 1984): 31-55.

9. L.E. Stager and S.R. Wolff, "Child Sacrifice at Carthage," *Biblical Archeology Review* 10, no. 1 (March/April 1982): 31-55.

10. The pronunciation of some of the letters of the Hebrew alphabet has changed over the years. The sixth letter was pronounced "waw" in biblical Hebrew but is now pronounced "vav" in Sephardic Hebrew.

11. Speiser, "Genesis," *The Anchor Bible* 1:xxii-xliii.; Brown et al., *The Jerome Biblical Commentary* 1:13-17.

12. *Encyclopedia Brittanica* 13 (Chicago: William Benton Publisher, 1967):85.

13. Alcalay, *The Complete Hebrew-English Dictionary,* s.v. "charsit" and "charoset."

14. Brown et al., *Jerome Biblical Commentary* 3:44; 77:76-92

15. Alcalay, *The Complete Hebrew-English Dictionary,* s.v. "Ba'al."

16. Ibid., 2143, 279.

17. de Vaux, "Religious Institutions," *Ancient Israel* 2:417- 418.

18. Bokser, *The Origins of the Seder,* 58, emphasis mine.

19. Eban, *Heritage: Civilization And The Jews,* 69-73.

20. Orthodox Jews and many evangelical Christians do not accept the Four Sources theory as the basis of the Penteteuch.

21. Brown et al., *The Jerome Biblical Commentary* 3:12.

22. Speiser, "Genesis," *Anchor Bible,* 1:8-13.

23. Glatzer, *The Passover Haggadah,* 55-56.

24. Silverman, *Passover Haggadah,* 64.

25. Brown et al., *The Jerome Biblical Commentary,* 68:121.

26. Cornfeld, *Josephus: The Jewish Wars,* 450-451.

27. Raphael, *A Feast of History,* 81,82.

28. Ben-Dov, *In the Shadow of the Temple,* 117-119, 149-153.

29. Glatzer, *Passover Haggadah,* 57.

30. Brown et al., *Jerome Biblical Commentary* 75:142-165.

31. I worked as camp steward for Kaiser Macco Aggregates at the American Camp at S'Dom Israel. The company was involved in building dikes and evaporation pools at the southern end of the Dead Sea, both for the extraction of minerals and the production of electricity.

32. *Encyclopedia Brittanica* 7:116-17.

33. Alcalay, *The Complete Hebrew-English Dictionary,* col. 2809.

34. This section on the tana'im and the Mishnah is taken from Brown et al., *The Jerome Biblical Commentary* 68:119-121.

35. Bokser, *The Origins of the Seder,* 37-49.

36. Tomas de Torquemada, 1420-1498, Inquisitor General of the Spanish Inquisition, began by suspecting converted Jews of practicing Judaism in secret and therefore of being a severe threat to Catholicism. Torquemada and the Inquisition went on to torture and kill many who were suspected of practicing Judaism and, in 1492, to expel the rest.

# TWO

# "Going Up to Jerusalem"

"Of Jerusalem's beauty during the Herodian period, the Talmud tells us: 'Whoever has not seen Jerusalem in its splendor has never seen a lovely city.'"[1] The Talmudists remembered the Holy City as "Jerusalem, the Golden." Part of that memory alluded to the great quantity of gold used to decorate the Holy Temple and many of the palaces and public buildings. But they may have also been referring to the natural stone used to build the ordinary homes. The buff or beige stone could easily be described as "golden," especially at certain times of the day.

The Jews were not alone in their appreciation of the Holy City's beauty and splendor. "Lest this seem a parochial judgment, we have the confirming view of the famous Roman scholar Pliny the Elder, who referred to Jerusalem as 'by far the most renowned city in the Orient, and not of Judea only.'"[2] Much of the credit for its magnificence belongs to King Herod the Great, who ruled from 37 B.C.E. until his death in 4 B.C.E.; "however, the period which bears his name continues to 70

A.D. when the Roman legions crushed the First Jewish Revolt and destroyed Jerusalem." [3]

> As king, Herod aspired to glorify both his kingdom and his name. He was among the most extreme admirers of Hellenistic-Roman culture, and his desire to gain a standing for Jerusalem imbued his capital with a decidedly Hellenistic flavor. This found expression in the dominant architectural style of the buildings and their monumental proportions, as well as in a lifestyle, which called for theaters, gymnasiums, hippodromes and "the games" — a cosmopolitan atmosphere and a luxurious court. This was neither entirely new nor unique in Jerusalem, where Hellenistic influence had already taken a hold among the Jews of the city under the Hasmoneans.[4]

Herod had the complete support of the priests and the Hellenistic wealthy noble families who comprised the Sadducee party. Only in their religious life were they strictly and rigidly Jewish. King Herod and the ruling Hellenists made Jerusalem a city of shining white stone, with magnificent accents of rich, oriental gold.

Jesus may have been referring to Jerusalem when He said, "A city set on a mountain cannot be hidden" (Mt 5:14 NAB) Jerusalem rests upon the crest of the central mountain range of Israel. The city sits on two large hills that range from 2,255 feet to 2,400 feet above sea level. The northern section of the eastern hill is called Mount Moriah and was the site of the Temple. To the south of the Temple Mount is the Ophel, the oldest part of the city. It is now called "The City of David." The eastern hill is bounded by the Kidron Valley on the east with the Mount of Olives beyond it. On the south, the Kidron Valley meets the Hinnon Valley running from the west. The ancient pool of Siloam is located here. This pool supplied water to King David's city. King Hezekiah had a tunnel dug from the spring of Siloam to bring water inside the city walls.

The eastern and western hills are divided by a long shallow valley called Tyropoeon (Valley of the Cheese Makers), also known as the "lower city." Most of the common folk lived and worked here. The western hill is bound on the west and south by the Valley of Hinnom, the infamous "Gehenna" where the city's garbage was dumped and burned. The area also featured public toilets. The Kidron and Hinnom Valleys formed a natural defense for the city. The southern walls of the city were built above these two valleys. To the north, the eastern and western hills joined and extended onto a plateau or plain where there was no natural barrier. As the city grew, a succession of walls was built there to enclose the northern expansion. In times of war, these northern walls had to be especially fortified. On the western hill, which was very broad, stood the palaces of King Herod and the high priest. Here also were the homes and mansions of the priests, the wealthy, and the aristocratic families. Opposite Herod's palace, to the east, was the "upper market." This was the international marketplace where articles from around the world were sold to the rich. Further to the east, across from the main gate to the Temple Mount, was the palace of the Hasmonean kings who ruled over Judea from 135 B.C.E. until it was conquered by Pompey in 63 B.C.E.[5] South of the Hasmonean Palace were the Greek theater and the Hippodrome, where the chariot races and the Greek and Roman spectacles were held. Just north of the Hippodrome, in the Tyropoeon Valley next to the Temple Mount, were the shops where the pilgrims could purchase the birds and animals for sacrifice. They sold the necessary religious articles, such as seven- and eight-branch menorahs and mezuzahs for the doorways and gates of homes. Inside the city gates, especially on the west and north, there were many other markets, each with their own specialties.

Many important trade routes ran through the city. Jerusalem was also an industrial center for stonecutting, pottery, and glassworks. The stonecutters were not only busy carving the monumental pillars and decorations for the buildings that were constructed throughout the city, they were also experts in the arts of mosaics, stone vessels, serving trays, and tables. The pottery workers were experts in both the native and the popular Grecian styles. The glassworkers were well known throughout the Roman Empire; they were especially famous for glass medallions that enclosed etchings in pure gold leaf. They were masters of the art of glass blowing, which was a new technique at that time, as well as the traditional art of glass molding. An enormous glass vessel was found in the ruins of Jerusalem by archaeologists, along with many multicolored jars and vases and thousands of *kohl* sticks, which were used to apply an ancient version of eye shadow called "kohl."[6] Under the archaeologists' spades, the ruins of ancient Jerusalem are revealing a once beautiful, busy, and cosmopolitan city.

## Pilgrim's Process

But Jerusalem was so much more! Even her name suggests her importance. Yerushalayyim (pronounced: yay-roo-shah-LYE-yeem) is in the dual form (the Hebrew language has singular, dual, and plural forms). Although the city was also known in its singular form, Yerushalem (Foundation of Shalem), the dual was preferred. *Shalem* means "completeness, wholeness, and peace." The city's name, in its dual form, emphasizes its prominence as both the political and religious capital of Israel. It is, especially, a place of pilgrimage. "Three times a year, then, every male among you shall appear before the LORD, your God, in the place which He chooses: at the feast of Unleavened Bread (Pesach/Passover), at the feast of Weeks (Shavout/Pentecost), and at the feast of Booths (Sukkot/Tabernacles)" (Dt 16:16 NAB). To make the annual pilgrimage to Jerusalem was "to go up" (*aliyah*) to the mountain of the Lord. "To go up on pilgrimage" (*aliyah le-regel*) was "to make pilgrimage" (chag).[7]

For the pilgrims arriving from the west and from overseas, it was a 2,500-foot climb from the coastal plains up through the mountains and forests. It was an even greater climb for those arriving from the east and the valley of the Jordan. From near the Jordan river, the pilgrims had to climb 3,800 feet on a winding road through hot and barren hills above a wilderness of deserts and wastelands. This route was unpleasant and dangerous. Gangs of thugs would waylay the weak and rob them, sometimes killing them. Near Jerusalem the valleys and hills became green at last, and the pilgrims passed through villages of friendly folks. Then they gained sight of the Mount of Olives with its terraces and gardens. It was this route that Jesus usually took on his pilgrimages to Jerusalem.

The pilgrims always came in groups, and they came singing. Psalms 120 through 134 are called the "Songs of Ascents" or Shirim HaMa'alot. Tradition says that the Psalms represent the fifteen steps from the Court of the Women to the Courts of Israel and of the Priests where the Temple itself stood. The Levites chanted these same Psalms on those steps as they assisted in the sacrifices and ceremonies that took place in the Court of the Priests.

Pilgrims came to the city by the thousands. The Talmud even records a Passover celebrated by three million! An elaborate system of waystations and inns existed to accommodate these great throngs as they ascended in song to Jerusalem. Over the centuries the city had been built to accommodate all of these people. Immediately after the return from Exile, the rebuilt Jerusalem was small and so were the number of pilgrims. At that time there was enough lodging within the city and enough room within the Temple courts for everyone to sacrifice and eat their Passover supper there. But in the second century B.C.E., Jerusalem began to grow into a city that would soon become many times the size it had been at the time of David and Solomon. At the same time the number of Jews living outside of the Holy Land grew phenomenally. Historians estimate that in those times more than six million Jews lived outside of Israel compared to two million who lived inside. And the Jews of the Diaspora came in pilgrimage to Jerusalem in amazing numbers. During the period of time from the third to the second century B.C.E., the ever-increasing number of worshipers eventually made it impossible for everyone to prepare and eat the Passover in the Temple courts. By the end of the first century B.C.E., Jerusalem could no longer supply enough lodgings for the multitudes of pilgrims. The authorities designated an area about one sabbath-walk's distance from the city as a legal lodging area for pilgrims. (A sabbath's walk was as far as a person could walk on the Sabbath—about two miles from one's home.) This included some important villages, such as Bethany, where Jesus stayed when He came to Jerusalem. The Passover Supper, however, still had to be eaten within the city itself. Courtyards and rooftops had to be assigned to groups of pilgrims. "Although it is written, 'It must be eaten in one and the same house' (Ex 12:46 NAB), nevertheless they eat it (the pascal lamb) in their courtyards and on their rooftops" (Tosefta Pesach 6.11).[8] The Talmud also noted that two or more groups sharing the same area were required to ignore each other. This preserved each group's identity as a "family unit" (BT Pesachim 86a). Several families could share Passover together, but they had to band together into identifiable groups. Large groups of families formed into Passover associations (chavurot) and always celebrated their Passovers together. However, groups of strangers and groups not formally banded together could not mix.

By mid-first century B.C.E., the estimated population of Jerusalem was 80,000. Josephus said that Jerusalem's population was 120,000, but some historians consider that number more symbolic than accurate. Twelve is the number of the tribes of Israel and twelve times 10,000 would have represented a great number.[9] Josephus is usually very accurate in his calculations, and it might have been that he was counting the population of the extended Jerusalem that included those villages within the sabbath's walk. Some historians  believe that the population may have been as high as 150,000. Whichever number is correct, the city swelled to ten, fifteen, and possibly twenty times its size during the pilgrimage festivals. The logistics must have been horrendous! In our century, the only comparison is the annual *hadj* to Mecca. That city does not seem capable of supporting the incredible number of pilgrims who converge on it every year, but it does. And so did Jerusalem. "Hadj" and "chag," it is interesting to note, come from the same Semitic root.

Elaborate preparations had to be made by the residents of Jerusalem. First of all, every group had to register with the priests to secure the number of paschal lambs they would need. Then they had to arrange with one householder for a place to stay and, more than likely, with another for a room in which to eat the Passover supper. The householder could not charge for the use of the rooms by the pilgrims for the seder, but traditionally the pilgrims gave the skins of the paschal lambs to the householder as a token of their gratitude. These arrangements had to be made as much as a year in advance.

## The Holy Temple

The main road from the east, over the Mount of Olives, was the one Jesus usually took when he traveled to Jerusalem. Coming from this direction, he would enter the city by passing though the Temple courts. He would ascend the Temple Mount from the Kidron Valley and pass through the Golden Gate, which opened onto the Court of the Gentiles through the Porch of Solomon. The Court of the Gentiles was an enormous and magnificent enclosure. It was a trapezoid, wider on the north than on the south, and more than 1,250 feet around its perimeter. This made it much larger than any other temple in the Greco-Roman world — three-and-a-half times as large as that of Jupiter Heliopolitanus at Ba'albek in Lebanon and twice the size of the Roman Forum. It was truly one of the wonders of the classic world.

The Court of the Gentiles was completely surrounded by porticoes or porches. On the eastern, northern, and western sides, these porches were approximately 150 feet deep. Marble columns, forty feet high and made of the whitest marble, supported the flat roofs. The ceilings were paneled in luxurious cedar. The porches were built on a platform that made them appear even loftier. These porches were places for assembly and study as well as worship. The portico on the east, directly opposite the Temple, was known as the Porch of Solomon. Here is where Jesus taught and where the first Christians met for study and preaching (Acts 2:46).

The southern portico was particularly grand. This two-story complex built by Herod the Great when he enlarged the Temple was called the Stoa Basilike or Royal Portico — Chanuyot in Hebrew. It consisted of 162 columns, thirty feet high and four-and-a-half feet wide, each cut from a single stone. Each was topped by a Corinthian capitol. Within the Royal Portico, there was a large basilica or assembly hall, consisting of a central nave and two side aisles. According to the Talmud, forty years before the destruction of the Temple, the Sanhedrin moved its meeting place from the Chamber of Hewn Stone, on consecrated ground within the Court of the Priests, and took its seat in the basilica of the Chanuyot.[10] Josephus describes the Chanuyot in his *Antiquities XV* as a beautiful edifice "more deserving of mention than any under the sun." The Royal Portico and its basilica, because they were late additions, were not considered "consecrated ground." Secular activities, such as the selling of animals for sacrifice and the changing of pagan coins for the obligatory "Temple shekel" could take place within them.

The entire Court of the Gentiles was paved with thousands of thick limestone blocks, some of which are still in place. On the southwest corner of the Temple Mount, where the western porch met the Royal Portico, there was a tower-like structure called the Pinnacle of the Temple. From here the priests would signal the beginning of special events such as the New Moon, the Sabbath, and the sacrifices. Recent excavations below the Temple Mount have uncovered one of the stones of this structure pushed down by the Romans. On it were engraved the Hebrew words, "(Belonging) to the place [literally, house] of trumpeting...."[11] These signals were made either by silver trumpets or by the *shofar*, which was a ram's horn. The priests were in charge of the calendar; they determined when each month began. After physically sighting the new moon, they would signal from the Pinnacle of the Temple that Rosh Chodesh or a New Month had begun. On the Mount of Olives, a signal fire would be lit alerting those beyond the sound of the trumpet. More signal fires would be lit to advise those living in Galilee and beyond the Jordan River, as far as Bablyon. This system, however, had a problem. Between Judea and Galilee lay Samaria. The Samaritans loved to throw the system off by lighting bogus fires that would cause those in Galilee and beyond to light their fires a day too soon. Long before the first century, the Jewish authorities gave up trying to stop the Samaritans. To compensate for this disruption, they decreed that Jews living outside of Judea had to celebrate two days of every major Jewish holiday, except Yom Kippur, so that at least one of the days would be the right one. In Galilee, and throughout the Diaspora, Passover became an eight-day celebration instead of seven. It began with two nights of seder instead of one. This law, from the time of Jesus, is still in effect. Jews living outside of Israel celebrate two nights of seder and an eight-day Passover. Those living in the Israel have only to celebrate one night of seder and a seven-day feast.

The great Court of the Gentiles could be entered from eight gates.[12] On the south, from the open area of the Ophel, worshipers ascended broad stairways, past the low building containing public mikva'ot, and onto a terrace that ran the full length of the great supporting wall. There were two gates in this wall called the Hulda Gates. The one on the left was a double gate; the one on the right was a triple gate. From the Hulda Gates, a series of steps led upward onto the Royal Portico. Pilgrims and worshipers ascended to the Court of the Gentiles through the triple gate and descended from worship through the double gate. On the west there were four more gates. On the southwest corner, under the Pinnacle of the Temple, a monumental stairway mounted on a great pier ascended from the Tyropoeon Valley up to the Royal Portico. It is now called Robinson's Arch after the man who discovered its remains. North of Robinson's Arch was another gateway some 28 feet high. It opened onto the valley, then ascended through a series of stairs and galleries to the Court of the Gentiles. The Mishnah, Middot 1,3, calls this the Kophonos Gate. North of the Kophonos Gate, a very large viaduct formed a wide bridge that connected the upper city with the western porticos of the Temple. The viaduct carried water from springs near Hebron to the Temple area. The viaduct was part of the main thoroughfare of the city, which ran due west from the main gate of the Temple to the main gate of the city. There was also access to the viaduct from the Tyropoeon Valley by a broad L-shaped staircase similar to Robinson's Arch. Worshipers crossing this viaduct bridge entered into the Court of the Gentiles through one of the most imposing Temple gates. The doors of the gate were covered with plates of silver. Even the sockets on which they rotated were covered with silver. North of this gate, there was another gate, now called the Warren Gate after its discoverer. Like the Kophonos Gate, it opened onto the valley, and from it worshipers ascended to the Court of Gentiles through a series of stairways and galleries. On the north, the Temple courts were entered by a single public gate that passed a number of pools: the Stuthion Pool, the Sheep Pool, and the Pool of Israel.

Another gate on the north side of the Temple was one the Jews did not like to think about. This was the gate into the impregnable Roman fortress called the Antonia. The four towers of the Antonia overlooked the Temple courts and allowed the Roman authorities to watch over most of the activity taking place there. They could and did send Roman soldiers through the gate of the Antonia to suppress any disturbance. The Romans had no compunction about mixing the blood of worshipers with that of their own sacrifices (Lk 13:1).

There was only one gate through the Porch of Solomon, the eastern portico. This gate, facing east toward the rising sun, was huge and ornate. It was, and still is, the famous Golden Gate, although the present Golden Gate stands over the one Jesus entered.[13] For Jews, Christians, and Moslems, this is the holy gate.

> The Final Judgment of mankind and the messianic associations of Jewish, Christian, and Moslem traditions are linked with this gate. In the Middle Ages, Jews prayed there as they do now at the Western or Wailing Wall. Christians have always associated the Golden Gate with Palm Sunday as well as with the second coming of Jesus. Moslems wanted to be buried near it because the Koran connects Allah's final judgment with this gate. Over the centuries...the Jewish and Christian presence near the gate shrank, while the Moslem cemetery enlarged along the city's eastern wall to the gate's very portals.[14]

The Gospels record that when Jesus entered Jerusalem triumphally, he descended from the Mount of Olives, crossed the Kidron Valley and then ascended to the Temple through the Golden Gate (Mk 11:1- 11). Inside the present Golden Gate, there is a Byzantine structure, possibly a chapel, that contains columns taken from the ruins of Herod's Royal Portico, the Chanuyot. The fame and recognition that the eastern gate still has gives us an inkling of just how beautiful the Golden Gate must have been when Jesus entered Jerusalem through it. Its name suggests that its doors were plated with sheets of gold.

Through these eight magnificent and ornate gates, thousands entered the Temple for worship, study, and sacrifice. The Court of the Gentiles alone could hold many thousands of people. Even Gentiles, hence its name, could enter sections of this court and marvel at this extraordinary structure. In the northern third of the Court of the Gentiles, opposite the Golden Gate, stood an even more imposing series of complexes. These were the sacred sanctuaries of the Temple itself. The whole complex was called in Hebrew the Azarot. It was surrounded by two raised terraces. The first, which filled nearly two thirds of the Court of the Gentiles, was a platform outlined by a balustrade and latticed railing. This balustrade was about five feet high and had, at regular intervals, stone slabs on which warnings were written in Greek and Latin, "No foreigner [Gentile] is allowed within the balustrade surrounding the sanctuary and the court enclosed. Whoever is caught will be personally responsible for his ensuing death." Two of these slabs have been found, one in 1871 and the other in 1935. They are now in museums.[15]

Fourteen steps led up from the first terrace to a second, narrower terrace. These terraces with the warning balustrade protected the outer wall of the sanctuary called the *cheyl* (rampart). The outer wall of the cheyl was some 65 feet high and constructed of white stone overlaid with gold plate. It was said that from a distance the cheyl looked like a mountain covered with snow. Nine gates — four on the north side, four on the south, and one on the east — passed through the walls of the cheyl into the inner courts of the sanctuary. The western side of the Azarot was the back of the Temple edifice itself and therefore had no gate. Each gate had five steps leading up to it from the surrounding terrace. The nine gates were overlaid with gold and silver. The four gates on the north and the four southern gates were each 50 feet high and 25 feet wide. Each gate had double doors. The gate that opened into the Court of the Women from the east, opposite the Golden Gate, was some 80 feet high and about 65 feet wide. Its decorations were even more magnificent than the others. The gold and silver plates on its doors were very thick. Its doorposts and lintels were luxuriously decorated. This gate was deservedly known as the Beautiful Gate.

When Jesus and his disciples entered the Temple through the Golden Gate to participate in the worship and sacrifices, they ascended the two terraces surrounding the cheyl. They ascended five more steps and passed through the Beautiful Gate and into the Court of the Women (Mk 12:41-44). The Court of the Women was a large square; however, much of its space was taken up by gateroom towers that stood in each corner and to either side of the four gates that opened into it. Each gateroom was a tower 50 feet square and some 66 feet high. At the left side of the Beautiful Gate, the gateroom was called the Chamber of the Nazirites. To the right the gateroom was called the Chamber of Wood. Across from this and opposite to it was the Chamber of Lepers, and across from the Chamber of the Nazirites was the Chamber of Oil. There were porches or galleries around the three sides of the court. Because of the gateroom towers, these galleries and the court itself were in the shape of a cross. One of these gaterooms also contained the treasury. In the gallery outside of the treasury stood thirteen trumpet-shaped receptacles for the collection of alms. During the centuries of the Second Temple, Jews had to pay a Temple tax of a half-shekel or a whole shekel. In addition, the pilgrims made free will offerings of gold and silver for the enrichment of the holy place. Gifts from wealthy pilgrims could be large. Two Jews from Alexandrian Egypt donated the magnificent Nicanor Gate that opened from the Court of the Women into the Court of Israel and the Court of the Priests.

According to the Talmud, great communal functions were conducted in the Court of the Women. The court did not exclude men — it was open to anyone in a state of Levitical purity — but women could not pass beyond it. From here, worshipers could observe the sacrifices through the Nicanor Gate. The Court of Women served as a secondary sanctuary or outer court to the inner sanctuary of the priests. However, it was actually smaller than the inner court. All communal functions relating to the divine worship were conducted there. Upon completion of the sacrificial rites on the Day of Atonement (Yom Kippur), the high priest read the Torah before the people in the Court of the Women.[16] Once every seven years, on the Feast of Tabernacles (Sukkot), either the high priest or the king read the Torah there before the assembled worshipers.[17] There, too, the people gathered to witness and rejoice in the torchlight procession of the priests and Levites in the magnificent ceremony of the Simchat Beth Ha-shoeva (Rejoicing at the Source of Water), when water was drawn from the Spring of Siloam and brought in jubilant procession into the Temple for use in the ceremonies and libations of the Temple ritual. That ceremony occurred on the second night of Sukkot.[18] The Talmud says that anyone who had not seen the Ceremony of the Pouring of Water had never seen a joyous and impressive celebration.

From the Court of the Women, fifteen steps ascended to the Nicanor Gate. Those fifteen steps were fairly shallow and were shaped as a complete half-circle like a miniature amphitheater.

The Levites stood on these steps when they sang the fifteen Songs of Ascents[19] and the Hallel on the pilgrimage feasts. The Nicanor Gate, even larger than the Beautiful Gate, was made of Corinthian bronze and was considered more valuable and more ornate than all of the other gates. It was named after its wealthy donors from Alexandria. Only men could enter the Court of Israel through the Nicanor Gate. The Court of Israel was also known as the Court of the Men. The Court of Israel opened onto the Court of the Priests where the daily and festival sacrificial rites were conducted. Only the priests and Levites could enter the Court of the Priests, which was slightly higher than the Court of the Men. However, worshipers in the Court of Israel had a clear and unobstructed view of all of the ceremonies in the Court of the Priests. They also had an unobstructed view of the magnificent facade of the Temple itself.

The Court of the Priests was a rectangular, porticoed enclosure that completely surrounded the Temple. In the open area before the facade of the Temple stood the slaughterhouse, the bronze laver, and the great altar of sacrifice. Within the portico, along the southern wall, was the Lishkat Ha-Gazit (Chamber of Hewn Stone) where the Sanhedrin met before it moved to the basilica of the Royal Portico.

On the right, facing the facade of the Temple, stood the slaughterhouse. Alongside it was a large, marble table and stone posts with hooks from which animals could be hung for skinning and butchering. The sacrificial animals had to be killed with a sharp knife as quickly and as painlessly as possible. Levites cut the throat through both carotid arteries, collected the blood in basins, and then poured the blood onto the sides of the altar of sacrifice. They washed and salted the meat, as a rite of purification, before taking them to the altar. Sometimes they added various spices "as a pleasing fragrance."

To the left and south of the slaughterhouse was the great Altar of Sacrifice. The dimensions at its base were 82 feet by 82 feet.

It was made of undressed stones because "iron was made to shorten a man's life, whereas, the Altar was erected in order to lengthen a man's years."[20] The altar rose in a series of indentations, much like a Maya pyramid. A platform around the top allowed the priests and Levites to tend the fire and the sacrifices. On the four corners of the top of the altar, there were rising projections called the "horns of the altar." The top of the altar was a large sunken area where a perpetual fire burned. Over that firepit was a bronze grate upon which the sacrifices were placed. Some sacrifices were completely consumed in a burnt offering, but most were roasted and then shared in a communion meal. Priests and Levites climbed to the altar via a ramp, made of the same undressed stone, from the south side of the altar.

Behind and to the west of the Altar of Sacrifices stood the great bronze laver. This bronze bowl, sitting on the backs of twelve life-size bronze oxen facing the four directions, held the huge amount of water needed for the purification rites and libations. After the daily sacrifice, the water was used to clean the Court of the Priests.

Both Josephus and the Talmud give descriptions of the morning sacrifice. Upon awakening, the priests and Levites washed and then completely immersed themselves in the ritual bath. Then they dressed in linen drawers. Over those they wore a long, white linen tunic that covered them from their necks to just above their feet. They secured the tunic with sashes of variegated work and colors. They wore conically shaped linen hats with a heavily brocaded band at the bottom (Ex 28:40-43). The priests then left their quarters, which were underneath the Temple courts, and ascended through passageways that were lit by clay lamps placed in niches along the walls. They passed in doublefile through the portals of the Chamber of Hewn Stone and formed a large circle inside. Then they drew lots to determine their duties. The presiding chief priest directed a priest to go up onto one of the towers surrounding the inner courts. He was then asked, "Does the light of dawn in the east spread as far as Mount Hebron?" If the answer was yes, the chief priest ordered a ewe lamb brought up from the pen of ewe lambs in the Chamber of the Hearth, which was located below the Royal Portico. The ewe lamb was taken to the slaughterhouse where its throat was slit and its blood drawn into a basin. Then it was skinned and dismembered. The parts were salted and placed on the marble table. The priests returned to the Chamber of Hewn Stone where they all recited the first three verses of the Sh'ma, Judaism's great confession of faith,

> Hear, O Israel! The LORD (YHWH) is our God, the LORD (YHWH) alone! Therefore, you shall love the LORD (YHWH), your God, with all your heart, and with all your soul, and with all your strength. Take to heart these words which I enjoin on you today. Drill them into your children. Speak of them at home and abroad, whether you are busy or at rest. Bind them at your wrist as a sign and let them be as a pendant on your forehead. Write them on the doorposts of your houses and on your gates (Dt 6:4-9 NAB).

The priests drew lots twice more, once to decide who would carry the censers and spread the incense over the altar and again to decide who would place the sections of the sacrificial lamb, first over the lower level of the ramp leading up to the high altar and then up to altar itself. A priest hurled a gong-like instrument called a *margrefa* onto the pavement of the Court of the Priests, and the clatter alerted all of the priests and Levites to attend to the morning song sung by the Levites and to the communal sacrifices. The lay worshipers assembled, the men in the Court of Israel and the women in the Court of Women near the open Nicanor Gate. Ninety-three officiating priests stood in a group on the south, at the foot of the ramp leading up to the altar. They carried censers, torches, fire pans, tongs, and other paraphernalia. They blessed the worshipers with the ineffable

Name of the LORD (YHWH). They poured libations of wine for the meal oblation and brought sheets of matzot for the high priest. As the officiating priest bent to pour the libation, the deputy high priests raised a standard and signaled the leader of the Levitical band to strike the cymbals and for priests to blow the silver trumpets. The Levites sang the prescribed daily Psalms and portions of the Torah. As they finished each verse, they stopped for the priests to blow a musical fanfare on the silver trumpets. The worshipers bowed in prayer.[21] While the ministering priests prayed and the Levites attended the sacrifice on the top of the altar, other priests blew trumpets as the choir of Levites sang to the accompaniment of a variety of instruments.[22] The awe-inspiring ceremony lasted several hours.

After the morning sacrifice, the priests were kept busy the rest of the morning with offering sacrifices for individual worshipers. There were guilt or sin offerings, atonement offerings, appeasement offerings, and thanksgiving offerings. The offerings might be a lamb, a turtledove, or a young pigeon when brought by the poor. Such sacrifices went on for the rest of the day.[23]

Among the worshipers one morning were Joseph and Mary, who had brought their infant son, Jesus, for the obligatory rites of ransoming back their firstborn.

> When the days were completed for their purification according to the law of Moses, they took him up to Jerusalem to present him to the Lord, just as it is written in the law of the Lord, "Every male that opens the womb shall be consecrated to the Lord," and to offer the sacrifice of "a pair of turtledoves or two young pigeons," in accordance with the dictate in the law of the Lord (Lk 2:22-24; Lv 12:8 NAB).

Joseph had also to pay a ransom price to the treasury to buy Jesus back from the Lord. When the morning sacrifice was over, they brought Jesus to the Nicanor Gate and presented him to one of the officiating priests. Joseph handed the two turtledoves, or pigeons, to the assisting Levite and followed him through the Court of Israel. Joseph stopped just short of the step that led up to the Court of the Priests. Mary watched from the Nicanor Gate. The Levite took the two birds to the marble table of the slaughterhouse and slit their throats. He drained their blood into a small basin made of silver or gold. One of the minor priests took the basin from the Levite and, crossing over to the side of the Altar of Sacrifice, he poured the blood onto its side. The Levite plucked all the feathers from the two birds, washed them with water and then rubbed them with salt. The Levite was then joined by one of the priests who accompanied him up the ramp to the top of the altar. While the Levite laid the birds over the grate to be consumed by the fire, the priest chanted the prescribed prayers. The prayer of the priest was a familiar blessing known to everyone.

> Blessed are You, O LORD (YHWH) our God
> King of all creation,
> Who gives life to us
> and sustains us
> and has brought us to this season.

Mary and Joseph and all of the people responded. In the Temple ceremonies, the simple "Amen" was not used. All prayers were concluded with the Temple Doxology,

> Praised be his name
> whose glorious kingdom
> is forever and ever.
> Amen![24]

If the Temple Doxology sounds familiar, it is because it passed into the liturgy of the Orthodox church. There it became attached to the Lord's Prayer where it was found by the translators of the King James Bible, who did not recognize it as a doxology. It then became firmly fixed in the Protestant Lord's

Prayer. It has now been accepted into the Liturgy of the Roman Catholic church.[25]

After Joseph returned to Mary and Jesus at the Nicanor Gate, they were met by the prophetess Anna (Lk 2:36-38) and Shimeon who uttered this beautiful prayer,

> Now, Master, you may let your servant go
>   in peace, according to your word,
> for my eyes have seen your salvation,
>   which you prepared in sight of all the peoples,
> a light for revelation to the Gentiles,
>   and glory for your people Israel (Lk 2:29-32 NAB).

According to a pious tradition going back to at least the fourth century C.E., the Altar of Sacrifice stood above the spot where the Dome of the Rock now stands. But recent investigations of the Temple Mount have suggested that the altar stood some 300 feet north of the Dome of the Rock.[26]

Dominating the Court of the Priests was the most splendid edifice in the whole world — the Holy Temple itself. The facade was more than 160 feet across and 160 feet high. In the center of the facade, there was a doorless gate 115 feet high and 40 feet across. It opened onto and gave a clear view of the Porch of the Temple. Twelve steps ascended from the Court of the Priests to the Porch of the Temple. The entire interior of the porch was plated with pure gold. Its grandeur represented the vast expanse of the heavens. Since the facade faced due east, the rays of the rising sun would strike that expanse of gold and would force the worshiper to look away. The building behind the facade was narrower than the facade by some 66 feet, although it had the same height. The interior of the Temple was fully visible through a golden door some 90 feet high and 26 feet across. Above the door were golden grapevines holding grape clusters as tall as a man. The sanctuary inside was a two-story room 100 feet tall, 66 feet deep, and 33 feet across. This room was called the Kodesh (The Holy Place). At the far end of this room, there was a huge curtain called the Veil of the Temple that separated off the Kodesh Ha-kodashim (Holy of Holies). The curtain was a Babylonian tapestry of marvelous craftsmanship. It was embroidered with threads of blue, scarlet, purple, and fine linen. Blue represented the sky; scarlet, fire; purple, the sea; and fine linen, the earth. The design of the Temple veil represented the panorama of the heavens with its sun, moon, and stars.

The interior of the Kodesh was paneled in fine cedar and included three of the most famous works of art: The great seven-branched Menorah, the Altar of Shew Bread, and the Altar of Incense. The golden Menorah stood on an octagonal base that supported a straight shaft as tall as a man, from which curved six branches — three from the right side and three from the left side. The branches from each side curved up to the same height as the central shaft. Upon each of these was placed an oil lamp. Josephus said that the seven lamps symbolized the seven then-known planets. Upon the Altar of Shew Bread were placed twelve loaves or sheets of matzot. They represented the Twelve Tribes of Israel. In the Book of Leviticus (24:5-9), this is called the Bread of Presence. The Altar of Incense, also gold, burned frankincense, stacte, onycha, and galbanum. To these were added myrrh, cassia, spikenard, saffron, mace, costus, cinnamon, and salt. An herb was mixed with all of these to make the smoke rise vertically. The golden Altar of Shew Bread and the great Menorah stood to either side of the Altar of Incense. The Arch of Titus in Rome depicts these three great works of art being carried in the triumphal victory parade celebrating Emperor Titus' capture of Jerusalem.

Only priests chosen by lot could enter the Kodesh and maintain these holy objects.

> Once, when it was the turn of Zechariah's class and he was fulfilling his functions as a priest before God, it fell to him by lot

according to priestly usage to enter the sanctuary of the Lord and offer incense. While the full assembly of people was praying outside at the incense hour, an angel of the Lord appeared to him, standing at the right of the altar of incense. Zechariah was deeply disturbed upon seeing him, and overcome by fear (Lk 1:8-13, translation mine).

Behind the veil was the Kodesh Ha-kodeshim or Holy of Holies. The room was 33 feet in height, depth, and width: a perfect cube. It was unapproachable, inviolable, and invisible to all except the high priest, who could only enter it once a year on the Day of Atonement (Yom Kippur). On that day he would burn incense on the spot where the Ark of the Covenant was supposed to have stood. To enter the Holy of Holies, the high priest had to lift the veil and pass under it. The room inside was completely dark except for the light from the burning coals in the fire pan he was carrying. There were no windows or other sources of light in this most sacred sanctuary. The Holy of Holies of this Second Temple was empty. The ark was lost at the time Solomon's Temple was destroyed. Some priests hid it from the Babylonian conquerors, and after the Exile no one could find it. On the Day of Atonement, the high priest simply put the firepan, the burning coals, and incense on the spot where the Ark of the Covenant should have stood.

The Holy of Holies was also known as the Debir from the Hebrew verb, *dabar*, which means, "to speak, command, accomplish something." The Kodesh Ha-kodashim was considered the "Place of Oracle" as well.

The Holy Temple was also known as the Beyt Mikdash (Dwelling Place of the Holy One). Here is where God had established his house among his people or, in the Hebrew idiom, had "pitched his tent among his people." From there, God called his people to come to Him and celebrate with Him the joyous feast days. His Holy Temple made all of Jerusalem holy. It gave to the physical dimensions of the Holy City far more important spiritual dimensions. That is why its name is in the dual form: Yerushalayyim. It is the site of both a capital city encompassing the heart of people and a Temple enshrining the soul of a nation. To this day, Jews everywhere remember that once, and someday again, magnificent city that Jesus knew.

Ten portions of beauty descended to the earth,
Jerusalem received nine,
and the rest of the world one![27]

## NOTES

1. Mazar, "Excavations Near Temple Mount Reveal Splendors of Herodian Jerusalem," *Biblical Archaeology Review* 6, no. 4 (July/August 1980): 44, quoting Babylonian Talmud, Succah 51b).

2. Ibid., 45, quoting Pliny's *Natural History,* 70.

3. Ibid., 47.

4. Avigad, *Discovering Jerusalem,* 81.

5. Judas Maccabeus defeated the Seleucid king, Antiochus IV Epiphanes, and won for the Jewish people complete religious and some political freedom from the Greek kingdom of Syria. His family became the priest-kings of Judea. The name of the Hasmonean dynasty was derived from the family name of Judas, which was "Hashmon" or "Asamonaeus" in Greek.

6. Avigad, "A Craft Center for Stone and Glass," *Biblical Archaeology Review* 9, no.6 (November/December 1983): 45-65.

7. Alcalay, *The Complete Hebrew-English Dictionary,* col. 1905.

8. Jeremias, *The Eucharistic Words Of Jesus,* 43.

9. The same kind of computation is found in the Apocalypse, the Book of Revelation. In chapter seven, it says that the number of the servants of God is 144,000. 12 is the number of the tribes of Israel and, again, 12 is the number of the tribes of the New Israel. The number 1,000, or "elef" in Hebrew, means "community," "family," and "tribe." In the Hebrew sense, then, the servants of God are a great and royal tribe. That is, 12 times 12 times 1,000 equals 144,000.

10. Ben-Dov, *In The Shadow Of The Temple,* 124-127.

11. Aaron Demsky "When The Priests Trumpeted The Onset Of The Sabbath," *Biblical Archaeology Review* 9, no. 1 (November/December 1986): 24-37.

12. Ben-Dov, *In The Shadow Of The Temple,* 135-147.

13. James Fleming, "The Undiscovered Gate Beneath Jerusalem's Golden Gate," *Biblical Archaeology Review* 9, no. 1 (January/February 1983): 24-37.

14. Ibid., 24.

15. Ben-Dov, *In The Shadow of The Temple*, 102.

16. Cornfeld, *Jospehus: The Jewish Wars*, 356 n. 199 [b].

17. Ibid.

18. S. Safrai, *The Jewish People in the First Century*, 866-867.

19. Cornfeld, *Josephus: The Jewish Wars*, 357 n. 206 [a].

20. Ibid., 360, n. 225 [b].

21. Ibid., 350, nn.

22. Ibid.

23. Ibid.

24. Eric Werner, *The Sacred Bridge*, 277.

25. Ibid., 278: *Talmud Yerushalmi (The Jerusalem Talmud)* of the Minim,

At the close of every Benediction in the Temple they used to say, "For everlasting." But after the Sadducees — the heretics — had taught corruptly and said that there is but one world (no resurrection), it was ordained that they should say, "From everlasting even to everlasting."

Gemara: "Why is this so? Because one does not respond 'Amen' in the sanctuary. How do we know that one does not respond 'Amen' in the Sanctuary? Because it is written, 'Stand up and bless the Lord (YHWH) your God, from everlasting even to everlasting,' and let them say 'Blessed be Thy glorious Name this is exalted above all blessing and praise.' Is it possible that all the blessings had only one praise? Scripture teaches us that (they) exalted for each blessing and praise, etc."

26. Historians are no longer sure what the famous rock might have supported during the time of the Second Temple. It may have been the foundation of a large platform from which the Torah was read to crowds too large to fit into the Court of the Women. "A reasonable conjecture is that the rock was the Stone of Claimants (Mishnah Ta'anit 3:8) from which announcements of lost and found property were made." Asher S. Kaufman, *Biblical Archaeology Review* 9, no. 2 (March/April 1983): 41-59.

27. Eban, *Heritage: Civilization and the Jews*, 98.

# THREE

# *A Week of Preparation*

Now the Passover of the Jews was near, and many went up from the country to Jerusalem before Passover to purify themselves (Jn 11:55 NAB).

Six days before Passover Jesus came to Bethany, where Lazarus was, whom Jesus had raised from the dead (John 12:1 NAB).

Jesus stayed at the house of Simon the Leper, which may well have been the home of Martha, Mary, and Lazarus. Since Martha[1] and Mary[2] were living with Lazarus,[3] their brother, we can assume they were unmarried. Simon the Leper might have been their father or grandfather. The house would have held his name, as founder and patriarch of the family, until a more famous descendant came along. Then the house would be renamed "House of so-and-so," for instance, Beyt El'azar. As a leper who had the means to take care of himself and his family, Simon would have been forced by law to live east of Jerusalem — that is, downwind from the city. Ancient people believed leprosy could be spread by the wind. Bethany[4] was situated on the eastern slope of the Mount of Olives and was within a sabbath's walk — about two miles — of Jerusalem.

We can guess from the bits of evidence in the Gospels that Martha, Mary, and Lazarus were Pharisees. The rabbis had their strength in the lower and middle classes. While Martha, Mary, and Lazarus were certainly not poor (they were wealthy enough to afford a private family tomb), there is no reference to servants. In fact, Martha is always described as busy with cooking and housework. Like most rabbinical Jews, they had Hebrew and Aramaic names, although these are recorded in the Gospels in their Greek forms. The clearest evidence, though, is Martha's statement to Jesus, "I know he [Lazarus] will rise, in the resurrection on the last day" (Jn 11:24 NAB). The Pharisees believed in the resurrection of the dead while the Sadducees did not and denied it (Lk 20:27).

Jesus arrived in Bethany six days before the Passover simply because there was so much to do before the festival. He did not come alone; he brought his whole family with him. By law, Passover had to be observed by *l'bay-avot* or "by the whole household." This included all men, women, and children (Ex 12:3,4,47). Jesus' entourage included his mother and her sister, Mary Magdalene, the Twelve Apostles and their mothers, wives, children, and grandchildren, plus the disciples and their family members. The entourage of a few hundred people or more made up a chavurah or Passover association. It was just like thousands of other such groups who came to Jerusalem at the same time.

## Housecleaning for Passover

Jesus had made arrangements well in advance with the village of Bethany to have lodging set aside for all of the members of his chavurah. When they settled in, they joined members of the regular households in the necessary preparations for the feast. There was much work to be done.

The pilgrims had arrived right in the middle of intensive housecleaning. By law, no leaven, no product of leavening, and nothing that could become leavened could exist in the household for the seven days of the feast (Ex 12:15). This was a strict commandment. The scribes or *soferim*[5], who were the authorities on the fine points of the Law, taught that the offending *chametz* (leaven) could be lurking in the dust in the numerous nooks and crannies of the houses and buildings. The whole house had to be cleaned and scrubbed. This cleaning took several weeks and required help from everyone, even the children. The cleaning and scrubbing ended on the evening before the day of the Passover sacrifice when the father of the house conducted the official "search for the leaven." The mother prepared by putting some bread crumbs on a window sill or in the corner of each of the rooms. The father began the search by reciting the blessing:

> Blessed are You, O Lord (YHWH) our God,
> King of all creation,
> Who has sanctified us with your commandments
> And commanded us that we must remove all leaven.

The father would then search the whole house with a wooden scoop and a feather. The older sons would accompany him. One would hold a lighted lamp to aid in the search. When they found the offending chametz, they would remove it by sweeping the crumbs onto the wooden scoop with the feather. When the search was over, the father would carefully bind the chametz and the feather onto the wooden scoop with an ample piece of cloth so that nothing could escape. With the conclusion of the search, and when all of the crumbs were securely bound onto the scoop, all of the men would gather together and recite:

> May all of the leaven in my possession
> Which I have not seen or removed,
> Be regarded as non-existent and considered
> As the mere dust of the earth.

The next morning, the men would build a small fire in the courtyard of the house or in the street out in front. The father would then put the scoop and its contents on the fire and burn them up. If there were more than one group searching the house—and some of the houses were very large—then each group would place their bound scoops on the fire at the same time. When the chametz was burned up, they would make the final declaration:

> May all leaven in my possession,
> Whether I have seen it or not,
> Or whether I have removed it or not,
> Be regarded as non-existent and considered
> As mere dust of the earth. [6]

## Kashering

The preparation was far from complete. All of the pots and pans and eating utensils had to be cleaned and purified as well. And there were enough pots and pans to keep Martha and the Marys busy for some time. In a Jewish household, there were two complete sets of pots and pans and eating utensils for ordinary use because of the commandment against boiling a kid in its mother's milk (Ex 23:19 & Dt 14:21). Keeping this commandment, according to the rabbis, required separating dairy meals from meat meals. Meat could never be mixed with dairy products. To further insure this, families kept separate cooking and eating utensils for dairy meals and meat meals. For Passover, though, the household needed to keep the rule against mixing dairy and meat *and* the special Passover rule against contaminating anything with chametz. The wealthy simply un-packed a separate set of utensils used exclusively for Passover. But for ordinary folks, that simple luxury was not possible. They had to clean and purify what they had for the festival.

In the courtyards of the houses at Bethany, the men built large fires. Over one of the fires, they boiled water in a large cauldron. The women brought them all the pottery and stone pots, bowls, and trays. They had to do this in two shifts. One shift for the dairy meal items and the other shift for the meat meal items. The men lowered the stoneware into the boiling water and left them there until they were scalded clean of any leaven. In the meantime, two other groups of women brought out all of the metal utensils and trays to men at other fires. By turns, these men placed the metal utensils on those fires and kept them there until they glowed from the heat and were purged of all possible chametz. The local scribes supervised these fires and cauldrons to be sure that the laws of ritual purity were being strictly ad-hered to. In Martha's and Mary's house, Jesus was the rabbi and he himself supervised this "kashering" or "rendering kosher."

Nahman Avigad writes in his book, *Discovering Jerusalem*, that archaeologists were astonished at the number and variety of stone cooking and eating vessels found in their Jerusalem excavations.

> The answer to this lies in the realm of Halakhah, in the Jewish laws of ritual purity. The Mishnah includes stone vessels among those objects which are not susceptible to uncleanness. (Kelim 10,1; Para 3,2)...When a pottery vessel, however, became ritually unclean through contact with an unclean substance or object, it had to be broken and withdrawn from use.[7]

Stone vessels could be made kosher again by boiling.

# The Passover Registration

On the tenth day of the month of Nisan, four days before Passover, some of the men had to go to the Temple in order to register the number of people in their chavurah and to purchase the paschal lambs necessary for the group's sacrifice and seder. "On the tenth of this month every one of your families must procure for itself a lamb, one apiece for each household" (Ex 12:3 NAB). All of the scalding and searing of the utensils had to be completed by this time so that the courtyard could be used as a corral for the paschal lambs. Those from Galilee who had been sleeping in the courtyard moved in at this time with those on the roof. The extra crowding would last for four nights.

Very early in the morning, soon after sunrise, the men chosen for this task purified themselves in the mikveh and set out for the Temple. Jesus probably put Peter, James, and John in charge as usual. The men chosen did not have to be the head of households — in fact they could be servants — but there had to be at least one from each family. The process would take most of the day. When they arrived in the Court of the Gentiles, they headed for the Royal Portico where the priests and their clerks had set up tables for registration. In the Middle East, forming an orderly queue was not then the custom and still is not in places today. Mobbing and shouting was the procedure. The Galilean pilgrims and the men from Bethany pushed their way into the crowd, shouting and maneuvering, hoping to catch the attention of one of the clerks. Finally, an official signaled for them to come forward to his table. The officials preferred that groups register one paschal lamb for every ten persons, but they allowed registration of one lamb for as many as a hundred people if the group was too poor to afford more. The object was to have enough lamb for each person to receive at least one bite-size piece — "the size of an olive." The official gave the men a token authorizing them to purchase their paschal lambs. They might also have assigned the men a time and a Temple gate whereat they were to await the signal to enter the Temple courts for the Passover sacrifice.

After working their way out of the first throng, the men joined the mobs around the moneychanging tables in the Royal Portico. They had with them the ordinary coin of the realm, Roman money, whose idolatrous images could not be used in the Temple. This had to be changed into Temple shekels before any transaction could take place. Unfortunately, the high priest enforced his own rate of exchange upon the moneychangers. At the end of the day, the priests collected their percentage of the profits made by the exchanges, a practice that made the priests very unpopular with most of the people.

Once the men had their Temple shekels, they were able to go to the enclosures where the paschal lambs were kept. Local shepherds, acting under religious and secular laws, had brought their yearling lambs to the Temple for inspection several days earlier. Before the inspection by the priests, the shepherds had washed the lambs in one of several pools available for this purpose. One was the Sheep Pool north of the Temple, and another was the stream that flowed through the Kidron Valley. After the priests had picked out the unblemished ones suitable for sacrifice, they placed them in special pens for several days to make sure they were healthy. Because lambs could be disqualified at the last minute, more lambs had to be quarantined than would actually be sacrificed. Lambs were disqualified if they became injured just before the sacrifice, if the slaughterer bungled the job and failed to kill it quickly, or if the blood did not flow properly and freely from it.

When their purchases of the certified lambs were completed, the men finally could go back to Bethany and relax. Exhausted as they must have been, they were still joyful. Procuring lambs for Passover was not only naturally satisfying, but it was an exhilarating religious experience. The paschal lambs would become a part of them and their families for the next four days so that the people would be giving up something of themselves to God at the Passover sacrifice. Those lambs would die so that all of them could live in Holy Covenant with the God of Israel.

Today, Christians tend to see the Covenant as something separate from Passover. But in Jesus' day, Jews realized that the Covenant regulated every detail of the Passover sacrifice and seder supper. You could not celebrate Passover without observing the commandments of the Covenant and, therefore, it was the Covenant that gave Passover its fullest meaning. As the scribes had written, "To eat Passover without contemplating the Torah would be to eat like the animal that eats at the feed trough!"

The disciples led their lambs through the streets of Bethany. The children ran out to meet them, clapping their hands and singing and hugging their lambs. The older youths looked on with their parents' loving approval. When they arrived at the courtyards of the houses where they were staying, the children excitedly showed the animals where the food was and the corral where they were to sleep. The men of the families taught their children to be very careful, so that they did not excite the animals and cause them to panic. A guard was set up to watch constantly over the lambs; thus the animals were properly taken care of and stood less chance of suffering an injury and being disqualified.

## Clothing

The last days of the preparation arrived at last; however, there was still more to be done. The family heirlooms that were used only at this feast were now unpacked and cleaned and polished. There were large trays and platters, special oil lamps, decorative cloth coverings for the special matzot used in the ritual, hand-embroidered linen tablecloths, and the special, white linen robes that everyone was required to wear in honor of the

Passover sacrifice. They had to be unpacked and washed. Those white robes represented the priestly role everyone had in the feast of Passover.

The white robes worn by the men, women, and children had two parts. Everyone wore a long-sleeved, white tunic (*itzt'lah*) that covered the whole body from shoulder to ankle. They were usually made of linen and were modeled after the linen garments worn by the priests and Levites in the service of the Temple. The tunics were gathered at the waist with either a linen-cloth or linen- cord belt (*chagorah*) that was wound many times around the waist. Young boys, twelve years and under, wore a white cloth hat (*kipah*) that was similar to, but larger than, a modern yarmulke. The women and girls wore a veil that covered their head and shoulders. Men and youths, thirteen years and older, wore a kipah or a turban (*tz'nifah*). In addition, they placed over their heads and shoulders a very large shawl or outer garment (tallit). The tallit draped down from their shoulders to their waists in front and to the calves of their legs behind. The wearing of the tallit was a commandment.

> The LORD (YHWH) said to Moses, "Speak to the Israelites and tell them that they and their descendants must put tassels [*tzitzit*] on the corners of their garments, fastening each corner tassel with a violet cord [*t'khelet*]. When you use these tassels, let the sight of them remind you to keep all the commandments of the LORD (YHWH), without going wantonly astray after the desires of your hearts and eyes. Thus you will remember to keep all my commandments and be holy to your God. I, the LORD, am your God who, as God, brought you out of Egypt that I, the LORD, may be your God" (Nm 15:37-41 NAB).

The tallit that Jesus, his male disciples, and all religious Jews of the time wore in public was quite large. It was rectangular with fringes along the shorter sides and the tassels or tzitzit attached to each corner. Pharisees wore the tallit in one of two ways. Some men placed the tallit over the head and draped it over the shoulders. The tallit was wide enough to cover the arms, but for freedom of movement, it was often folded up onto the shoulders. Two ends of the garment, with their tassels, hung in front to below the waist. The two other ends draped from the shoulders in back to about calf length, with the second two tassels hanging in back. Other men preferred not to wear the tallit over their heads. Instead they draped it over their shoulders, with the sides folded up away from their arms, with two tasseled ends hanging just below their cinctures in front, and the rest draped down their backs to just beyond their thighs. For those who draped the tallit over their shoulders only, the kipah served as the necessary head covering. Otherwise the kipah or turban served merely to hold the tallit in place.

Since the wearing of the tallit was a commandment, its weaving and making came under strict rules. Materials could not be mixed. The warp and woof on the loom had to be of the same fabric. If the tallit were made of wool, then the warp and woof on the loom, the fringes and the tassels had to be nothing but wool. These outer garments were made of wool, cotton, or linen.

The religious Sadducees wore much smaller outer garments and frequently draped them in the manner of the Greek stole. They would let one end, with its two tassels, hang from the left shoulder in front. From the left shoulder, the garment was passed across the back and under the right arm, then across the chest and back over the top of the left shoulder and then falling down the back, with the other two tassels dangling below the waist in back. A clasp of some sort could be used to hold it in place on the left shoulder.

All religious Jews covered their heads with the tallit when they recited their morning prayers, prayed in the synagogues, or worshiped in the Temple. The scribes and other devout Jews preferred to wear the tallit over their heads at all times. For them, every act was an act of prayer — eating, walking, studying, or conversation over some point in the Law. This was how they understood the Sh'ma. The love of God had to be on their minds, at all times. To not wear the tallit was considered to be naked.

> Take to heart these words which I enjoin on you today. Drill them into your children. Speak of them at home and abroad, whether you are busy or at rest. Bind them at your wrist as a sign and let them be as a pendant on your forehead (Dt 6:6-8 NAB).

Wearing the tallit over the head was especially important when one was privileged to read from the Torah scrolls because it was understood that God spoke directly from Torah.

The tassels that hung from the four corners of the tallit were not simple decorations. The tzitzit, as they are called in Hebrew, are worn in fulfillment of the commandment found in Numbers 15:37-41 and Deuteronomy 22:12. The rabbis wrote, "Scripture looks upon him, who fulfills the commandment of the tzitzit, as if he was in the company of the Shekhinah (The Holy Presence of God)."[8] The commandment required that the thread that tied the tassel together must be dyed royal blue (t'khelet). This thread was a reminder that the Jews are a "holy nation" to God (Ex 19:6 NAB). The wearing of the tassels was a constant reminder that Jews were to "Be holy, for I, the LORD (YHWH), your God, am holy" (Lv 19:2 NAB).

Four threads – three white and a long, royal blue one – were used in the making of the tzitzit. The long blue thread was called the *shamesh* or "servant" of the others. The four threads were drawn through a small hole or eyelet at one of the four corners of the garment and brought together at the hem. A single knot was tied close to the hem so as to form a tassel of eight threads, the blue thread hanging much below the other seven, which were adjusted to be of the same length. The shamesh was tightly wrapped seven times around the other seven, and then a double knot was tied. Then the shamesh was wrapped eight more times around the others, and another double knot was tied. Then the shamesh was wrapped eleven more times around the others and another double knot was tied. Finally, it was wrapped thirteen more times around the white threads and the final double knot was tied. The remaining lengths of the eight threads were allowed to hang as a regular tassel. Today, the tzitzit on the prayer shawls are tied exactly the same way except that all of the threads are white. After the destruction of the Jewish nation by the Romans, the people were no longer able to obtain the royal blue for the shamesh. To substitute for that loss, sky blue bands or stripes are now woven into the cloth at the two ends of the tallit.

These knots and wrappings come from the gematriya, the Jewish study of numbers. In the Hebrew alphabet, the letters *aleph* through *tet* are counted as 1 through 9. *Yod* through *tzade* are counted as 10 through 90. The last four letters, *qoph, resh,* *shin,* and *tow (tov)* are counted as 100, 200, 300, and 400. Applying that information to the tzitzit reveals the following: The shamesh was wrapped 7 times around the others, knotted, and then wrapped 8 more times and again knotted. 7 plus 8 equals 15. The first two Hebrew letters of the tetragrammaton "YHWH" also equal 15. However, their precise numerical value are not used in the number of the first 2 wrappings out of reverence and respect for the Divine Name. The blue thread is next wrapped 11 times around the 3 white threads to represent *waw* (vav) and *hey* because waw (6) plus hey (5) equal 11. Taken together, then, this configuration represents the tetragrammaton "YHWH." The final 13 times the shamesh was wrapped around the white threads has the same numerical value as the Hebrew word *echad,* which means "1." The letters in echad — aleph (1), *chet* (8), dalet (4) — add up to 13. Consequently, the series of wrappings, 7 +8 +11 +13, equals "YHWH echad" (pronounced "adonay echad") or "The Lord is one" from the Sh'ma (Dt 6:4).

There is more. The numerical value of the word, tzitzit, is 600. That is, tzade (90), plus yod (10), plus tzade (90), plus yod (10), plus tow (400) equals 600. The eight threads and five knots of the tzitzit equal thirteen. And that brings the total numerical value of the tzitzit to 613, which is the total number of commandments in the Torah. This numerical significance of the tzitzit gives meaning to the statement in the Talmud that the wearing of the tzitzit is of equal merit to the observance of the whole of Torah![9]

The Book of Numbers 15:39 reads in Hebrew as *ure'item oto u'zkhartem et kol mitzvot YHWH* ("And you shall look upon [the tzitzit] and remember all of the commandments of the LORD [YHWH]"). The Hebrew word "oto," which refers to the tzitzit, is a pronoun that means "him" (Hebrew has no "it"). Thus, the passage means that looking on the tzitzit is the same as looking on "Him," (YHWH). This sheds some light upon a poignant incident recorded in the Gospels.

> A woman suffering hemorrhages for twelve years came up be-
> hind him and touched the tassel (tzitzit) on his cloak (tallit). She
> said to herself, "If I can only touch his cloak, I shall be cured."
> Jesus turned around and saw her, and said, "Courage, daughter!
> Your faith has saved you." And from that hour the woman was
> cured (Mt 9:20-22 NAB).

The poor woman was an outcast even among her family and friends. Her constant hemorrhaging made her ritually unclean. She could not eat at the same table as others. She had to eat alone, sleep alone, and be on guard lest she pass on her unclean-ness to others. She could not join others in the celebration of the Sabbath, Passover, or other holy days. She could not touch Jesus because that would make him ritually unclean. By touch-ing only the tzitzit of his tallit, she protected his ritual purity. But by touching the tzitzit, she touched "Him" and his power went out from him, healing her (Lk 9:43-48; Mk 6:25-34). It was another recognition of Jesus as "Him" who is the Lord.

The white garments that Jesus and his disciples wore at Passover are still with us today. The first Christians wore those same white garments when they were baptized on Pascha (Easter) and Pentecost. They can still be recognized in the white garments worn by many Christians when they are baptized by immersion. The tunic worn underneath the tallit has evolved very slightly into the alb[10] worn by priests, ministers, and bishops at the celebration of the Eucharist. The tallit has undergone greater modifications and has evolved into the stole worn by priests. The chagorah or cincture has remained much the same, though shortened so that it goes around the waist only once or twice. The kipah became the small cap that is now worn only by bishops, cardinals, and popes.

Naturally, the white garments of Passover have been retained by the Jewish community as well. In many observant Jewish homes, the father wears a white garment called a "kittle" when he leads his family in the seder. It is traditional that the men wear white kipot or yarmulkes at Passover in memory of the time when the Temple was standing and they would be dressed in white. The outer garment has been modified into the shawl (tallit or tallis) worn in the synagogue and at morning prayer. When Emperor Hadrian began his persecution of the Jews and attempted to stamp out Judaism by outlawing circumcision, Sabbath observance, and the study of Torah, he made it impossible for Jewish men to continue to wear the tallit in public. It had to be modified so that it could be hidden and carried to a place of worship in secret. Consequently, it was transformed from a full garment to a shawl that could be folded, put in a pouch, and taken out only when it was safe.

The wearing of the prayer shawl fulfills the commandment to wear an outer garment with four tassels. The prayer for putting on the tallit is essentially the same as the one Jesus would have said.

Bless the LORD, O my soul!
O LORD (YHWH) my God, You are very great.
You are robed in glory and majesty.
You are wrapped in light as in a garment.
You spread the heavens out like a curtain.

I am wrapping myself in the tasseled garment
in order to fulfill the commandment of my Creator.
As it is written in the Torah;
"They shall make fringes for themselves on
the corners of their garments
throughout their generations!" [Nm 15:38].

Even as I cover myself with the [tallit] prayer shawl
in this world, so may my soul deserve to be
robed in a beautiful garment in the world to come,
in Paradise.[11]

## Tassels of the Head

One more commandment completes the picture of Jesus and
his disciples celebrating Passover. This one concerned the men.
The observance of this commandment set the Pharisees off
from the Sadducees who, except for some of the priests, had
adopted Greek and Roman hairstyles and dress. The commandment says, "Do not clip your hair at the temples, nor trim the
edges of your beard" (Lv 19:27 NAB). This meant the religious
Jew must not trim, cut, or shave the beard and the sideburns.
All devout Jewish men had full beards, and they let their
sideburns hang along the sides of their faces in the manner of
the Chasidim today. Originally, the sideburns may have simply hung to the sides of the face, but the Pharisees, perhaps influenced by a Greek culture that considered curls an
enhancement of manly beauty, adopted the practice of curling
their sideburns as well. The sideburns hanging as forelocks to
either side of the face were called *tzitzit ha-rosh* (tassels of the

head) and were as much a sign of piety as the tzitzit that hung on the four corners of the tallit. Jesus wore his tzitzit ha-rosh in the style of a rabbi, that is, prominently framing his face. He would have had a full beard that he parted in the middle with his fingers. The rest of the hair on his head was parted in the middle along the top of his head, then combed down and gathered in a braid at the back of his neck. This was the common fashion of Jewish men in the first century, according to the scholars Gressman and Daniel-Rops.[12] The style allowed men to keep control of their hair under the numerous head coverings required by religious law and tradition.

## Palm Sunday Remembered

While the preparation activities were going on, much talk and speculation made the rounds in Bethany and Jerusalem. Some great events had happened earlier that foretold this pilgrimage feast as something extraordinary. Those events were Jesus' triumphal entry into Jerusalem, his driving out the moneychangers from the Temple, and his raising Lazarus from the dead. Everyone wanted to plan their activities so that they could include a visit to Martha's and Mary's and get a glimpse of Lazarus and the great prophet, Rav Y'shu'a Ha-Notzri (Rabbi Joshua of Nazareth), whom more and more people believed was the much longed-for Messiah. Who but "He Who Comes" could have raised back to life a man who had been dead for three days? The very title they knew him by fanned the flames of their expectations. Ha-Notzri, the Nazarene, reminded them of the prophecy of Isaiah, "But a shoot shall sprout from the stump of Jesse, and from his roots a bud shall blossom" (Is 11:1 NAB). The Hebrew word for "bud" is *netzer*. The people made a play on words with that prophecy, something that was very popular in both Hebrew and Aramaic. Inspired by Isaiah's prophecy, the people changed *hu netzri*, which means, "He is the bud" into *hu notzri,* which means "He is the Nazarene." Matthew records that popular ha-netzri-ha-notzri prophecy in 2:23.

Many within the Holy City had witnessed the miracle of Lazarus and the news of it had spread among the arriving pilgrims very quickly. The Jewish people were hungry for a Messiah who would liberate them from Roman domination and restore the royal line of kings descended from David. The prophets had said that "He Who Comes" would appear at the gates of Jerusalem during Passover. The high priest and those Sanhedrin members who supported Roman occupation, on the other hand, felt their worst fears were being realized (Jn 11:47-48). The people were in such a condition of excitement that they could be whipped into an open rebellion very quickly and easily. This time, it would not be a small group that would be easily suppressed, but a mass uprising of the whole population. The Romans had given the Sanhedrin the responsibility for preventing just such a rebellion. They had to respond to this emergency.

> So chief priests and the Pharisees convened the Sanhedrin and said, "What are we going to do? This man is performing many signs. If we leave him alone, all will believe him, and the Romans will come and take away both our land and our nation." But one of them, Caiaphas, who was high priest that year, said to them, "You know nothing, nor do you consider that it is better for you that one man should die instead of the people, so that the whole nation may not perish" (Jn 11:47-50 NAB).

The common people were not aware of the plots and schemes of the Sanhedrin. If they had known, they would have been furious. Instead, they awaited the next sign demonstrating that Jesus was indeed the Messiah. Jesus supplied them with that sign when he made his triumphal entry into Jerusalem and then attacked the authority of Caiaphas and the chief priests. His driving out the moneychangers and animal sellers from the

Courts of the Holy Temple met with popular approval. Besides liberating them from the cruel Roman rule, the people expected the Messiah to cleanse the Temple of corruption and greed. The messianic entry into Jerusalem had put Rome on guard and the driving of the money changers out of the Temple openly challenged the authority of the high priest and elders. The air was full of expectations.

The popular and triumphal entry into Jerusalem by Jesus was actually an open act of sedition. The people did not greet Jesus with cries of approval and acclaim but with petitions to liberate them and lead them in open rebellion against the domination of Rome and the betrayal and corruption of the Sanhedrin. "Hosanna," or more accurately "Hoshi'a Na!" means "Please, salvation now!"[13] It was a battle cry for liberation. The crowd was proclaiming Jesus as "He Who Comes" and the "Son of David" or the Messiah, the "king of Israel" (Mt 21:9; Mk 11:9,10; Lk 19:38; Jn 12:13). Their words paraphrased some dramatic verses in Psalm 118:

> O LORD (YHWH), grant salvation!
> O LORD (YHWH), grant prosperity!
> Blessed is he who comes in the name of the LORD
> (YHWH),
> we bless you from the house of the LORD (YHWH).
> The LORD (YHWH) is God, and he has given us
> light.
> Join in procession with leafy boughs up to the horns of
> the altar (Ps 118:25-27).

This was from the Hallel, the psalms sung at Passover. The palm branches mentioned in John 12:13 were the Lulav used to bless the Sukkah on the Feast of Tabernacles and were associated with the dedication of the Holy Temple.

## The Home of John Mark

Similar preparation activities had been taking place in the house of John Mark in Jerusalem where the Passover supper would take place. John Mark's home was situated within the city walls, on the southern section of the western hill, which is now called Mount Zion. Unfortunately, the building no longer exists, having been destroyed along with the rest of the city in the summer of 70 C.E. It has been replaced by the "Cenacle," which was built by the Crusaders on the traditional site many centuries later. John Mark and his family were Sadducees. His name and the site of their home leads us to believe that. The Sadducees were wealthy Jews who adopted the cosmopolitan Hellenistic-Roman life style. Only a wealthy Sadducee family would own a home sufficiently grand to have an upper room large enough for Jesus to celebrate the Passover supper with all of the disciples and their families that had come with him to Jerusalem. At home, the family of John Mark were practicing Jews. But in public, they dressed and acted very much like the Greeks and Romans that lived among them. The men attended the gymnasium[14] and the public Roman baths. The family attended plays at the Greek theater and chariot races at the Hippodrome. They would also appear at the popular dinner parties and banquets of their gentile friends. There they would sample those foods strictly forbidden by the Mosaic Law. At home, their kitchen was probably kosher, and there they ate only the permitted foods in the prescribed ways. They had elaborate bathing facilities that contained both bathtubs for bathing and a large mikveh for the rites of purification. They took the practice of their religion seriously at home but took the prevailing Greco-Roman culture equally seriously when outside of the home.

The family of John Mark spoke fluent Greek. They also spoke Hebrew and Aramaic. Aramaic, however, was for speaking to servants and slaves. Hebrew was for worship in the

Temple. At the Sadducee synagogue, the prayers and readings were probably in Greek. Even the Torah scrolls were written in Greek and were called the Pentateuch (The Five Books). Because they had a religious lifestyle at home and a secular lifestyle in public, they had private and public names. The private names, for use in the home and at the synagogue, were Hebrew or Aramaic names, like John (Y'hochanan, meaning "Yahweh is gracious"). Their public names were Greek (Marcos) or Roman (Marcus). They cleverly integrated their Jewish outer garments into their secular attire; however, they wore the prescribed white garments at Passover. In spite of the tzitzit harosh commandment, Sadducee men had clean-shaven faces, no forelocks, and head hair curled in the Greek style. Like Romans, they considered the beard to be barbaric. Sadducee women wore kohl, a heavy black makeup, around their eyes in the Egyptian style. They might have rinsed their dark hair with henna, a fashion trend that was very popular at that time. They fashioned their hair and their clothes to conform with the latest styles and fashions arriving from Rome and Alexandria.

As sophisticated and as Romanized as they were, Sadducees still loved Passover very much. They may have philosophized about it and allegorized the narration to bring it into line with the best Greek philosophy, as did Philo of Alexandria, but that did not diminish their attachment to it. The home of John Mark and his family was just as busy as that of Martha and Mary. John Mark's parents, however, had servants to do all the cleaning. They owned separate and complete sets of cooking and eating utensils for use at Passover; thus they did not have to go through the ordeal of scalding and scorching to purify those items. Many costly utensils of gold, silver, brass, and bronze would grace their seder tables — and they had the finest linen tablecloths to cover them. They had servants who could go to the Temple to secure the paschal lambs. They might have gone to the Temple for the Passover sacrifice itself if they wished to, but the Law permitted them to send servants for this as well.

The atmosphere in the home of John Mark was not as jubilant as it was in the homes of Bethany. John Mark's family was well known to the high priest, his family, and servants, and they would have known and been apprehensive about the high priest's decision to arrest Jesus when the opportunity arose. However, they probably expected an arrest attempt to come only after the week of Passover, so as to avoid inciting the mobs of pilgrims. For the feast, at least, they expected him to be safe. They were sincere disciples of Jesus, in spite of the Pharisees' disdain of their lifestyle, and they were honored when Jesus approached them months before for the use of their upper room. Because they were so well aware of the dangers for Jesus, they arranged a signal that would allow the disciples to find their house without having to ask directions. One of their male servants would go to the public fountain in the lower city and fetch water from it (Mk 14:13). He would stand out among the women, who customarily carried the water jars. His clothing as well would distinguish him as a servant to a wealthy family in the upper city, and the disciples could easily recognize him and follow him to the home of John Mark's family.

Jesus needed a large room to accommodate his chavurah. Wealthy families had such rooms on the roofs of their houses and they placed them at the disposal of large chavurot. All of the buildings had flat roofs, built that way to collect all of the rain water, which was then funneled into cisterns below the buildings for use in the many rites of purification. Most of the rooftops had awnings placed over them after the rainy season, and latticed walls could be put up around them for privacy, converting them into pleasant rooms where the families could retreat from the summer heat. The rooftops caught any breeze that blew in from the distant sea to the west. Those upper rooms were connected to the courtyards of the houses by outside stairways. That made them ideal for use by the Passover pilgrims. Those guests had free access to the upper rooms without disturbing the families and guests within the house.

During the enormous activity taking place on the first day of Passover, Jesus and his disciples could easily slip into the main courtyard of John Mark's house and ascend the outside stairs to the upper room. As was the custom, the family had furnished the rooftop room with tables, couches, rugs, cushions, lamps, and braziers to light if the night became cold. The disciples brought everything else that they needed. As similar activities were taking place in every house and building in Jerusalem, there was little danger of anyone noticing Jesus and his disciples entering John Mark's home. All of their Sadducee friends would be too busy preparing for their own Passover to notice who might be using the upper rooms of their neighbor's house. All of the priests of the Temple would be involved from sunup to well past sundown in the extraordinary number of sacrifices required on the day of the Passover sacrifice.

## NOTES

1. Martha in Aramaic is Marta and means "lady."
2. Mary (Hebrew: Miryam) is from the Egyptian *mrjt* and means "beloved."
3. Lazarus in Hebrew is El'azar and means "God has helped."
4. Bethany, in both Hebrew and Aramaic, is Beyt Anniyah and means "House of Anniyah."
5. The scribes or soferim (from *sofer* or "book"), were the rabbis. Today, "Rabbi" is both a title and the correct form of address. In the first century, the correct title was "Scribe," but the correct form of address was "Rabbi" (my master, from *rav* or "master").
6. Silverman, *Passover Haggadah,* xi.
7. Avigad, *Discovering Jerusalem,* 182-183.
8. Pinhas H. Peli, "Torah Today," "Curbing Our Lustful Eyes," *The Jerusalem Post* (week ending June 28, 1986), 18.
9. Birnbaum, *Ha-Siddur Ha-Shalom,* 4.
10. From the Latin, *alba,* for "white."
11. Birnbaum, *Ha-Siddur Ha-Shelom* , 4.

12. Kenneth E. Stevenson and Gary R. Habermas, *Verdict on the Shroud* (Wayne, PA: A Dell/Branbury Book, 1987), 44; Daniel-Rops, *Daily Life in the Time of Jesus*, 345, 346, 480.

13. Pope, Marvin H. "Hosanna—What It Really Means," *Bible Review* 4, no. 2 (April 1988): 16-25.

14. The Greek gymnasium derived its name from two Greek words, *gymnazien,* "to train," and *gymnos,* "naked." The Greeks traditionally trained for and practiced athletic events in the nude.

# FOUR

# The Day of
# the Passover Sacrifice

## The Ritual Bath

It was now the fourteenth of Nisan, and Passover formally began at sunset that evening. It was "the first day of the Feast of Unleavened Bread, when they sacrificed the Passover lamb" (Mk 14:12 NAB). By sunset, every man, woman, and child had to be ritually pure for the celebration. This required everyone to immerse themselves in a mikveh (plural: mikva'ot). Thousands upon thousands of pilgrims engulfed the city and surrounding villages. All available open space was covered by tent camps. Times had to be assigned to accommodate the crowd.

Like other middle-class and wealthy homes, the house of Martha, Mary, and Lazarus probably had a private mikveh. Even so, with family and guests occupying every room of the house and sleeping on the roof and in the courtyards, arrangements had to be made to insure that everyone had their alloted time to perform the proper ritual. Men went first because they had the first responsibilities to perform. Then the women bathed, and afterwards they helped the children. The ritual had to be done correctly. The person had to wash thoroughly before entering the mikveh. Meticulous attention had to be taken so that every part of the body was clean. Nothing could come between the purifying waters of the mikveh and the body. The cleansing waters had to reach even to the hair roots, under the fingernails, and into every crease, fold, and wrinkle of the skin.

Nahman Avigad writes of the amazing number of cisterns, baths, and pools uncovered from the time of the Second Temple. Mikva'ot required very special construction.

> According to the Halakhah, the Jewish religious law, a ritual bath must hold no less than forty seahs (about 750 liters or 198.13 gallons) of spring water or rain water, drawn directly into the bath. Since this was not always practicable, impure water could be made suitable by bringing it into contact with ritually pure water. For this purpose, a special "store pool" of at least forty seahs capacity was often installed adjacent to the ritual bath, to hold pure rainwater. The wall between the two pools contained a connecting pipe, through which the waters could come in contact, thus making the bath water suitable for ritual immersion.[1]

Lis Harris describes the present-day ritual of the mikveh in *Holy Days*.[2] Before entering into the ritual bath, she had to thoroughly clean herself, even using dental floss and Q-Tips to insure that absolutely nothing came between her whole body and the purifying waters. When she immersed herself three times, she was supervised by a professional attendant who was responsible for seeing that the ritual was performed correctly. Although no toothbrushes or dental floss have been discovered in the excavations of first century Jerusalem, a number of bath tubs were found near some of the mikva'ot for use in bathing beforehand. When Harris immersed herself, she felt a deep sense of communion with her mother, grandmother, and generations of Jewish women who had preformed the ritual before her. A devout Jewish woman, according to Harris, explained how, after immersing herself following childbirth, she could return to her husband again as a "bride" and as a "virgin." I could not help but think of Jesus' mother, Mary, of Martha and Mary, of Mary Magdalene, and of all of the women disciples and what they must have experienced when they immersed themselves in the mikveh. The first Christians were baptized for the most part in the mikva'ot.[3]

## The Morning Prayers

The morning of the fourteenth of Nisan dawned in Bethany upon a day full of intense activity. There was so much that had to be done to prepare for the great feast that would begin at sunset. While the women headed for the kitchen to prepare the morning meal, all of the men washed and then gathered about Jesus for morning prayers. The boys thirteen years of age and older were expected to join with the men. They gathered together either in the courtyard of the house or on the roof and faced west toward the Holy Temple. Placing their outer garments over their heads, they accompanied Jesus as he lead them in the opening prayers, which they began by confirming their obedience to the commandment to wear the tallit or tasseled garment and by praising God for placing his dwelling place among them:

> How goodly are your tents, O Jacob, your habitations, O Israel! By your abundant grace I enter your house; I worship before your holy shrine with reverence. O LORD (YHWH), I love your abode, the place where your glory dwells. I will worship and bow down; I will bend the knee before the LORD (YHWH) my Maker. I will offer my prayer to You, O LORD (YHWH) at a

time of grace. O God, in your abundant kindness, answer me with your saving truth![4]

Then, gathering the two front tassels of their outer garments in their hands before them, they continued,

> Blessed are You, O LORD (YHWH) our God,
> King of all Creation (Ha'Olam),
> Who has sanctified us with your commandments, and
> commanded us to enwrap ourselves in the fringed
> garment. May it be your will, LORD (YHWH) our
> God and God of our Fathers, that my observance of
> this Commandment of the tzitzit be considered as if I
> fulfilled it with all its particulars, details and implica-
> tions, together with the six hundred and thirteen com-
> mandments that are related to it.
> Amen.[5]

Then, dropping their outer garments to their shoulders, all of the men began to attach their phylacteries or *t'fellin*. Each man had two of these, one for his forehead called the *t'fellin shel rosh* or or "head phylactery" and a second for his left arm and hand called the *t'fellin shel yad* or "hand phylactery." The head phylactery was a small, dark or black, wooden or leather box with four compartments each containing separate handwritten strips of parchment on which were inscribed one of four biblical passages. Two were from Exodus (13:1-10 and 13:11-16); two were from Deuteronomy (6:4-9 and 11:13-21). From the t'fellin shel rosh hung two leather straps for attaching it to the head. On the phylactery was written the Hebrew letter "shin," representing one of the Hebrew Names of God, Shaddai or "The Almighty." The hand phylactery was smaller and contained only one compartment into which was inserted one handwritten parchment scroll. The same four biblical quotations were inscribed on it but in four parallel columns. In each of these four quotations there is the commandment that they are to be a sign on the hand and reminder on the forehead. The men attached the t'fillin shel yad to their left arms by wrapping one of its leather straps seven times around their left arm from wrist to elbow, while reciting this blessing,

Blessed are You, O LORD (YHWH) our God,
King of all creation,
Who has sanctified us with your commandments, and
commanded us to wear the t'fillin.

They then placed the t'fellin shel rosh upon their foreheads and bound it to their heads with the two leather straps. Again they placed the outer garments over their heads as they recited a prayer,

Blessed are You, O LORD (YHWH) our God,
King of all creation,
Who has sanctified us with your commandments and
commanded us concerning the commandment of the
t'fillin.
Blessed be the Name of His glorious majesty forever
and ever. Supreme God, You will imbue me with
your wisdom and your intelligence. In your grace
You will do great things for me. By Your might, You
will cut off my enemies and my adversaries. You
will pour the good oil into the seven branches of the
menorah so as to bestow Your goodness upon Your
creatures. You open your hand, and satisfy every
living thing.

They all took the second strap of the t'fillin shel yad, called the *retzuah*, and wrapped it three times around the middle finger of the left hand while reciting the beautiful prayer,

I will betroth You to myself forever!
I will betroth You to myself in righteousness and in justice, in kindness and in mercy.
I will betroth You to myself in faithfulness, and You
shall know the Lord! May it be Your will, O LORD

(YHWH) our God and God of our Fathers, that my
observance of this commandment of the t'fillin be
considered as if I fulfilled it with all its particular
details and implications, together with the six
hundred and thirteen commandments that are related
to it.
Amen.[6]

The Law required that they wear their t'fillin every day
during their morning prayers, except on Sabbaths and festivals
because these were considered to be signs in their own right of
the covenant relationship between God and the Israel.

Now properly attired, robed in faith and marked with the sign
of God on their foreheads and upon their hands, the men continued with the lengthy morning prayers, which consisted of
numerous prayers, blessings, psalms, and readings from Scriptures. References were made to God's glory residing in his Holy
Temple and to the sacrifices made to Him there.

## The Work Begins

After their morning prayers, the men removed their t'fellin,
wrapped them up, and placed them in special cloth pouches to
protect them. They filed inside the house for breakfast, which
the women had prepared for everyone. They washed their
hands again, before touching food, and took their places by sitting at the tables. If the breakfast of the first century was anything like a typical one in modern Israel, it consisted of yogurt,
various cheeses, some dried, smoked, and preserved fish, and
some fresh vegetables such as lettuce, scallions, endive, and
celery. Ordinarily, there would also have been fresh-baked
bread, but as this was the day of the Passover sacrifice and the
time for burning up all of the chametz, religious Jews refrained
from eating any kind of bread, although it was technically per-

mitted until just about noon when the signal was given that all "leavening" must have been burnt by then.

During breakfast they discussed their various assignments for the day. Jesus chose men to go into the city and meet with the male servant of John Mark's family, who would lead them to the house where Jesus had made arrangements for the Passover Supper. These disciples had to go early in order to report back to the rest of the group before noon so that everyone would know where to go that afternoon and evening. Some of the men would be assigned to burn the chametz after breakfast.

A larger group of the men would be chosen for the sacred duty of taking the paschal lambs to the Holy Temple for the Passover sacrifice. Those men had to have some training in these responsibilities, because if they made a mistake and failed in carrying out their duties properly, their lambs would be disqualified and declared "unclean." For each paschal lamb, no less than three men had to be assigned: one to do the actual killing and skinning, while the other two assisted. Some of the younger men might have gone along to learn their future responsibilities. These men would enter the mikveh before they went up to the Temple. It was customary for the rabbi to be first to take the ritual bath, but Jesus might very well have waived that honor and given it to those men.

The rest of the men would be pressed into the service of carrying all the food to Jerusalem as the women finished preparing it. An enormous amount of supplies had to be taken from Bethany up to Jerusalem for the Supper — everything, in fact, except for the slain paschal lambs brought from the Holy Temple.

While some of the men burned the chametz on bonfires out in the street, the women disciples washed the morning dishes and stacked them away. They were very careful to keep them completely separate from those to be taken to the home of John

Mark; this kept the items for Passover safe from any contamination.

At the same time, some of the men built a fire in the special oven that would be used to bake the matzot or unleavened bread for the seder. The women sent some of the other men to a special bakery to buy some select matzot called "watched matzot" or *matzah shemurah* that would be used in the ritual itself. These were prepared under the most meticulous conditions, as they had been "watched over" by religious authorities from the time the grain was planted, through growth and harvesting, and especially during grinding of the flour, mixing, shaping, and baking to insure exact conformity to every law of ritual purity. These matzot were expensive, so only a few would be purchased to be placed before the host for Jesus to share with them at the time required by the ritual. The women would bake enough matzot for the rest of the meal so that everyone could eat their fill. The extra matzot were especially important for the children. The very little ones were often bored during the long recital of the *maggid* or "narration" and some extra matzah could keep little hands and mouths busy.

The men also purchased special wine. A dark red wine was especially desirable, and it could be sweetened with a "sugary" syrup made from the reduced juice of grapes. Everyone would eat and drink until they were stuffed in the congenial atmosphere of the great Holy Day.

If, for some reason, the men could not burn the chametz right after breakfast, they had until close to noon to do so. The eyes of Jerusalem were on the roof over one of the main Temple gates where the priests had put two loaves of regular bread. As long as both of the loaves remained in place there, there was time to complete the burning, and eating the ordinary bread was still permitted. Towards noon, one of the loaves would be removed and that was a signal that there was very little time left, for when the last loaf was removed it meant that no leaven could exist in the Nation of Israel (BT Pesachim 11b). Anyone caught with any leavened substance after that was subject to a public flogging.

## Preparation of the Meat

Some of the men roasted the chaggigah from the previous day's sacrifice. Unlike the paschal lamb, this meat of the festival offering could be either roasted or boiled. For the Passover seder, however, nothing could be boiled, so this meat would also be roasted and served along with the roasted flesh of the paschal lambs. For the second day of Passover, however, in honor of the second passover sacrifice of the priests, the chaggigah could be boiled as well as roasted, or even cooked over a grill. Most likely, it would have been boiled because that was easiest for the cooks after the strict regulations governing the preparation of food for the Passover seder.

The preparation of the meat was not simple. The commandment states, "since the life of every living body is its blood, I have told the Israelites: You shall not partake of the blood of any meat" (Lv 17:14 NAB). All blood had to be extracted from all meat, and that was done in three stages. First, the animals were slaughtered by specially trained men, usually young rabbis, called *shochtim*. They kept their knives razor sharp so that the kill was instantaneous. No nicks or imperfections were permitted in their blades. With one smooth and quick stroke, the shochet sliced through the two main arteries on either side of the animal's throat so that it went into immediate unconsciousness. The carcass was then raised so that all of the blood drained out of it. Only when the draining was complete could the carcass be butchered for food. The second step took place after the meat was purchased. The meat was soaked in cold water for a considerable time in order to draw out the residual blood. Then, after draining the meat, the third stage was accomplished by heavily salting the meat with coarse salt and letting it stand for a half hour to draw out the last possible blood from the meat. And yes, at each step of the way, the men would bless God, thank Him for his commandments, and acknowledge that they were fulfilling his commandments for the proper preparation of meat. Only after this lengthy process could meat be cooked for eating.

## Baking the Bread

Special clay ovens, made for Passover use only, were used to bake the unleavened bread. Many of them have been uncovered in excavations in the Holy Land. These ovens have also been found in the ruins of synagogues throughout the Diaspora, such as the one at Ostia near Rome. Since they were used only to bake the Passover matzot, they could be kept ritually clean from any contamination that might render them useless for baking pure, clean, unleavened bread. Only pure water and pure flour could be used in the making of the matzot. Matzah could be made from either wheat or barley flour. In the first century, however, barley flour was preferred because Passover was associated with the barley harvest that occured at that time and also because the Hebrew name of spring, aviv, was taken from the word for "new ears of barley" or *abib*.

Three of the women disciples would have been assigned the task of making the matzot (BT Pesachim 48b). One poured the pure water into the flour in the mixing bowl while the second mixed it into a dough and then kneaded it to proper consistency. The third disciple shaped the dough into round, flat loaves and placed these into the hot oven to quickly bake. The whole process from mixing to baking took less than half an hour so that there was no possibility of any leavening taking place. After baking, the matzah loaves were stacked and wrapped to be taken up to the city. The matzot of the first century were not like the thin, flat, crisp, machine-made ones that we are familiar with today. They were thicker, softer, and chewier. They frequently cut designs into them with special tools.

## Preparation of "Greenstuff"

All this preparation required good supervision. Mary, the Mother of Jesus; Martha, their hostess; Mary Magdalene; and the mother of the sons of Zebedee were the natural leaders among this group of disciples. They were the keepers of the cherished recipes of the community of Jesus' followers and of their traditions. They were the organizers and synchronizers of all the kitchen activity. They shooed the children and men out of the way, especially the ones out for samples of everything.

While some of the men were roasting the chaggigah for the extra meat, and a few of the women were mixing and baking the matzot, others were busy preparing the other foods required by the ritual of the seder. Some of the mothers and daughters worked on the fresh vegetables that would be needed. Among those were lettuce, chervil, endive, and, most important of all, the horseradish or maror. These were all mentioned in the Mishnah as necessary if a person was to fulfill his or her obligation at the supper (TB Pesachim 39a).

Along with the lettuce and horseradish, other green and bitter herbs might have included parsley, radishes, celery, and watercress. All of these came under the general category of "greenstuff" or *karpas*. Carrots and beets were also favorite vegetables that could be served at the Passover supper. However, peas and beans, such as lentils and fava, were forbidden at the Passover seder because, in their dry states, they could become fermented or leavened.

Leafy lettuce was very important to the meal. Along with the unleavened bread, it was used to pick up food from the serving trays for eating. In the days of the Temple, there were no dishes or forks and spoons; people ate with their hands from the trays they shared. One of the subtle and little known dietary laws required that only the right hand be used when eating. That was because the left hand was used for cleaning oneself after elimination, which rendered that hand unfit for use at the table. Many Americans visiting the Middle East have shocked their hosts by reaching for their food with the left hand. Belching is a nice touch at the Mediterranean table, but using the left hand is still a serious taboo. And that taboo was very strong in the first century, despite all the ritual washings of the hands.

There were two traditional ways to prepare the maror. One way was to slice the horseradish into thin pieces. The other way was to pound it into a paste and then add wine, honey and salt. Some puree of cooked beets might also be added to it to turn the paste a brilliant red. The slices of horseradish were used for dipping the "bitter herb" as called for in the ritual. The puree was one of the condiments served with the paschal lambs. Hot mustard might also be one of these condiments. Both methods of preparation were very difficult. Horseradish has a nasty habit of burning the eyes and taking the breath away. In preparing the maror for the seder supper, the mothers and daughters were forced to take turns in groups. When one group could no longer breathe, another group would take over, and in turns, they would struggle until the disagreeable work was achieved. There must have been a lot of laughter as these crying and gasping ladies rushed for the doors, wiping their bloodshot eyes, overflowing with copious tears. The bitter herb was appropriately bitter to remind everyone of the bitter slavery that the Egyptians inflicted upon the Israelites in Egypt.

The horseradish was prepared in two ways because of a religious tradition that food must be taken from its raw or natural state, and processed into a prepared or finished state that conformed to the dietary laws. Horseradish comes under this commandment of Passover observance. Therefore, it was per-missible to eat the horseradish raw, but it also had to be prepared from its natural condition into a state of fulfillment and completeness, as kosher.[7]

## Making the "Clay"

The women also had to prepare the charoset or "clay." In the Mishnah, the rabbis disputed whether charoset was required by the Law or not. It was not mentioned in the Torah. But it had been a specialty of the Passover supper for so many centuries that many felt that it must have always been a part of the seder. Since charoset is eaten with maror as a way of cutting the bite of the horseradish, perhaps the obligation developed out of the commandment to eat the bitter herb (Ex 12.8). Whether there was a commandment or not, Passover would be incomplete without that delicious pureed compote of fruit and nuts called charoset.

The transformation of the charoset from its natural state to its kosher state also took a lot of hard work. It was almost as hard as preparing the maror, but it was a much more pleasant task. Charoset is a puree of fruits and nuts. The fruits were predominantly apples and raisins. To these were sometimes added dates, some citrus, and the popular pomegranate seeds. Traditionally, the nuts were walnuts and almonds. But to those other nuts could be added. At the time of the Temple, this "clay" was made by pounding the fruits and nuts in large, stone mortar bowls with a stone pestle. It could also be finely chopped in a wooden bowl with a metal chopper. Again, three women probably worked on its preparation. One added fruit and nuts while another pounded them into a paste with the pestle or chopper, and the third stirred the puree until all of the ingredients had been reduced to a paste. God was thanked and praised, meanwhile, for the "fruit of the trees and vines." When all had been reduced to a paste, wine, honey, and such spices as cinnamon would be added to the puree and mixed until the whole thing was the consistency of mud. The charoset represents the clay that the Israelites used to make the bricks for pharoah.

The recipe for charoset was usually a lovingly held family tradition. For the Last Supper, Jesus' mother, Mary, probably supervised the making of the charoset according to her own favorite family recipe.

## Forbidden Foods

We can be sure that all of the above-mentioned foods were served at the Last Supper. They are all referred to in the Mishnah, which is a written record left to us by those rabbis who remembered how things were before the destruction of the Holy Temple and Jerusalem in the year 70 C.E. All of the libraries went up in flames and the disciples of the rabbinical schools were slain by the sword in the wholesale destruction of the Jewish Nation. But the survivors set down in writing all the things they could remember of the oral laws and traditions. The Mishnah is our window into the real world of the first century in Judea and Israel.

In the Mishnah, there is no mention of any other food that might be permitted for the Passover supper, except for beets and rice. Many foods were forbidden, however. No wheat, barley, spelt, rye, or oats could be eaten during the week-long festival. In recipes that ordinarily used wheat or barley flour, finely ground matzah had to be substituted. Also prohibited during the seven or eight days of the Feast of Unleavened Bread (Chag HaMatzot) were any other items that could be made from grains, such as Babylonian kutach (a porridge), Median beer, Idumean vinegar, Egyptian zithom (a kind of beer), dyer's broth, cook's dough, scribe's paste, women's cosmetics (made with flour), and all items made with flour or flour paste (BT

Pesachim 42a). Rice was not forbidden, and there was no explanation as to why not. Today, Ashkenazic or European Jews believe that rice is forbidden, while the Sephardic or Middle Eastern Jews believe that it is permitted and include rice dishes in their seders.

But from all of the foods that are mentioned as permitted or obligatory for Passover, you can see that the Last Supper was a gargantuan feast that was served in two courses and concluded with a ritual "dessert" called the afikoman.

## The Passover Sacrifice

As midday approached, the trumpet blast from the pinnacle of the Temple announced the beginning of the evening sacrifice. That was the final signal for the men assigned to sacrifice the paschal lambs to gather at the Temple gates. Earlier that morning, everyone had gathered around their lamb and had placed their hands upon its head to officially recognize that the offering was theirs. This ritual was also meant to symbolically pass some of their personalities onto these paschal lambs. They were offering themselves to God through the sacrifice of these animals. The men, having bathed in the ritual bath (mikveh) and now clothed in their white robes and white outer garments, lifted the Passover lambs onto their shoulders and carried them off to the Holy Temple. On their way they joined a great mass of men participating in the same ritual.

The sight of hundreds of thousands of men, all in white, with lambs draped about their shoulders, captured the imagination of the ancient world. The image of what we now call "The Good Shepherd" appeared in classic art. Both the Greeks and Romans created statues of their popular gods, Apollo and Eros, with lambs draped across their shoulders. Ironically enough, it was these very statues of Apollo and Eros that became the models for the first statues of Jesus when, centuries later, images were allowed in Christian art. It was necessary for the disciples to carry their lambs in this way to avoid having them injured by the great crush of the crowd. Since there were at least three men with each lamb, they all could take turns and share the burden, and the paschal lambs were docile and uncomplaining, which made the burden easy.

By noon, an immense sea of white radiated out from the Holy Temple Mount in all directions. It was a surging sea of singing and gentle bleating. The men sang the Psalms of Ascents and psalms from the Hallel. Inside the Temple, all of the priests and Levites bathed in the ritual baths and dressed in their finest linen robes. Lots were thrown by the high priest to determine which divisions were to be assigned the numerous responsibilities of the sacrifice. At about the "ninth hour," near our noon, those Levites not assigned to the choir and orchestra went to the numerous outer gates of the Temple courts and took charge of them.

The Passover sacrifice had to be offered in three divisions (BT Pesachim 64a) according to an interpretation of Exodus 12:6: "You shall slaughter it, the whole assembly of the congregation of Israel." The priests reasoned that *qahal* or "assembly" represented one group, *adat* or "congregation" represented another, and Yisrael or "the people of Israel" represented the third. It took three hours or more for these three groups to complete their sacrifices.

In chapter five of the Babylonian Talmud, tractate Pesachim, the Mishnah gives a vivid account of that paschal offering in the first century. At about noon, the Temple gates swung open and Jesus' disciples entered with the first group. As they pushed forward with their lambs, the crush must have been tremendous. Passing through the Golden Gate, they entered a very large passage and climbed many steps up to the enormous Court of the Gentiles. That great, open-air plaza covered over one million square feet of stone-paved surface. The disciples were met with an extraordinary sight. The Court of the Gentiles was completely filled with row upon row of priests radiating out from the nine gates into the inner sanctuaries or *hekal* of the Temple. All of the priests held large basins made of precious metals. One row of priests held gold basins, the next held silver, the next held gold, the next silver, and so on in alternating rows of silver and gold. At the feet of each priest in the open court there were thin, smooth staves, probably banded in the same precious metal as their basins. The priests standing in the porticoes surrounding the Court of the Gentiles did not have these staves; hooks in the walls and on the pillars would serve the same purpose. The disciples, along with the vast crowd of men, quickly filled up the court by following one of the lines of priests until they found their place before one of the priests. As they waited for the immense court to fill up, they could hear the orchestra of the Levites playing their instruments on the steps of the Nicanor Gate in the Court of the Women. When the Temple court was full, the Levites in charge of the Gates closed them and kept them closed the whole time that the first gathering, called the "qahal" or "assembly," offered to God their Passover sacrifice. When the gates were closed, other priests signaled the sacrifice to begin by blowing a ram's horn, or shofar. The pattern was one long blast, three short blasts, and one long concluding blast. The Levite choir began to sing the Hallel, which is the section of Psalms from 113 through 118. Between each psalm, other priests sounded silver trumpets in a musical interlude. The Levites would complete the whole Hallel twice during the first hour of sacrifice and repeat it a third time if necessary.

When they heard the blasts of the shofar, each group of disciples stepped forward with their lamb to position themselves directly in front of the priest. They all placed their hands upon the head of their paschal lamb. Then, while the others held the animal, the disciple assigned to be the shochet quickly sliced through the neck, severing both of the carotid arteries. The animal dropped instantly into unconsciousness. The priest caught its blood in the basin while the disciples lifted the carcass up so that all of its blood would flow freely into the basin. After all of the blood had drained from the animal, the priest stood back in line and waited for the other priests to return to their places in the line. When ready, all of the priests passed their basins along the line toward the Inner Court of the Temple where the great Altar of Sacrifice stood. As the filled basins were received by the priests positioned around the great Altar of Sacrifice inside the Court of the Priests, they poured the blood of the paschal lambs against the sides of the altar. The "life of the animal," the blood, belonged to God. This was the first of God's portion. Below the Altar of Sacrifice, large cisterns cut into the native rock received all of that blood.

Trays made of the same precious metals as their basins were then passed out to the priests in the outer court. While the priests in the Inner Court were pouring the contents of the basins against the sides of the altar, two of the disciples in each group picked up the smooth stave at the priest's feet and placed it across their shoulders. The disciples suspended the carcass of their lamb from these staves. While the two held the animal up, the others skinned it. The skins of these paschal lambs were to be given to the father of John Mark as a courtesy for allowing them to use a room in his house for their seder supper. Hosts and landowners were not permitted to charge for the use of their property by the pilgrims, but the animal skins functioned as a donation in lieu of any payment.[8]

When they finished skinning the carcass, the shochet slit open the animal's belly and removed the two kidneys with their surrounding fat. These were the *emurim* or the "fat of the lamb." They were also sacred to the LORD (YHWH) and became the second portion of the paschal lambs given to God. Through these two portions, God became a participant in and member of every Passover supper to be celebrated that night. The disciples placed the kidneys and surrounding fat of their lambs upon the trays held by the priests. All of the emurim were now passed to the priests in the Inner Courts. That evening, after all of the Passover sacrifices of the people were completed, all of these kidneys and their fat would be salted and mixed with herbs and then burned by the priests upon the altar, presenting "a sweet fragrance to the LORD (YHWH)." That evening, the fragrance of these immolated emurim would mix with the aroma of the roasting Passover lambs wafting up from every courtyard and street of the Holy City.

When everyone was ready, the disciples wrapped their lambs back in the skins and again placed them upon their shoulders. The Levites again opened the Temple gates and the first assemblage left that holy place while the next assemblage awaited its turn to enter the Temple courts.

What a sight the disciples and that throng of men leaving the Temple gates made upon those still waiting outside — and upon the people who followed these disciples. While sacrificing their paschal lambs, the men in white robes had become soaked in blood. That image was applied to the Passover sacrifice of our Lord, Jesus Christ, and was the origin of the line, "They have washed their robes and made them white in the blood of the Lamb" (Rv 7:14 NAB). As long as that blood remained moist it was no obstacle to their fulfillment of the sacred obligations. No contamination had yet occurred. But once the blood had become completely dried, it would render them as "unclean." Before that happened and before they could join the others in the celebration of the Passover feast, they had to remove their bloodstained robes, wash again, and dress in another set of white garments.

## Roasting the Lamb

Once sacrificed, the Passover lambs could not be taken outside the recognized boundaries of the Holy City of Jerusalem. Instead of returning to Bethany, now out of bounds, the disciples were led directly to the house of John Mark where the rest of the disciples were waiting for them. At the house, the disciples unwrapped their lambs and presented the skins to the head of the household, who graciously accepted them. Then others assisted them with the preparing of the carcass for roasting. Some of the residual blood that had drained into the cavity of the carcass was collected into a bowl. One of the disciples would apply some of the blood to the lintel and two doorposts of the room where they would be eating, with some branches of the herb hyssop. The carcass itself had to be thoroughly washed to remove all traces of any other blood, then salted heavily and set to rest and drain.

The regulations governing the cooking of the Passover lambs were many and strict. "That same night they shall eat its roasted flesh with unleavened bread and bitter herbs" (Ex. 12:8 NAB). The Hebrew words translated as "roasted" are emphatic here. They are *tzli-esh*, which means "roasted with fire." The rabbis took these words seriously. Chapter seven of the Mishnah, Pesachim, begins with, "How is the Passover-Offering roasted? We bring a spit of pomegranate wood and thrust it into its mouth right down as far as its buttocks,...One may not roast the Passover-Offering either on a metal spit or on a grill" (BT Pesachim 74a). All of the rabbis agreed that the Passover lamb must be roasted entirely by the direct heat of the flames of the fire. Metal spits or grates could not be used because some of the cooking would be done by the heat of the metal instead of the heat of the flames. The innards of the animal also had to be exposed to the direct heat of the fire and not stuffed into the animal's cavity. Rabbi Joses, the Galilean, disagreed on this point, but the majority decreed that if the innards were stuffed into the cavity, the cooking method would be "seething." "Seething" means moist cooking from the heat inside the animal, and therefore not by the direct heat of the fire. This was not permissable.

All of the authorities agreed that the lamb must be attached to a wooden spit and placed directly over the hot coals so that all dripping would cause a distinct sizzling and flashing of the fire. Actually, two spits were used and these were probably of the preferred pomegranate wood. Pomegranate wood imparted a subtle and pleasant flavor to the meat. The longer spit was thrust through the mouth and buttocks and beyond to where the back feet were attached. The front legs were then spread out to the sides where they were attached to the second spit, which formed a cross, and thus the meat was suspended above the pit of burning coals to roast. An oven could be used, and sometimes was out of necessity, but extra precautions had to be taken. The animal still had to be roasted over burning coals and not by the heat of the oven walls. In fact, if in the process some part of the animal accidentally touched the walls of the oven, then that portion became contaminated and had to be cut off (BT Pesachim 75b). Basting of the animal was one of the few things that was permitted.

The roasting of the paschal lambs was the responsibility of the men and older youths. A tradition that has lasted over two millennia, it was the occasion for much male comradery. Fortunately, beer was not permitted at Passover. There were a number of prayers that had to be said, both in the preparation of the lamb for cooking and in the act of roasting it as well. The commandments had to be obeyed and fulfilled, but that did not make the chore somber. Passover was a joyous time, a time for visiting between groups and the greeting of old friends and newfound acquaintances. There was a lot of singing and praising God. It was also the time for fathers to instruct their sons on the proper way to roast the lambs, and perhaps to pass along some family secrets on just what herbs and spices were the best to use in preparing the "piece de la resistance" of their Passover feast.


## Final Preparations

While the men were occupied in the courtyard or street with the roasting of the paschal lambs, the women were busy upstairs with the final preparations for the supper. The tables had to be covered with their best linen table clothes. The tables, some of wood and some of stone, were square and rested upon either a single pedestal or on three legs. On three of their sides were arranged wide dining couches, each of which could hold three or four persons reclining on their left sides, supporting their heads upon their left arms and hands. The fourth side of each table was kept open for the serving of food.

The metal lamps were polished until they sparkled, filled with olive oil, then placed upon stands throughout the large room. The metal serving trays were polished with vinegar and salt until they shined. There were also serving trays made of stone and of stone mosaic. Some of the serving trays were oval, but many others were rectangular. They came in two popular styles. One style was a plain tray, much like our silver serving trays, except they were much larger because they had to hold an entire roast lamb. The other style had bowl-like depressions around the sides to hold the condiments of Passover, such as the salt water, ground horseradish, vinegar, mustard, and especially, the charoset. When the plain serving trays were used, the condiments were served alongside in metal and stone bowls.

The food that had been brought up from Bethany was now arranged upon the various platters and serving trays. The freshly baked matzot were also placed on trays and covered with specially embroidered cloths, ready to be placed on each table. The "watched matzot" they had purchased were placed on a distinctive tray, covered with an especially beautiful cloth that Jesus' mother had brought with her, and set aside for the head table where Jesus would recline. These coverings for the matzot were traditionally handmade by wives and mothers, and some of them could well have been heirlooms.

In the center of the upper room there was a very large metal or pottery vessel that was heated to supply the diners with hot water. It was customary, at that time, to add hot water to the wine to cut its possible roughness or bitterness and to bring the wine from its natural state to its finished kosher state. Stone and metal cups were arranged on all of the tables with an especially large and elegant one of gold or silver set at Jesus' place.

Jesus' mother and Martha took charge of the arrangement of the room. The couches and tables were supplied by John Mark's family. The women enjoyed as much good cheer and socializing as did the men down below. The atmosphere was little different than that of a modern holiday — except for the numerous prayers that had to be said, the many times the hands had to be washed, and the many other obligations that had to be met. As was the case for any popular Holy Day, everyone joined in the singing of many popular and sacred songs. That was especially true of favorite Psalms. Over to one side, older brothers prompted the young boys with the Four Questions that they would be required to ask during the supper. Some of the older children, not otherwise employed by their mothers, stood on the outside stairway to watch the sky and let the women know when the sun approached the horizon. At sunset, that day would be over and all their chores had to be completed. The festival lamps would be lit and the great feast of Passover would begin.

Concerning these final hours, the Mishnah states, "On the eve of Passover close to *minchah* (the usual hour of the evening sacrifice) a man must not eat until nightfall. Even the poorest man in Israel must not eat on the night of Passover *until he reclines*" (BT Pesachim 99b, emphasis mine). At that hour, the time of minchah, the twelve apostles and many of the male disciples were with Jesus reciting the evening prayers. Unlike the morning prayers, the evening prayers were said indoors. As they recited their prayers, the men rocked back and forth from the waist. This practice involved the whole person, their thoughts, words, and actions in their prayers.

The greatest obligation to be met before sunset was to be in a state of levitical purity before beginning the supper. Leviticus 15:16 says, "He shall bathe his whole body in water...." That verse refers to men in a state of "uncleanness" and a method of becoming ritually "clean" and is followed by others concerning the states of "uncleanness" for women and methods for their ritual purification. Based on these verses, the rabbis required everyone to be "ritually clean" before eating on Passover. Bathing the "whole body" in water was interpreted strictly: "This intimates that nothing must interpose between his [or her] flesh and the water. 'In the water' means in the water of a mikvah. 'All his flesh' implies sufficient water for his [or her] whole body to be covered therein" (BT Pesachim 109a). Those disciples that did not purify themselves earlier did so now. Those disciples who had allowed blood from the sacrificed lambs to dry on their robes and who therefore had become unclean bathed themselves again.

## NOTES

1. Avigad, *Discovering Jerusalem*, 139.
2. Harris, *Holy Days*, 146-148.
3. William Sanford La Sor, "Discovering What Jewish Mikva'ot Can Tell Us About Christian Baptism," *Biblical Archaeology Review* 13, no. 1 (January/February 1987): 52-59.
4. Birnbaum, *Ha-Siddur Ha-Shelom*, 3.
5. Ibid., 6.
6. Ibid., 5-10.
7. Fredman, "The Created Society," *The Passover Seder*, 75.
8. A. Baraita (b. Meg. 26a; Tos. M. Sh. 1.12f [87.9]) comments that since Jerusalem was considered a national possesion, it was not per-

missible to rent rooms in the Holy City to the Passover pilgrims for a financial consideration. It was, however, customary for the pilgrims to recompense the householder by giving him the hides of the paschal lambs. Cf. Mann, "Rabbinic Studies in the Synoptic Gospels," *Hebrew Union College Annual* 1 (1924):343, n. 64, and Jeremias, *The Eucharistic Words of Jesus,* 44.2.

# FIVE

# *A Necessary Digression*

"Know the Truth, and the Truth shall make you Free" is just as true of the Bible as it is true of the person of our Lord Jesus Christ. As the real world of Jesus becomes clearer to us, we will begin to be able to reunite ourselves and put away the destructive myths that still so divide us. That is the reason for this chapter. Many centuries ago Christianity became cut off from its roots in Judaism. As soon as that happened, serious divisiveness appeared in the Christian family, and the new and everlasting Covenant of Christ's love was abandoned. The church relinquished the concept of itself as the family of God and reorganized itself along the lines of the Roman hierarchical government. Gentile pride was convinced that the civilizations of Greece and Rome were much superior to that of Judea, and the church repudiated its Jewishness. When that happened, misinformation replaced truth and facts, and the Gospels became a source of disunity because love had gone out of them.

Among the many misconceptions, three particularly divisive ones need to be set straight before we can discuss the Last Supper.

## MISCONCEPTION #1: Jesus Celebrated the Last Supper With Only the Twelve Apostles

Now that we have a clearer picture of how Passover was celebrated in the first century and an appreciation of the commandments and rabbinical laws that regulated its observance, we can take another look at the popular belief that Jesus celebrated the Last Supper alone with the Twelve Apostles. First, where is the biblical evidence? What do the Gospels say? Matthew 26:19-20 says, "The *disciples* then did as Jesus had ordered, and prepared the Passover. When it was evening, he reclined at table with the *Twelve*" (NAB, emphasis mine).

Luke 22 describes much the same. Peter and John are in charge of the preparations, but they would need a great number of people to help them. In verse 11, Jesus states that he desires to eat that Passover with his "disciples," but in verse 14 it says, "When the hour came, he took his place at table with the *apostles*" (NAB, emphasis mine).

Two groups are mentioned in both Gospels: The "disciples" (*mathetai*) and the "Twelve" (*dodeka*) or the "Apostles" (*apostoloi*). Clearly, the disciples prepared the supper, and when they had completed their very involved responsibilities by sunset, Jesus reclined at table with the Twelve Apostles.

Even though all four Gospels emphasize that the Twelve Apostles were present, this must not blot out the reality that other disciples were also present. In fact, an all-male seder would have been unlawful and invalid unless circumstances, such as wartime, made it impossible for men, women, and children to be together. The reason for the emphasis on the

Twelve Apostles is that Jewish tradition required twelve witnesses to inaugurations of divine institutions (See Ex 24:4).

On a local radio talk show last Easter, the host was discuss-
ing the Last Supper and the Passover with a rabbi. The rabbi
wondered how the Last Supper could have been a Passover.
"Where were the women and children?" he wanted to know.
Where indeed? The divine commandment states clearly that
Passover must be observed "by the whole family." ("l'bayt
avot" or "by the household of the parents")[1] (Ex 12:3,4).

Did the Apostles come up to Jerusalem on pilgrimage with
their wives and children? If you put the Last Supper into the
perspective of a first-century observance of Passover, the overwhelming evidence is that they did indeed come to Jerusalem
with their wives and children. And the biblical evidence cor-
responds. Matthew states that at the crucifixion, "There were
many women there, looking on from a distance, who had followed Jesus from Galilee, ministering to him. Among them
were Mary Magdalene and Mary the mother of James and
Joseph, and the mother of the sons of Zebedee" (Mt 27:55,56
NAB). Mark adds even more information, "There were also
women looking on from a distance. Among them were Mary
Magdalene, Mary the mother of the younger James and of
Joses, and Salome. These women had followed him when he
was in Galilee and ministered to him. There were also many
other women who had come up with him to Jerusalem" (Mk
15:40,41 NAB). Luke supports Mark with, "all his acquaintances stood at a distance, including the women who had followed
him from Galilee and saw these events" (Lk 23:49 NAB). And
John's Gospel says, "Standing by the cross of Jesus were his
mother and his mother's sister, Mary the wife of Clopas, and
Mary of Magdala" (Jn 19:25 NAB). When these four quotations are brought together, it becomes very clear that Jesus and
his Apostles came up to Jerusalem from Galilee, on pilgrimage,
with their mothers and wives "who attended to their needs,"

such as cooking the Passover supper. With mothers and wives also came children, for it was the duty of families to celebrate Passover in such a way that they could instruct their children on the significance of the celebration and encourage them to ask questions (Ex 13:8) (BT Pesachim 116a).

We not only have a clear record in the Gospels that there were women at the Last Supper, we actually have some of their names recorded for us. However, there is one other passage in the Scriptures that we ought to examine because it is so often overlooked, yet so revealing. In the first chapter of the Book of Acts, the disciples have met again in the upper room to pick from among themselves someone who would replace Judas as one of the Twelve Apostles. Peter addresses the assembled ("there was a group of about one hundred and twenty persons in the one place") as brothers: "Therefore, it is necessary that one of the men who accompanied us the whole time the Lord Jesus came and went among us, *beginning from the baptism of John until the day on which he was taken up from us,* become with us a *witness to his resurrection*" (Acts 1:15,21,22 NAB, emphasis mine). Jesus had given his Twelve Apostles the responsibility of organizing about themselves a quorum or *minyan* of ten fellow disciples and "brothers." These 120 men made up the School of Jesus, the Beyt Y'shu'a. The Twelve Apostles were the elders of Jesus' school. This was in the well-established tradition of all renowned rabbis of that period, such as the School of Shammai, Beyt (Beth) Shammai, and the School of Hillel, Beyt (Beth) Hillel. These disciples were the students (Hebrew *talmidim,* Greek *mathetai,* Latin *discipuli,* from which we get "disciples") of the Rabban Jesus (Jn 13:13). They were responsible for memorizing their teacher's and master's every saying and teaching. The Twelve Apostles, as elders, were the official memorizers (tana'im), responsible for preserving and passing on to others their teacher's and master's parables and instructions. As a school or bayt, they constituted a legal extended family and were a legitimate household under the requirement of Exodus 12:3,4 that Passover be celebrated by "family" and "household."[2]

These 120 disciples were the companions of Jesus and the Twelve "beginning from the baptism of John until the day on which he was taken up from us [at his Ascension]" (Acts 1:22 NAB). That meant that they were with Jesus on that most important day, the 15th of Nisan, when he celebrated the Last Supper, was arrested, tried, and crucified. They were expected to celebrate the Passover with their rabbi (teacher and master), and, according to the Law of Moses and the teaching of the rabbis, they were obligated to appear at the Passover supper with their wives and children. We actually have the names of the two other disciples: "Joseph called Barsabbas, who was also known as Justus, and Matthias" (Acts 1:23 NAB). Matthias was chosen by lot to replace Judas, "and he was counted with the eleven apostles" (Acts 1:26 NAB). He took his place as one of the twelve official witness to the Lord's resurrection (Acts 1:22).

The disciples of a typical school (bayt) of a renowned first-century rabbi, under the tutorage of the school's elders, memorized their master's every word, action, and decree. As three typical examples, the disciples of Gamaliel remembered that "Rabbi Gamaliel used to say, 'Whoever does not make mention of these three things on Passover does not discharge his duty, and these are they: the Passover-Offering, Unleavened Bread, and Bitter Herbs'" (BT Pesachim 116a,b). The disciples of Hillel recalled the actions of their master at Passover: "It was related of Hillel that he used to wrap them together [paschal lamb, bitter herb, unleavened bread], for it is said, *they shall eat it with unleavened bread and bitter herbs*" (BT Pesachim 115a, emphasis mine). The disciples (tana'im) of Shammai and Hillel had memorized the decrees of their master on how far the first part of the Hallel should be recited at the

Passover supper: "How far does he [the leader of the seder] recite it? Beth [School of] Shammai maintain 'until as a joyous mother of children,' while Beth [School of] Hillel say 'until the flint into a fountain of waters'" (BT Pesachim 117a).

The elders and disciples of Jesus' school did exactly the same thing. They preserved what their master said, as in "so now I say it to you. I give you a new commandment: love one another...This is how all will know that you are my disciples, if you have love for one another" (Jn 13:33-35 NAB). They remembered his actions at the Last Supper: "When the hour came, he took his place at table with the apostles. He said to them, 'I have eagerly desired to eat this Passover with you before I suffer, for, I tell you, I shall not eat it [again] until there is fulfillment in the kingdom of God'" (Lk 22:14-16 NAB). As for passing on a decree in his master's name, Paul writes, "For I received from the Lord what I also handed on to you, that the Lord Jesus, on the night he was handed over, took bread, and after he had given thanks, broke it and said, 'This is my body that is for you. Do this in remembrance of me'" (1 Cor 11: 23,24 NAB).

Jesus was the shepherd, teacher, and overseer of his school. He was assisted in the care and keeping of his school by the twelve elders, who were also responsible for the feeding, teaching, and caring of all the disciples. They in turn were assisted by their wives and the wives of the other disciples in the cooking, washing, and cleaning necessary (Mt 27:55; Mk 15:41: Lk 23:49). The model that Jesus established was perpetuated by the Apostles as they established other church communities, or families. Over those communities they placed a pastor (shepherd) as bishop (overseer), who was assisted by a number of elders (presbutoroi), probably twelve in number, who were responsible for feeding, teaching, and caring for the disciples (students) and followers (Acts 14:23; 20:28; 21:18; 1 Tim 3:1-15; Tit 1:5-9; 1 Pet 5:1-4).

The School of Rabbi Jesus would also constitute a Passover association called a chavurah,[3] a necessary fact of life at that time. Individuals and small groups did not have the clout to secure the necessary lodgings and deal with the authorities. As a bayt, the community constituted a legal family, and for that reason Peter addressed the men as "brothers."[4]

Now that we know that the first-century Passovers were indeed crowded, the large community that accompanied Jesus on his pilgrimage and was present with the Lord at the Last Supper makes sense. His school was entirely typical.[5]

## MISCONCEPTION #2: "The Last Supper was not Passover"

"The most disputed calendric question" in the New Testament, according to Scripture scholar Raymond Brown, is whether the most significant day in Jesus' life was the 15th of Nisan (Passover) or the 14th of Nisan and, correspondingly, whether the Last Supper was the Passover meal or not.[6]

I believe that many scholars have not done their homework. They seem to avoid, at times, the simple fact that the books of the Bible are Jewish books and that their writers were Jews. This includes the books of the New Testament, even the Gospel of Luke. These books, though written in Greek, were translations of Hebrew concepts and ideas that were originally expressed in either Hebrew or Aramaic. When New Testament scholars find a seeming contradiction between John's Gospel and the Synoptics, they should go to the rabbis, who are experts on Jewish thought, for solutions. Too often they don't, and we have scholars who insist that the Synoptic Gospels are wrong and that the early church made a false assumption about the Last Supper coinciding with Passover.[7]

All four Gospels agree that the day of Jesus' death was a Friday.[8] And they therefore agree — because during Jesus' time, the day was reckoned from sunset to sunset—that Friday included the whole of the Passion in the narrower sense: the Last Supper, Gethsemane, arrest and trial, crucifixion and burial.[9]

All four Gospels also agree that the Last Supper took place in Jerusalem, which is where the Passover supper would have been held (BT Pesachim 85b).[10] They all agree that the Supper was held at night, which is when the Passover supper would have been held (Ex 12:8), as distinguished from the normal main meal, which at that time would have been eaten in the late afternoon. At the Last Supper, everyone reclined at table (BT Pesachim 99b).[11] Jesus warns about his betrayal by Judas in all the Gospels.[12] All describe Jesus' prediction of Peter's denial before the "cock crows."[13] All four Gospels agree that Jesus did not return to Bethany that night, as was his usual custom. In spite of the crushing crowd and the threats on his life, he remained within the legal boundaries of the Holy City of Jerusalem in accordance with the decree of the rabbis, who taught, "the first Passover [the 15th of Nisan] requires the spending of the night [in Jerusalem]" (BT Pesachim 95b). After the Last Supper, he walked only as far as Gethsemane.[14] The fact that Jesus did remain in Jerusalem after the Last Supper should be accepted by scholars as undeniable evidence that all four Gospels are describing the 15th of Nisan, the night when the paschal lambs were eaten.

There are other agreements among the Gospels that one might miss because of an inability to "think Jewish." All four refer to the "fruit of the vine," although each one does so in its own way.[15] Wine was the drink of Sabbath and festival meals. There are four cups or glasses of wine required by the ritual of the Passover supper (BT Pesachim 99b), and Luke's Gospel refers to Jesus' reciting the Kiddush (Lk 22:17,18) and sharing the first cup with his disciples. The Synoptics have Jesus instituting the New Covenant,[16] whereas John's Gospel has Jesus instituting the New Commandment,[17] which is the fundamental and indispensable principle of the New Covenant. John's Gospel includes the vital information that everyone at the supper was in a state of Levitical purity required for the celebration of Passover on the 15th of Nisan (BT Pesachim 109a).[18]

Scholars seem to ignore or diminish the importance of church tradition in this debate. For example, Raymond Brown writes: "The Synoptics or their tradition, influenced by these Passover characteristics, too quickly made the assumption that the day was actually Passover."[19] That "tradition" was the oral tradition of the Apostolic Church. The preaching and teaching of the church was entirely oral until the Jewish Revolt of 66-70 C.E. Only after that did the church find it necessary to write down the Gospel of Christ. The Evangelists found it necessary to write down the sayings of Jesus at the same time, and for the same reasons the rabbis collected and wrote down the Sayings of the Sages in the Talmud.

The "tradition" in the Synoptics that the Last Supper was Passover was the *universal conviction of the whole church!* Nowhere does John openly and clearly refute that tradition. Scholars agree that John was aware of Mark and was in some way acquainted with Luke.[20] Moreover, John continued to be a champion of that Passover tradition; he was referred to by Eusebius as a supreme example among the bishops of the Middle East who continued to celebrate the Last Supper and the Resurrection (Pascha) on the same day each year as the day the Jews observed Passover. In his letter to Victor, the bishop of Rome who wanted all the churches to convert to the "Sunday only" celebration of the Pascha (Easter), Polycrates writes that the bishops of Asia insisted on preserving the custom they had received from the apostles. Polycrates specifically points to Philip and John the Beloved, who not only began his Paschal Festival on the 14th of Nisan without deviation, but wore the mitre of the high priest at the celebration of the Eucharist.[21] If John agreed in his subsequent actions with the universal tradition of the church, then why would he disagree with or refute that tradition in his Gospel?[22]

Some scholars have a real problem with the clause, "before the feast of Passover," in John 13:1; they question the date of the Last Supper because of John 18:28, "Then they brought Jesus from Caiaphas to the praetorium. It was morning. And they themselves did not enter the praetorium, *in order not to be defiled so that they could eat the Passover*" (NAB, emphasis mine); and John 19:31, "Now since it was *preparation day...*" (NAB, emphasis mine). These verses in the fourth Gospel seem to imply that the Last Supper took place on the 14th of Nisan, the day before Passover. But there are answers for those who object to the date of the Last Supper being the 15th. One answer to the first objection would be a more accurate translation of John 13:1. The answers to the two great objections are found after further research into the way Passover was actually observed during the time of the Second Temple and into the Aramaic idioms used at that time.

1) In his notes on his translation of John 13:1 in the Anchor Bible (vol. 29a), Ray Brown writes, "*It was just before the Passover feast. This is a free translation.*" However, it should be noted that, literally, the opening verse of chapter 13 begins with a prepositional phrase, followed by the subject, which is followed by two participial phrases, and then the main verb and the main part of the sentence: "And before the feast of the Passover, Jesus, knowing that his hour had come for him to move from this world to the Father, loving his own in the world, he loved them to the end."[23] Ray Brown admits that his translation is not a literal one. But it does show his conviction that the date of the Last Supper was the 14th, the day before Passover. A much better translation is found in the New American Bible, "Before the feast of Passover, Jesus knew that his hour had come for him to pass from this world to the Father. He loved

his own in the world and he loved them to the end" (Jn 13:1
NAB). It seems clear to me that what John was saying is that
Jesus was aware *even before the feast of the Passover* that his
hour had come. What John wrote does not conflict in any way
with the witness of the Synoptic Gospels that the Last Supper
was on the 15th of Nisan. The conflict arises in the way the
translators translate the verse. If the translator believes that the
Last Supper was not Passover, he translates John 13:1,2 to confirm that conviction. If the translator believes the Last Supper
was the Passover, he translates those verses to confirm that conviction.

The conflict arises from translating completely out of context with John's train of thought throughout his Gospel. John
carefully builds up to that momentous Passover as the Supper
of the Lamb of God, especially in verses 11:55, 12:1, and 12:12.
(Remember also that the Messiah is to appear at Passover.) But
then to have his message aborted by a mistranslation is quite
regrettable.

Besides, Jesus and his disciples could not have gotten away
with a private and anticipatory celebration of the Passover seder
on the night before Passover. Such a celebration would have
been a serious breach of Mosaic Law.[24] It would, in any case,
have been impossible to hide on the night when thousands of
Jews were searching every room in the city for the forbidden
chametz. Moreover, in the first-century idiom, the phrase "to
eat Passover" meant "to eat the paschal lamb." The procure-
ment of lambs for the Passover Supper was under the strict control of the priests, and that would have made it impossible for
the disciples to get unauthorized lambs for the Last Supper.

2) There are serious questions about the trial of Jesus before
the high priests and the Sanhedrin that lead some scholars to
believe that the Last Supper could not have been held on the
15th of Nisan.[25] Some point to a rule that the Sanhedrin could

not meet on Holy Days. Actually, the Law that "None may sit in judgment on a Feast Day" militates against a trial on the 14th as much as it does for one on the 15th, and as far as I am concerned, even more so. The Passover sacrifice on the 14th was the most solemn sacrifice offered in the Holy Temple, and that required the presence and officiating of the high priest, chief priests, and all the available priests. The 14th of Nisan was the busiest day of the entire year for the high priest and priests of the Temple. There would be no time for them to be involved in anything else but the Passover sacrifice! Besides that, there were exceptions to this regulation.

> Deut. 17:12,13 prescribes the death penalty for anyone who opposes the decisions of the priests and judges of the High Court in Jerusalem. As a deterrent such a case was to be made public: "And all the people shall hear, and fear, and not act presumptuously again" (Deut. 17:13). Since "all the people" were assembled together in Jerusalem only on the occasions of the three pilgrimage feasts, it follows from Deut. 17:13 and the parallel texts Deut. 21:20,21; 13:11-12 that the executions in those cases designated by the Torah as the most serious offenses were – despite the rule against executions on a feast day – to be carried out *baregel,* "during the feast."[26]

Therefore, in cases deemed to be national emergencies, the Sanhedrin could and did meet. The accusations against Jesus – he was a false prophet (Dt 18:20), a blasphemer against God and his Temple (Mk 14:58, 62), and a proclaimed Messiah (Mk 14:61,62) – gave ample justification to the Beyt Din HaGadol to believe that it was faced with an insurrection of mass proportions. The high priest, Caiaphas, was deadly serious when he proclaimed, "You know nothing, nor do you consider that it is better for you that one man should die instead of the people, so that the whole nation may not perish" (Jn 11:49,50 NAB). The high priest was well aware of how the Romans reacted to any challenge to their authority, even on a feast day, and of how that reaction could be swift and bloody.[27] On one Passover, more than a thousand worshipers died in the Temple when the people rioted after a Roman soldier "mooned" them from the parapets of the Antionia. Now they were faced with a crisis of monumental proportions.

The stories of miracles coming out of "Galilee of the Gentiles" could be easily dismissed as popular credulity. But now, some people of authority in Jerusalem had witnessed the raising of Lazarus from the dead (Jn 11:31-45).[28] That had caused widespread acceptance of the miracle by the people of Jerusalem and the arriving pilgrims. Next came Jesus' triumphal entry into Jerusalem. The masses proclaimed him Messiah, that is "The Anointed King of the Jews," and had shouted "Hosanna!" which was not a shout of approval but a battle cry. The Hebrew *hoshi'ana!* actually means "Liberation Now!" or "Save us Now!" and were the slogans of a popular revolt against Rome. Finally, when Jesus drove the moneychangers from the Temple,[29] he directly challenged the authority of the chief priests. A challenge to the authority of the Sanhedrin was also a direct challenge to the authority of Rome.

At that time, the Sanhedrin was a quisling institution under complete Roman control. The office of high priest, which was supposed to be for life, was actually bought and sold by the Romans. Ananias, who was the patriarch of the high priestly family at that time, held the office from C.E. 6 to 15. He was succeeded as high priest by five sons, a grandson, and his son-in-law, Caiaphas (Brown et al., *Jerome Biblical Commentary* 63:159[12]). Joseph Caiaphas was appointed high priest by the Roman procurator Valerius Gratus in 18 C.E. and removed from office by another, Vitellius, in 36 C.E. The pontificate of Caiaphas was longer than the administration of Pontius Pilate (25-27 C.E. to 35 C.E.), which shows that the two of them got along well together and cooperated in all important matters. In fact, Vitellius removed Caiaphas from the office of high priest just a year after Pilate was sent to Rome for trial over the slaughter of Samaritan pilgrims at Mount Gerizim. The implications are that Caiaphas was in collusion with Pilate in that and many other incidents.

If the Sanhedrin had not immediately acted on "a clear and present danger," the Roman garrison would have acted and with far greater and more disastrous consequences. But the Sanhedrin had another serious problem: Some of their own members had become sympathetic to Jesus (Jn 13:42; Mk 23:50). This meant that the full Sanhedrin of 70 to 72 members could not sit in judgment to bring in the desired verdict of "guilty." Actually, there was no need for the Sanhedrin to conduct a trial. Jesus had already committed a seditious act in his triumphal entry into Jerusalem. Anyone proclaimed the "king of Israel" (Jn 12:13 NAB) was an enemy of Rome and would be executed at the first opportunity. "King of the Jews" was the actual indictment under which Jesus was executed (Jn 19:19). The fourth Gospel states that Jesus was arrested by a combined force of Roman soldiers and Temple guards (Jn 18:3). That implies that Pilate was already involved in the case and would handle the actual trial and crucifixion. But the high priest and the Sanhedrin were also deeply involved in the arrest by sending Temple guards, who together with the Roman tribune, brought Jesus to the palace of the high priest, where both Annas and Caiaphas lived (Jn 18:12-14). The immediate need of Annas, Caiaphas, the chief priests, and elders of the Sanhedrin was to interrogate Jesus in the hope of extracting from him enough derogatory and blasphemous information to thoroughly discredit him with the people (Mk 14:63,64). It was not a trial that the Sanhedrin conducted, but an intense interrogation attempting to exonerate themselves with the people.

Joachim Jeremias records in his footnotes on page 79 of the book *The Eucharistic Words of Jesus* that the Sanhedrin actually did have the authority to put someone to death, and it is recorded that they did so in 100 B.C.E. They hung Jeshu, a disciple of Rabbi Joshua Ben Perachiah — on Passover — for practicing sorcery, leading the people into idolatry, and enticing them to apostasy — much the same charges as they had against Jesus.

If the chief priests and elders had all that time to conduct two trials, then the date of the "trials" must have been on the 15th. On the 14th, all of the priests, and especially the high priest, were occupied with the elaborate preparations and purifications for the sacrifices of the Passover. They were not only fully occupied with the Passover sacrifice from noon until after three, and with the emurim from late afternoon until well into the evening, but their entire morning was taken up with the morning sacrifice, the festival offerings (chaggigah) of the throngs of pilgrims, and the minchah or the evening sacrifice, all of which had to be completed before noon! There just was not enough time for them to gather the others for a meeting, let alone to gather the necessary witnesses. The 15th, on the other hand, was more relaxed.

3) The third argument against dating the Last Supper on the 15th of Nisan is based on two verses in John's Gospel: "Then they brought Jesus from Caiaphas to the praetorium. It was morning. And they themselves did not enter the praetorium, in order not to be defiled so that they could eat the Passover" (Jn 18:28 NAB), and "It was preparation day for Passover, and it was about noon" (Jn 19:14 NAB). The two verses present a problem for which there seems no resolution, but I found a solution for the first quotation where I expected — from a Jewish source. In *Passover Haggadah, A Messianic Celebration*, Eric-Peter Lipson writes:

> The obligatory Passover peace offering, the second chaggigah of the 15th Nisan — also referred to as "pesach" — must be distinguished from the paschal lamb itself and its accompanying chag-

gigah of the 14th (Deuteronomy 16:2-7, 16-17). In the Talmud a
question is asked, "What is the meaning of Pesachim?" The
reply is: "The Peace Offerings (sh'lamim) of Pesach" (Rosh
Hashanah 5a).[30]

There was the explanation all along, just waiting for someone to ask a rabbi. Jesus was condemned by the chief priests of
the Sanhedrin, who were responsible for the *second Passover
sacrifice* (Nm 28:16-25). Originally, this sacrifice was offered
along with the Passover offering (2 Chr 35:10-19; 2 Chr 30:21-
27). Together, these two sacrifices were known as "Pesach,"
and known as such from the time of Kings Hezekiah and Josiah.
The two sacrifices remained together as one until the first century, when they were separated because of the enormous number of Passover offerings. The second Passover sacrifice was
moved from the 14th to the 15th of Nisan; the eating of it from
the evening of the 15th to the evening of the 16th; then it was
repeated every day throughout the seven-day Feast. The people
could share in the second Passover sacrifice by their offering
of additional chaggigot. In the Torah, both the Passover offering and the second Passover sacrifice of the priests are called
"Pesach" (Dt 16:2 as well as in 2 Chr 35:7). Deuteronomy 16:2
(NAB) reads, "You shall sacrifice the Passover (Pesach) to
YHWH your God from the flock and from the herd (*tzon
uvakar*)." "Tzon" means "sheep, goat, flock," and *baqar*
means, "cattle, cows, herd, kine, oxen."[31] It is a clear reference
to the two Passover sacrifices that made up the one Pesach or
Pascha (Passover). "Tzon" refers to the first sacrifice of the
paschal lambs (Ex 12:5), while "baqar" refers to the second
and priestly sacrifice of Passover (Nm 28:16-19; 2 Chr 35:7-9,
12,13). Consequently, the priests' need to stay in a state of ritual
purity so that they might eat the second Passover sacrifice, also
called Pesach, on the night of the 16th does not in any way conflict with the Synoptics assertion that Thursday night was in
fact the 15th of Nisan. "To eat Passover" ("phagosi to Pas-

cha," Jn 18:28) meant just as much "to eat the priestly Pesach/Pascha" as it did "to eat the Passover sacrifice Pesach/Pascha." We must not forget that it was the chief priests and priestly elders of the Sanhedrin that brought Jesus to Pilate, *and not the Jewish people!*

Now, finally, to John 19:14 and "the Preparation Day for Passover." The Greek reads much more simply, *paraskeue tou pascha* or "the Preparation of the Passover." Here "paraskeue" most likely represents the Aramaic *arubta* or *arubat pascha.* Both Raymond E. Brown and Joachim Jeremias recognize that the phrase is equally applicable to Friday, the day before the Sabbath of Passover, as it is to the preparation day on Thursday. Josephus in his Antiquities uses "paraskeue" to designate "the Preparation Day for the Sabbath" (XVI.vi.2; #163).[32] The Synoptics use the same word as well for "the Preparation Day of the Sabbath. It is "paraskeuen" in Matthew 27:62, "paraskeue" in Mark 15:42, and "paraskeue" in Luke 23:54. All of them refer to the Friday preparation for the Sabbath of Passover. Moreover, C.C. Torrey presents the possibility that the phrase, "paraskeue tou pascha" could very well represent the Aramaic genitive *arubta di pascha* or "Friday of Passover Week." Even in early Aramaic, "arubta" had already been established as "Friday" (the day before the Sabbath).[33]

This use of "paraskeue" for "Friday, the preparation day for the Sabbath of Passover" is no small thing. The Sabbath of Passover is an extremely important day. It determines when the Feast of the Sheaf Offering of the First Fruits occurs and when Pentecost (The Fiftieth Day) is to be celebrated (Lv 23:9-11, 15,16). On the eve of the Sabbath, extra prayers are added to the celebration of Passover. So the 16th of Nisan, that year, took on added importance because it was the Sabbath of Passover. On the very next day, the day of the Resurrection, the priests and rabbis began the count of seven weeks and one day, or fifty days, until Pentecost.

Since the 15th of Nisan fell on a Friday that year, that fact made the first day of Passover a partial work day. Ordinarily, the 15th was a day of rest, a day of Holy Convocation or "Miqra-Qodesh" in Hebrew. But when the 15th fell on a Friday, the preparation day (for the Sabbath) of Passover, then all of the work forbidden on the Sabbath had to be done on the day before. That would include the lighting of lamps for light, the preparation of food to be eaten on the Sabbath, and the making of any necessary purchases before the solemn Sabbath of Passover. As a partial work day, that Friday, the 15th of Nisan, was the logical day for the trial and execution of Jesus.

There are three questions that have to be asked of those who do not believe the Last Supper was the Passover. Why would John describe a Passover setting if it were not the Passover supper? Where does the concept of Jesus as our Passover sacrifice originate if not from Jesus himself at the seder? "For our paschal lamb, Christ, has been sacrificed" (1 Cor 5:7 NAB) was already an established belief when Paul used it to exhort the Corinthians to moral behavior. And, if the Last Supper were not the Passover supper, what did Jesus mean when he announced "Do this as my anamnesis"? (1 Cor 11:24,25). Dangling in a void, "my anamnesis" could have meant any number of things, but when Jesus proclaimed his intentions to his disciples at the Passover supper, his purpose became very clear. The Passover supper is itself an "anamnesis" (BT Pesachim 116b). The Passover supper is the zikkaron/anamnesis of God, the Father, "This day shall be a memorial feast (zikkaron) for you, which all your generations shall celebrate with pilgrimage (chag) to the LORD, as a perpetual institution (*chukat 'olam*) (Ex 12:14 NAB). If Passover is the Father's memorial zikkaron-anamnesis, then it follows quite simply that the Eucharist is Jesus' memorial zikkaron-anamnesis!

Now, we have established that Thursday night was indeed Passover, the 15th of Nisan. We have also established that

Friday was the preparation day for the Sabbath of Passover and the day on which the priests offered the second Passover sacrifice, also called Pesach/Pascha, and the chaggigah for the supper of the 16th. So just what has John's Gospel been trying to tell us with its unique description of the 15th of Nisan of that momentous year?

John's Gospel in no way disputes the chronology of the Synoptics, but it does add much to our understanding of that eventful day. On Thursday, the 14th of Nisan, the disciples of Jesus sacrificed their paschal lambs and, at sunset, when the date changed to the 15th of Nisan, they ate the Passover with Jesus in the upper room in the Holy City of Jerusalem according to the Law of Moses. Later that night, the 15th of Nisan, Jesus was arrested and taken to the palace of the high priest. On Friday, the preparation day for the Sabbath of Passover, he was subjected to a pre-trial interrogation by members of the Sanhedrin, turned over to the Roman Procurator for trial, convicted, scourged, and crucified. He hung on the cross during those same three hours, noon to three, when the paschal lambs had been sacrificed the day before. But on this day, the Passover sacrifice (Pesach/Pascha) was a burnt offering (Nm 28:16-25) as well as a sin offering for the atonement of sins (Nm 28:22 NAB).

Yes, Jesus died as paschal lambs (chaggigot) were dying, but especially, he hung dying as portions of bullocks, one ram, and unblemished yearling paschal lambs were consumed in the flames of the burnt offering of Passover (Nm 28:19) and as a sin offering for the atonement of the people's sins (Nm 28:22). Moreover, Jesus was separated in quarantine, prepared for death, and executed under the watchful eyes of the chief priests like the paschal lamb, (Mt 26:57; Mk 15:31; Lk 23:33-35; Jn 19:18:12-14), something that could not have happened on the 14th. He was taken down from the cross as the Sabbath of Passover approached, when the priests and people would share, as

Pascha, the chaggigah of the 16th. He lay in the tomb throughout the Sabbath of Passover, but he rose from the dead on the first day of the week (Yom Rishon), the Feast Day of the Offering of the Sheaf of the First Fruits (Lv 23:10-12 and 1 Cor 15:20) and the first day of the *omer*—the count of fifty days until Pentecost (Lv 23:15,16).

## Misconception #3: "The Jews Killed Christ"

Many years ago during Good Friday services, I heard several impassioned sermons on how the crowds that came out to greet Jesus on Palm Sunday later turned against him and had him crucified. They were impressive sermons, but they were based upon a grave falsehood. The crowds that greeted Jesus on his entry into Jerusalem had nothing to do with his arrest and death!

Jesus was very popular with the majority of the Jewish people, and it was because of this popularity that a small but powerful minority wanted him dead. The Gospels are very explicit in naming those people. Even before Jesus entered the Holy City, he told his followers exactly who wanted him arrested and turned over to the Roman authorities: the chief priests, elders, and scribes of the Sanhedrin.[34] All four Gospels record that it was the Sanhedrin that plotted against Jesus and that they carried out their planning in secret because they feared that Jesus' arrest would cause a riot among the people.[35]

The misunderstanding about who was responsible for Christ's death arises out of a lack of awareness of the political and religious situation in the first century. The Romans were the cruel masters of the Holy Land. They had some support from the wealthy Sadducees, the cosmopolitan, Greek-speaking Jews who felt that membership in that Roman world was the necessary price of progress. Only on the matter of religion did the Sadducees separate themselves from the culture of Greece and Rome. Even here, though, they brought to their faith the logic, philosophy, and culture of the general civilization. Among the Sadducees were many Levites, the very wealthy, and the hereditary families of the priests and high priest. Unfortunately, among the leading priestly families, religion was the means to acquiring great wealth and power. The Romans used the rivalry among the priestly families to gain control of the Jewish nation. The Roman authorities sold the office of the high priest to the highest bidder, who held that office until it was sold to another. Those who held office in the Sanhedrin not only had to make their position worthwhile to the Romans, but they also had to assure them of their loyalty. It is no wonder, then, that this institution would have been threatened by any man whom the common people considered to be the Messiah or anointed king.

The majority of the religious people were Pharisees, who hated Rome and Roman rule. They disliked the Sadducees because they had sold out to the pagan, foreign culture. They hated and despised the families of the high priests, because, like the Borgias and Medicis who came later, they used religion to acquire wealth and exercise power. The people's feelings toward the high priests' families are recorded in the Talmud as "Woe is me because of the house of Boethus; woe is me because of their staves! Woe is me because of the house of Chanin [Chananyah, Annas], woe is me because of their whisperings! Woe is me because of the house of Kathros, woe is me because of their pens! Woe is me because of the house of Ishmael the son of Phabi, woe is me because of their fists! For they are High Priests and their sons are [Temple] treasurers and their sons-in-law are trustees and their servants beat the people with staves" (BT Pesachim 57a). They loathed the Sanhedrin because it had become the symbol of pagan, Roman rule. Unfortunately, neither the common people nor the Pharisees feared Roman power. They were inspired by the victory of the Maccabees over the Syrian Greeks and were sure that the Messiah was about to appear and lead them to victory over Rome and its polluting, pagan culture. Josephus and others record the many rebellions and riots that led up to the revolt of 66 to 70 C.E. Although the Romans crushed every rebellion, the people remained confident that at the right time, God would give them the victory. When Jesus appeared at the gates of Jerusalem at Passover time, they were convinced that their Messiah had at last arrived and their glorious hour had come! When the Sanhedrin heard the people's cry of Hoshi'a Na! they had to act swiftly in order to save themselves as well as the nation from a powerful Roman response.

All four Gospels clearly identify the guilty ones, and they were the chief priests and their followers (Mt 26:3-5; Mk 14:1,2; Lk 22:1,2; Jn 11:47-53). As if to leave no doubt about who wanted Jesus dead, John's Gospel records that the chief priests led that small, condemning crowd of their entourage in the cry, "We have no king but Caesar" (Jn 19:15 NAB). No ordinary Jew or Pharisee would ever, could ever utter such a blasphemy. The vast majority of the Jews would have happily cut out their own tongues than allow such a disgusting sacrilege to pass their lips. *Adonai Elohenu Melekh HaOlam,* "The LORD our God is the King of this Universe!"

There is a problem in John's Gospel, however, where Jesus identifies his enemies as "the Jews." The actual word is "Ioudaioi" or "Judeans," and I can't understand why it is still translated — wrongly so — as "the Jews." What we are dealing with here is an idiom that is easily understood by 20th century Americans. We have one almost like it: "Yankee" or "Yanks." To foreigners, all Americans are "Yanks," but we Americans know that only the people in the North are Yankees. Of course, Northerners consider that only New Englanders are Yankees, while New Englanders know that it is in Connecticut where you find the true Yanks. The term "Ioudaioi," for Judeans — or Jews — had a similar variety of usage at the time of Christ. To the Gentiles, all Hebrews were "Judeans," while the vast majority of Jews called themselves "Hebrews." Only those living in the vicinity of Jerusalem were actually Judeans, because the Holy City was in the province of Judea. The Hebrews of Galilee were actually Galileans and looked down upon by the Judeans.

John, however, is making an even more specific use of the idiom. Throughout his Gospel, "the Jews" are the religious authorities in Jerusalem: the Sanhedrin and their representatives.[36] John is using the idiom as a beautiful play on words.[37] The religious authorities are the leaders of the people and, as members of the Sanhedrin, are, indeed, "Judeans." But they are false leaders who have perverted the Holy Temple and its use. Jesus, on the other hand, is the true Judean, Messiah and lawful leader and king of his people, Israel. Although the Sanhedrin knows of him only as the Nazarene and Galilean, Jesus was born in Bethlehem of Judea, which also makes him a Judean. Moreover, he was born into the family of David of the tribe of Judah, and as the "Messiah The Son Of David," Jesus is the True Judean! Against him, the True Judean, the false Judeans plot and scheme.

It is true that the birth of Jesus at Bethlehem is not mentioned in the fourth Gospel, but the most persuasive tradition has been that Mary, the mother of Jesus, spent her final years in the Johannine community at Ephesus. That community would be the primary source of information on the Nativity. Luke, who records that he interviewed eyewitnesses (Lk 1:2,3), strongly implies that he got his information direct from Jesus' mother, because he relays to us intimate details of the Annunciation and twice states, "And Mary kept all these things, reflecting on them in her heart" (Lk 2:19,51 NAB). It was significant to the Jewish people that the Messiah — the Son of David — was born in Bethlehem ("The House of Bread"), which was the birthplace of King David (1 Sm 16:1,12,13; Mi 5:1).

The next question might then be: If the majority of the Jewish people were willing to follow Jesus, then what really happened on Good Friday? And why did God allow the great punishment to overtake all of them in the destruction of the whole nation? The answer to the first part of the question can be found in John 12:32-34. Jesus announces to the crowd that he is to be crucified. The people react with strong objections and confusion, "We have heard from the law that the Messiah remains forever" (Jn 12:34 NAB). Well versed in the popular biblical prophecy about "He Who Comes," the people believed that the Messiah was invincible. He could not suffer, be defeated, or die. They believed that all the prophecies about the "Suffering Servant" in Isaiah and in Psalm 22 applied to the sufferings of the nation of Israel, not to its Messiah. Therefore, when the common people saw Jesus being dragged through the streets, bleeding from the scourging, and tied to the crossbeam of a cross by the Roman soldiers, they "knew" that Jesus could not be their Messiah. The Messiah could not suffer and die! They simply turned away from him in humiliation, believing that they had been seduced once again by another false prophet who hoped to be king.

The reason for which the great calamity fell upon the Jewish people can be found in Josephus' *The Jewish Wars*. The people turned away from the Pharisees' wise council that they should not use force to gain independence; they turned their support over to the Zealots and Sicarii and their acts of terrorism and political assassination (Josephus, *Jewish Wars*, 166,167). *That political nightmare degenerated into a vicious civil war between the supporters of the Zealots Simon Bar Giora and John of Gischala, which raged within the walls of the Holy City as Titus ringed Jerusalem with his earthworks and war machines (Josephus, Jewish Wars, 267-286; 316-321).* The people had broken the Covenant with God. The Covenant meant that God would have love (chesed) for his people and protect them, so long as they had love (chesed) for each other. But the people had replaced that covenant/love for their neighbors (Lv 19:17,18) with hateful and murderous hearts. Not only had they gone to war with Rome, they had also engaged in a vicious civil war. If the Romans had not destroyed the nation, the people would have exterminated themselves by their constant infighting and murders and reprisals. Jews were hating fellow Jews and killing those who did not agree with them. Even while the Romans crushed the defenders of the Holy City, the civil and religious war raged on inside of the walls of Jerusalem and the Holy Temple. It was an insanity much as we see in Beirut, Lebanon, today.

There is also a more subtle and persistent form of anti-semitism that must be addressed before we can understand the whole of sacred Scripture. When Jesus confronted the Sanhedrin and the high priests with their misuse of God's Holy Temple, Jesus rejected the Temple and replaced its sacrifices, but he did not reject Judaism. He said,

> Do not think that I have come to abolish the law or the prophets. I have come not to abolish but to fulfill. Amen, I say to you, until heaven and earth pass away, not the smallest letter or the smallest part of a letter will pass from the law, until all things have taken place (Mt 5:17,18 NAB).

Not even the smallest letter of the Torah and prophets, the yod, nor even that very small part of the letter that distinguishes the letter *bet* ("b") from the *kaph* ("kh") or the dalet ("d") from the resh ("r") can be done away with until the messianic kingdom has been established all over the world, and all people everywhere are brothers and sisters under the fatherhood of God! Jesus praises those who practice and preach the commandments of the Torah and condemns those who violate them (Mt 5:19). He also condemns those Pharisees who had fractured Judaism into warring camps by their bickering over the fine shades and nuances of the law (Mt 5:20). He goes to the very heart of the matter about what he expects from Judaism and why he was so angry with many of the disputatious Pharisees and contentious rabbis. A prominent rabbi and doctor of the law once posed to Jesus a popular question among the scribes, "Which is the first of all the commandments?" (Mk 12:28 NAB).

Jesus then recited the Sh'ma, Judaism's great profession of faith.

> Hear, O Israel!
> The LORD (YHWH) our God,
> is LORD (YHWH) alone!
> You shall love the LORD (YHWH) your God
>     with all your heart,
>     with all your soul [*nefesh*],
>     with all your mind [*nefesh*],
>     and with all your strength
> (Mk 12:29-30 NAB; cf. Dt 6:4-5).[38]

But then Jesus added to the Sh'ma the Commandment from Leviticus 19:18 (NAB), "You shall love your neighbor as yourself," concluding, "The whole law and the prophets depend on these two commandments" (Mk 22:40 NAB). What Jesus demanded from Judaism, and from his followers, was to love God by loving their neighbor. "If anyone says, 'I love God,' but hates his brother, he is a liar; for whoever does not love a brother whom he has seen cannot love God whom he has not seen. This is the commandment we have from him: whoever loves God must also love his brother" (1 Jn 4:20-21 NAB). What Jesus condemned was the hypocrisy of those Jews who zealously demonstrated their love of God with their religious ostentation, but who abused and at times even killed fellow Jews who disagreed with them or disputed their teachings.

What Jesus repudiated was the Temple with its priesthood and sacrifices. Jesus demonstrated his anger against these with the action/parable of the fig tree. His curse of the fig tree was a part of the action of cleansing the Temple (Mt 21:12-20; Mk 11:12-21). Jesus had come to God's Holy Temple hoping for it to be the place that enshrined God's Covenant with Israel and a place that unified the nation. Instead, he found that it had been turned into a money-making machine for the priests and a national treasure held in ransom by the Roman authorities. Jesus expected to find his father's Holy Temple bearing the fruit of love of God and love of neighbor. He found, instead, the fruits of avarice and arrogance. Jesus' directing his anger at the tree, even though it was "out of season" for figs, means that we never know when God will call us to an accounting and his judgment. In the year 70 C.E., the Holy Temple was destroyed and dismantled. All sacrifices ceased and the priesthood was abolished.[39] All of the wealth of the Sadducees was plundered by the Romans. Only the Pharisees survived to save the Torah and the prophets and the 613 commandments of the Eternal Law. They built a new temple in which to enshrine the Covenant and that new temple is the Talmud.

If Christ had rejected the whole of Judaism, he would have repudiated the Ten Commandments because they are essential to Judaism. The eternal Covenant entered into by God and his people at Mount Sinai *is* Judaism. Anyone who says that "Judaism is over and done with" nullifies the Ten Commandments because the Torah and its 613 Commandments are Judaism, along with the Prophets and the Writings that make up the Hebrew Scriptures.[40] If Judaism is obsolete, then the Hebrew Scriptures are obsolete as well. They are no more than a relic of some past civilization. If Judaism has been abandoned, then why do we Christians proclaim that Jesus is the Christ, the Messiah, which means that we proclaim that he is the anointed king of the Jews?

> I do not want you to be unaware of this mystery, brothers, so that you will not become wise [in] your own estimation: a harden-

ing has come upon Israel in part, until the full number of the Gentiles comes in, and thus all Israel will be saved, as it is written...In respect to the gospel, they are enemies on your account; but in respect to election, they are beloved because of the patriarchs. For the gifts and the call of God are irrevocable (Rm 11:25-29 NAB).

Now I am speaking to you Gentiles. Inasmuch then as I am the apostle to the Gentiles, I glory in my ministry in order to make my race jealous and thus save some of them. For if their rejection is the reconciliation of the world, what will their acceptance be but life from the dead? If the first fruits are holy, so is the whole batch of dough; and if the root is holy, so are the branches.

But if some of the branches were broken off, and you, a wild olive shoot, were grafted in their place and have come to share in the rich root of the olive tree, do not boast against the branches. If you do boast, consider that you do not support the root; the root supports you (Rm 11:13-18 NAB).

We have been grafted onto the root of Judaism. If we reject that root, then we cut ourselves off from it and can no longer be nourished by it. Such has been the sad fate of the Christian church for all too long, and we languish on the bitter stump of paganism. We must reattach ourselves to the root God has provided for us and live!

Beside all this, if the destruction of the nation of Israel is the result of the crucifixion, then we Christians are in big trouble. Jesus prayed "Father, forgive them" for those responsible for his death. If God did not forgive them but instead vented his wrath on the many innocent as well as the few guilty ones, then what kind of intercessor do we have in Jesus if God ignores him when the chips are down?

## NOTES

1. The word "avot" is an inclusive word. It is based upon the word *av,* which means "father," but the word is given the feminine plural.
2. *Rabban* (Aramaic) means teacher, educator. "Rav" means teacher, master, and lord. *Rabbi* means my teacher, my master. The

title "Rabbi" is given to Jewish theologians or teachers of religious studies.

3. Raphael, *A Feast of History,* 81.

4. The first generation of Christian communities went far beyond the legal concept and recognized themselves as a real family, "children of God in their Lord Jesus Christ."

5. The Cenacle, built by the crusaders over what they believed was the Last Supper site, could not possibly have held that large an assemblage. I have the feeling that the upper room may have been the entire top floor of the house of John Mark. Such large and open top-floor rooms were a typical feature of first-century Jewish architecture. Whole families would retire to these spacious upper rooms during the long, hot summer months. Balconies and numerous latticed windows allowed any breezes that might arise to flow freely throughout the room. The family of John Mark was wealthy enough to have just that sort of room, one adequate for the large community that accompanied Jesus from Galilee.

6. Brown, "John (13-21)," *The Anchor Bible* 29a:555.

7. Ibid., 556.

8. Matthew 27:62; Mark 15:42; Luke 23:54; John 19:31,42.

9. Jeremias, *The Eucharistic Words of Jesus,* 15, 16.

10. Matthew 26:17-18; Mark 14:12-16; Luke 22:7-12; John 12:12.

11. Matthew 26:20: *anekeito meta ton dodeka,* "he reclined with the Twelve"; Mark 14:18-21: *erchetai meta ton dodeka kai anakeimenon ayton,* "he came with the Twelve, and they reclining"; Luke 22:14: *anepese, kai oi dodeka apostoloi syn ayto,* "he reclined, and the Twelve Apostles with him"; John 13:12: "*anapeson palin,*" "reclining again" (translations mine).

12. Matthew 26:21-25; Mark 14:18-21; Luke 22:21-23; John 13:21-30.

13. Matthew 26:31-35; Mark 14:27-31; Luke 22:31-34; John 13:36-38.

14. Matthew 26:36; Mark 14:26,32.

15. Matthew 26:29; Mark 14:25; Luke 22:17-18 (the reference here appears to be to the Kiddush of Passover); John 15:1-8 refers to Christ as the vine from Psalm 80:15,16 and as wisdom from Sirach 24:17. John's concept is preserved in the Didache, which refers to the Eucharist as "The holy vine of David your servant revealed through Jesus Christ."

16. Matthew 26:26-28; Mark 14:23-24; Luke 22:20.

17. John 13:34; 15:12,17.

18. John 13:10.

19. Brown, "John," *Anchor Bible* 29a:556.

20. Brown et al., *The Jerome Biblical Commentary* 63:17-23.

21. Eusebius, *The History of the Church,* 231.

22. There are other, less important arguments that the Last Supper could not have occurred on Passover, but these are handled well by Joachim Jeremias in *The Eucharistic Words of Jesus,* 15-84.

23. Brown, "John," *Anchor Bible* 29a:549.

24. Jeremias, *The Eucharistic Words of Jesus,* f4; G. Dalman, *The Words of Jesus,* (Endinburgh, 1909), 48.

25. I use the Jewish system of marking days from sunset to sunset. From sunset Wednesday to sunset Thursday was the 14th of Nisan. From sunset Thursday to sunset Friday was the 15th and the first day of Passover. Sunset Friday began the 16th and Sabbath of Passover.

26. Jeremias, *The Eucharistic Words of Jesus,* 78-79.

27. Cornfeld, *Josephus: The Jewish Wars,* 121, 122, 162.

28. John's Gospel implies that some of the witnesses to the raising of Lazarus were members of the Sanhedrin because he calls them "the Jews," its term for the religious authorities.

29. For theological reasons, John places that incident on a Passover some years earlier (Jn 2:13-17). However, he leaves us with a clue that the event actually took place at another time, as recorded in the Synoptic Gospels. At Jesus' entry into Jerusalem, John's Gospel says that "they got palm branches and came out to meet him" (Jn 12:13 NAB). Palm trees do not grow in Jerusalem, which sits upon the crest of a 2,000-foot mountain range. But palm branches, called the *lulav,* were a familiar symbol of Judaism. The lulav has been found frequently depicted on wall murals and in floor mosaics of ancient synagogues. Among other things, the lulav represented the dedication of Solomon's Temple, which occurred during Sukkot (1 Kgs 8:2; 2 Chr 5:3) and the rededication of the Temple under the Maccabees (Chanukah) when the people, "carrying rods entwined with leaves, green branches and palms,...sang hymns of grateful praise to him who had brought about the purification of his own Place" (2 Mc 10:7 NAB).

30. Lipson, *Passover Haggadah,* 5.

31. Alcalay, *The Complete Hebrew-English Dictionary,* cols. 2143, 279.

32. Jeremias, *The Eucharistic Words of Jesus,* 80; Brown, "John," *Anchor Bible* 29a:882 n. 14.

33. C.C. Torrey, "The Date of the Crucifixion According to the Fourth Gospel," *Journal of Biblical Literature* 50 (1931): 232- 237, 241; C.C. Torrey, "In the Fourth Gospel the Last Supper Was the Paschal Meal," *The Jewish Quarterly Review* 42 (1951-2): 237-250.

34. Matthew 16:21; Mark 8:31; 10:33,34; Luke 9:22.

35. Matthew 26:3-5; Mark 14:1-2; Luke 19:47-48; John 11:47-53.

36. See Brown, "John," *The Anchor Bible* 29:lxxi.

37. Puns and plays on words are common in the original Hebrew and Greek. They were used to help people memorize the passages. It is unfortunate that many of them are lost in translation.

38. See Deuteronomy 6:4-5, Matthew 22:37-38, and Luke 10:27. Jesus was reciting the great Sh'ma. Out of tradition, he recited it in Hebrew. That resulted in some discrepancy in the recording of it in the Synoptic Gospels as each author translated it into a Greek that would be comprehensible to his readers. The problem was with the Hebrew word "nefesh," meaning "being," which was frequently translated into Greek as "soul, life, spirit, mind, person."

39. In the ever-present hope that someday God will rebuild his Holy Temple, those descended from the Levitical and priestly families of the Temple period have kept their names. The Hebrew word for priest is *kohen*. Family names that contain the letters "k" (or "c"), "h," and "n" belong to the hereditary priestly families: Kohen, Kahn, Cohen, and Cohn, for example. Names built around "l," "v," and "y" belong to the hereditary Levitical families: Levy and Levin and Levine, for example.

40. There are some who believe just that, again with help from translators. Hebrews 10:9 from the NAB reads, "He takes away the first covenant to establish the second." The word "covenant" (diatheke) does not appear in the Greek, which reads more closely as, "He takes away the first, that the second he may set up, by which we are sanctified through the offering of the body of Jesus Christ once for all!" This is saying that "the first part," which was the daily sacrifices of the priests and the annual sin offerings of the Temple, are now removed and replaced by the one perfect sacrifice of Jesus Christ.

# SIX

# The Ritual of the Last Supper

## Blessing the Festival Lights

The younger children came running in from the outside stairway, exclaiming that the sun was about to set. Several of the women hurried to the various lampstands around the room. Jesus' mother, Mary Magdalene, and Martha surveyed the room and saw that everything was ready. All of the work in preparation had to be done by now, and it was. One of the children yelled that the sun was setting just as the blasts of the shofars from the pinnacle of the Temple announced that the day was over and that it was now Passover. The women at the lampstands lit the lamps, and then all of the women covered their eyes with the fingers of each hand. Jesus' mother led them all in singing, in Hebrew,[1] words that they each had learned from their mothers and that their mothers had learned from their mothers:

Blessed are You
O LORD (YHWH) our God,
King of all creation[2]
Who has sanctified us
through your commandments,
*(then removing their hands and looking at the flame)*
and commanded us
to light the festival lights
Amen.

The Festival had now begun, but a little while remained yet before everyone would recline for supper. The men, with Jesus, were still not there. The women sent the children outside to watch for them, reminding them to watch themselves as well and to stay clean. There were a few minutes for relaxing, but they strolled about the room to check on minor things and to admire the beauty of the scene. Their best linens covered the tables. Beautiful coverings and cushions were arranged over the couches. All of the metal objects — copper, brass, silver, and gold — glistened from their rigorous polishing. The olive oil-fed wicks cast a bright light over the whole room, accenting the decorations and arrangements, and gave to everything and everyone a festive feeling. Against one wall, the food was ready and the shiny serving trays were at their places, some filled with the roasted chaggigah, some awaiting the paschal lambs and their roasted giblets.

The women heard a commotion outside in the courtyard. The children had seen Jesus and Lazarus with the Twelve and the older disciples come through the gate, each one kissing the large mezuzah on the gatepost. They had come from a synagogue in the lower city where as Pharisees they were more welcome and not so easily recognized in the crowd. With the crush of the pilgrims, a synagogue would be the ideal place for the recital of the minchah or "evening prayers." All of the courtyards, rooftops, market areas, and other open spaces were filled with women and men preparing for the Passover supper.

They were preparing for it at the synagogue, too, but the main hall would have been left for the worshipers until the last minute. After the prayers, Jesus and his followers might have helped the synagogue community unroll rugs and place cushions around the room for those who would eat the seder there. Those who could not afford couches would recline on cushions on the floor, bedouin style. The women of that community were all the while in the kitchen and in the pilgrims' hall getting everything ready.

The men proceeded up the stairs, joyously singing. Jesus led the way, followed by the older men and then pairs of men carrying the paschal lambs on spits resting upon their shoulders. The children followed, laughing, clapping and dancing, skipping and singing. The procession broke out of the increasing darkness and chill into the bright, warm room where their mothers and wives greeted them with embraces and kisses. Eventually, all of the individual families coalesced together and a touching ceremony took place. Fathers and mothers gathered their sons and, placing their extended hands over their heads, recited the parental blessing for sons,

> May God bless you
> as he blessed Ephraim and Manasseh![3]

Then they gathered their daughters in the same way and blessed them with the blessing of the mothers of Israel,

> May God bless you
> as He blessed Sarah, Rebecca,
> Rachel and Leah.

After blessing all their children, the families broke up again, and everyone took their places upon the couches about the tables throughout the room.

The strict regulation among the orthodox of separating the men from the women at banquets was not enforced until several centuries later. Still, the men and women at the Last Supper might have separated for practical reasons. The men and older youths had to discuss the meaning of the seder at great length and in great depth. The women were responsible for keeping the ritual running smoothly. That meant that they, as well as the daughters and the younger boys, had to get up frequently throughout the evening to serve the food and remove the empty food trays. Therefore, so as not to interrupt the discourses, discussions, and disputations traditional at Passover, they would recline on separate couches, if not at separate tables. That did not mean, however, that the men ignored the women. Glances, words, touches passed between them all evening long, and the women were not above kibitzing when they knew more than their sons or spouses. Jesus encouraged the women among his followers to assert themselves to a degree that must have scandalized outsiders, and he counseled the men to accept them as equally as tradition allowed. The Law must always be tempered by Love, and Love must always give meaning to the Law.

## Kadesh: Sanctifying the Wine and the Day

> MISHNAH, Chapter 10: "And they should give him [the official host for the evening] not less than four cups of wine, even if he receives relief from the charity plate" (BT Pesachim 99b).[4]

Against the wall, where the food tables were located, a number of wineskins hung from hooks. These were the ordinary vessels for storing wine.[5] The wealthy could purchase wine-filled amphorae from the merchants who imported foreign wine, but the common people bought the locally produced wine preserved in the skins of cattle, sheep, and goats. For this purpose, the skins were coated inside and out with a natural pitch or resin. One of the forelegs was corked and served as a spout. As the wine was drawn from the skin, the area above the level of the liquid shrank dramatically and kept out invading air. The shrinking, however, caused that part of the skin to become very dry and brittle. Any attempt to refill a wineskin would be disastrous because the dry and brittle hide would simply split open and burst its contents onto the floor. Because that was the usual vessel for storing wine, the wine usually absorbed the flavor of the hide and the coating, and it acquired a rough taste, even when the wine itself was of superior quality.

Some of the male disciples carried a large bowl to one of the skins and filled it over half-full. They carried the bowl to Jesus, the official host of the Last Supper, who sampled its quality and flavor. Jesus then instructed the disciples on how much water to add to the wine (hot water was kept in a vessel in the center of the room) to make the wine pleasant tasting and palatable. The bowl held enough beverage so that everyone could receive one full cup. If the bowl was not large enough, other bowls were filled and mixed so that there was a generous amount of wine for all. More water and smaller portions were poured for the children.

In front of Jesus sat the kiddush cup over which he would pronounce the blessings of the evening. The Kiddush is the blessing recited on all Sabbaths and Holy Days. It is customary for the host, or father of the family, to share this cup with everyone. It was a beautiful gesture of family unity and solidarity. After they had supplied everyone with their first cup, the disciples in charge of the wine brought the bowl to Jesus' table and filled the kiddush cup. Naturally, this brought everyone's attention to Jesus, who was then expected to recite the Kiddush, which formally began the Passover supper. With all eyes on him, Jesus announced, "I have eagerly desired to eat this Passover with you before I suffer, for, I tell you, I will not eat it (again) until there is fulfillment in the kingdom of God" (Lk 22:15 NAB).[6]

Puzzled looks must have filled the room as people tried to grasp what Jesus meant. Actually, Jesus had made a solemn pronouncement that he would repeat throughout that evening. As a good teacher, he was introducing an idea that he would repeat and expand upon until his disciples understood him. He was inviting all of his followers to remain in table fellowship with him in the coming Kingdom. How that was to be done he would explain later in the context of the Passover supper.[7]

> MISHNAH: "They filled the first cup for him. Beth Hillel ruled: He recites a blessing over the wine first and then he recites the blessing for the Day" (BT Pesachim 114a).

"Then he took a cup, gave thanks" (Lk 22:17 NAB), and, as was the custom, he recited the Kiddush in Hebrew.

*(Sanctifying the Wine)*
Blessed are You, O LORD (YHWH) Our God,
King of all creation,
Creator of the fruit of the vine.

*(Sanctifying the Day)*
Blessed are You, O LORD (YHWH) Our God,
King of all creation,
Who has exalted us from all people,
and raised us up from speakers of all tongues,
and sanctified us with your commandments.
You have given us,
O LORD (YHWH) our God,
out of your love;
fixed seasons for rejoicing,
pilgrim festivals,
and Times for joy,
and this day
    The pilgrim Feast of Unleavened Bread,
    The time of our freedom,

A holy assembly,
The remembrance of our coming out of Egypt.
You have exalted us
And made us holy
From out of all peoples,
By giving us holy seasons
    for which to rejoice
    and be glad
As our inheritance.
Blessed are You O LORD (YHWH)
Who makes holy
    Your people, Israel,
    and the sacred times
(Haggadah shel Pesach).

As he concluded the Kiddush, he said, "Take this and share it among yourselves" (Lk 22:17 NAB). Then taking a sip from the kiddush cup, Jesus handed it to one of his disciples, who took it from table to table so that everyone shared from it. Although this took time, it had intense meaning for everyone. Table fellowship of family and friends has always been extremely important to the Jewish people; "breaking bread" together and "sharing the cup" were always signs of unifying relationships. A friend became a brother or sister in table fellowship.

As he handed the kiddush cup over to his disciples, Jesus repeated his proclamation, "...for I tell you [that] from this time on I shall not drink of the fruit of the vine until the kingdom of God comes!" (Lk 22:18 NAB).

His statement did not seem so startling and mysterious that time. Everyone thought they understood. "The Kingdom of God" was an idea they had grown up with and dreamed about: "When the Messiah comes," he will liberate his people from Roman and all foreign rule and establish a marvelous kingdom of fantastic earthly abundance and make the Israelites the new lords of this transformed world. However, Jesus was about to show them that he had something completely different in mind.

## Ur' Chatz: And the First Washing

One of the dietary Laws was that the hands must be washed before touching any food. When everyone had sipped from the kiddush cup, several male and female disciples got up and went for pitchers of water, small basins, and towels. They went to every table and, one by one, everybody extended their hands over the bowl. One of the disciples poured water over them and recited a short prayer, and the other person assisted by offering the towel to dry their hands. This first washing of the hands was almost informal and did not require the host to recite any prescribed prayer. Also, this first washing was merely a preparation for the hors d' oeuvres, or the first course of the Passover supper.

Jesus, however, turned this simple washing into a major event and a preparation for the solemn banquet of his kingdom:

> ...fully aware that the Father had put everything into his power and that he had come from God and was returning to God, he rose from supper and took off his outer garments. He took a towel and tied it around his waist [like a slave]. Then he poured water into a basin and began to wash the disciples' feet and dry them with the towel around his waist. He came to Simon Peter, who said to him, "Master, are you going to wash my feet?" Jesus answered and said to him, "What I am doing, you do not understand now, but you will understand later." Peter said to him, "You shall never wash my feet." Jesus answered him, "Unless I wash you, you will have no inheritance with me." Simon Peter said to him, "Master, then not only my feet, but my hands and head as well." Jesus said to him, "Whoever has bathed [in the mikveh] has no need except to have his feet washed, for he is clean all over; so you are clean, but not all." For he knew who would betray him; for this reason, he said, "Not all of you are clean."
> So when he had washed their feet [and] put his garments back on and reclined at table again, he said to them, "Do you realize waht I have done for you? You cL 'teacher' and 'master,' and rightly so, for indeed I am. If I, therefore, the master and teacher, have washed your feet, you ought to wash one another's feet. I

have given you a model to follow, so that as I have done for you, you should also do. Amen, amen, I say to you, no slave is greater than his master nor any messenger greater than the one who sent him. If you understand this, blessed are you if you do it" (Jn 13:3-17 NAB).

Even though all were taken aback by Jesus' waiting upon them as a slave, they still did not understand him. Perplexed by what they had seen and heard, the women and girls got up to serve the tables.

## Karpas: Greenstuff

MISHNAH: "They then set it before him (the first course). He dips the lettuce before yet he has reached the aftercourse of the bread" (BT Pesachim 114a).[8]

The women brought to each table a platter on which were arranged the roasted giblets and innards of the paschal lambs over beds of leaf lettuce. With these platters they brought bowls of saltwater and of vinegar for dipping the hors d'oeuvres. The roasted giblets were garnished with celery, chervil, parsley, and other green herbs representing spring. The saltwater symbolized the tears the Israelites had wept in Egypt. As they were eating, a dispute arose among the men about who was regarded as the greatest in the coming kingdom. Jesus rebuked them,

The kings of the Gentiles lord it over them and those in authority over them are addressed as 'Benefactors'; but among you it shall not be so. Rather, let the greatest among you be as the youngest, and the leader as the servant. For who is greater: the one seated at table or the one who serves? Is it not the one seated at table? I am among you as the one who serves. It is you who have stood by me in my trials; and I confer a kingdom on you, just as my Father has conferred one on me, that you may eat and drink at my table in my kingdom; and you will sit on thrones judging the twelve tribes of Israel (Lk 22:24-30 NAB).

Jesus continued in a somber vain, casting a shadow on the customary joy of the evening,

"I am not speaking of all of you. I know those whom I have chosen. But so that the scripture might be fulfilled, 'The one who ate my food has raised his heel against me.' From now on I am telling you before it happens, so that when it happens you may believe that I AM. Amen, amen, I say to you, whoever receives the one I send receives me, and whoever receives me receives the one who sent me." When he had said this, Jesus was deeply troubled and testified, "Amen, amen, I say to you, one of you will betray me." The disciples looked at one another, at a loss as to whom he meant. One of his disciples, the one whom Jesus loved, was reclining at Jesus' side. So Simon Peter nodded to him to find out whom he meant. He leaned back against Jesus' chest and said to him, "Master, who is it?" Jesus answered, "It is the one to whom I hand the morsel after I have dipped it." So he dipped the morsel and [took it and] handed it to Judas, son of Simon the Iscariot. After he took the morsel, Satan entered him. So Jesus said to him, "What you are going to do, do quickly."...When he had left, Jesus said, "Now is the Son of Man glorified, and God is glorified in him" (Jn 13:18-27,31 NAB).

His hour of glory had come!

The women disciples, noticing that everyone had finished with the first course, removed all the trays from the tables and made room for the entree. That took some of the stiffness out of the air. Someone began singing one of the popular songs of the seder, and everyone joined in. Breaks in the ritual and activities that took a long time—such as the washing of hands and the sharing of the kiddush cup—could always be pleasantly filled in with singing.

## Yachatz: Breaking the Unleavened Bread

Trays bearing the sheets of unleavened bread, or matzah, were now brought to the tables. Handmade cloth coverings, designed by the women, lay over the matzah; most of these were richly decorated and fringed. The special tray containing the three large sheets of the watched matzah was brought to Jesus' table. The appearance of more food delighted the children, but they were soon confused when their parents refused to let them eat any of it. Very small children might be allowed to have a little for obvious reasons, but the older children and adults had to wait.

Nowadays, at this point in the seder, the host breaks the center matzah in two. He takes half of this matzah and wraps it in a white cloth. Then he might ask all of the children to cover their eyes while he hides it. The children later try to steal the hidden matzah and force their father to buy it back from them for a price. He must have it, for it is the afikoman that must be eaten at the conclusion of the seder. In Jesus' day, however, a small piece of the paschal lamb was the last thing to be eaten. Whether a small piece of the watched matzah was also eaten with it is not clear.

Jesus took the tray of the watched matzah, uncovered the bread, and lifted the tray up to where all could see it. He announced in bold Aramaic the invitation to Passover, which was composed during the exile in Babylon:

Behold the bread of poverty
Which our ancestors ate
In the land of Egypt!

All who are hungry
Come and eat with us!
All who are needy
Come join us at the Passover sacrifice!

Now, we are here,
Next year, may we be in the Land of Israel!
Now, we are enslaved,
Next year, may we be a free people![9]

In the popular imagination of that time, the unleavened bread of Passover had become associated with the manna the Israelites had eaten in the wilderness. There was a belief that when the Messiah came, manna would fall again for all of the people to eat once more (in abundance) what they had learned to call "Bread from Heaven" (Jn 6:31). Jesus took advantage of that prevailing hope and announced to them that he was that heavenly bread. He repeated and then built upon his discourse to them at Capernaum. We only have his words at the Synagogue recorded, but they are enough.

> So Jesus said to them, "Amen, amen, I say to you, it was not Moses who gave the bread from heaven; my Father gives you the true bread from heaven. For the bread of God is that which comes down from heaven and gives life to the world."
> So they said to him, "Sir, give us this bread always." Jesus said to them, "I am the bread of life; whoever comes to me will never hunger, and whoever believes in me will never thirst" (Jn 6:32-35 NAB).

An obvious play upon the themes of the ha lachma, this might be called Jesus' invitation to the table fellowship of his Eucharist.

Jesus was taking, one by one, the meaningful symbols of the evening and appropriating them to himself. By using familiar actions and foods to teach his disciples about his relationship to them in the coming kingdom of God, he cast his instructions in indelible terms that they could never forget. Not even during the horror that would begin in several hours.

> MISHNAH: "They set before him matzah, lettuce (chazeret), and charoset and two other dishes, though the charoset is not

compulsory. Rabbi Eleazar Son of Rabbi Zadok said: 'it is compulsory.' And in the Temple they used to bring the body of the Passover Offering before him" (BT Pesachim 114a).

This time the young men got up to serve because it was time for the main course and the trays holding the whole, roasted paschal lambs and their condiments were heavy. This was one of the highlights of the evening, much like our bringing in the Thanksgiving turkey or the Christmas goose! Besides the marvelous pageantry, it meant the beginning of the wonderful storytelling of the maggid, wherein they would recount all the marvelous events of God's liberation of his people. Besides the trays of unleavened bread, bowls of charoset, and the bitter herbs, other condiments such as lettuce and celery were served with the paschal lambs and chaggigah. As with the roasted giblets, the meat of the roasted lambs was served on beds of leaf lettuce, which everyone would use for tearing off bits of meat with their right hands.

The room was now full of the sights and smells of bounty, but to the growing agony of the small children, no one was allowed to eat yet. For the children, however, it was at last the moment that they all especially loved.

> MISHNAH: "They filled a second cup for him. At this stage the son questions his father. If the son is unintelligent, his father instructs him to ask [the Four Questions]" (BT Pesachim 116a).

Jesus loved children (Lk 18:15-17). He must have called one of the youngest sons from each family to come to his table, for it was their responsibility to ask the Four Questions that began the evening's commentary upon the meaning of Passover. The Four Questions are traditionally sung because they are more easily learned as a song; they are sung in Hebrew because Hebrew is the traditional language of the Ma Nishtanah. Standing in a group before Jesus' table, they all sang together,

Why is this night different from all other nights?

For on all other nights we eat leavened and unleavened bread. Whereas on this night we eat only unleavened bread!

On all other nights we eat all kinds of herbs. On this night bitter herbs,

On all other nights we eat meat roasted, stewed, or boiled. On this night, roasted only!

On all other nights we do not dip even once. But on this night we dip twice! (BT Pesachim 116a).

The Ma Nishtanah is actually much shorter in Hebrew. For the English translation a number of words have to be added to make it understandable. When the boys finished, Jesus praised them and made them feel proud, as proud as their parents felt for them. It was a glorious moment to be in the spotlight like that, and the children looked forward to it and loved it. Older boys remembered their past moments of fame, and the even younger boys who were still too young to be called upon could look forward to their days of glory.

MISHNAH: "And according to the son's intelligence his father instructs him. He commences with shame and concludes with praise; and expounds from 'A wandering Aramean was my Father' (Dt 16:5) until he completes the whole section" (BT Pesachim 116a).

Those young boys then climbed onto the couches with their fathers in order to ask more questions and learn more about the seder.

Jesus began the long discourse of the maggid, or "retelling," by quoting from the same chapter of Deuteronomy that contains the Sh'ma:

We were once slaves of Pharaoh in Egypt, but the LORD (YHWH) brought us out of Egypt with his strong hand and wrought before our eyes signs and wonders, great and dire, against Egypt and against Pharaoh and his whole house (Dt 6:21,22 NAB).

If only the Holy One, Blessed is He, had not brought our ancestors out of Egypt, then we and our children, and the children of our children would still be enslaved by a Pharaoh in Egypt! Even if all of us were filled with wisdom and knowledge, and even if we were thoroughly versed in the Torah, even so, it would be our duty to tell of the Exodus from Egypt. Every repartition of the telling of this departure from Egypt is praiseworthy (Haggadah shel Pesach).

Thus says the LORD (YHWH), the God of Israel: In times past your fathers, down to Terah, father of Abraham and Nahor, dwelt beyond the River [Euphrates] and served other gods. But I brought your father, Abraham, from the region beyond the River and led him through the entire land of Cana'an. I made his descendants numerous, and gave him Isaac. To Isaac I gave Jacob and Esau. To Esau I assigned the mountain region of Se'ir in which to settle, while Jacob and his children went down to Egypt (Jos 24:2-4 NAB).

Blessed is He, who keeps his promise to Israel, Blessed is He. For the Holy One, Blessed is He, calculated the time He allotted until He would fulfill his promise to our father Abraham which He made (cut) in the Covenant between the animal halves. For it says, "Then the LORD (YHWH) said to Abram: Know for certain that your descendants shall be aliens in a land not their own, where they shall be enslaved and oppressed for four hundred years. But I will bring judgment on the nation they must serve, and in the end they will depart with great wealth" (Gn 15:13,14) (Haggadah shel Pesach).

Jesus then recovered the three watched matzot. Everyone then lifted their wine cups, including Jesus, who also had his own cup. He would not use the large kiddush cup again until much later. Everyone sang together a toast to the Almighty, who keeps his promises,

> And that promise has sustained our ancestors and us.
> For, not only one has stood over us to exterminate us,
> But in every generation others have stood over us to
>     destroy us.
> But the Holy One, Blessed is He,
> Has always delivered us from out of their hands
> (Haggadah shel Pesach).

Jesus assigned others to continue the lengthy maggid, which everyone knew by heart. Every male had learned the words in Hebrew school at the synagogue, and the older women who had heard the words since childhood also knew them by heart. Books and scrolls were costly and few in number, so the entire Haggadah had to be memorized. As an aid to memory, most if not all of it was chanted and sung. The last toast, the V'hi She'amdah, "And That Promise Has Sustained Us," is still sung in many homes.

The discourse continued with recitals of passages from Genesis 31 and Deuteronomy 26. Each phrase was then analyzed and elaborated upon. That form of commentary, called Midrash, was a popular pastime, which, in the right group, could go on for hours. It was an opportunity for the men to show how learned they were. The basic text was,

> [An Aramaean wanted to destroy my Father][10] ...who went down to Egypt with a small household and lived there as an alien. But there he became a nation great, strong and numerous. When the Egyptians maltreated and oppressed us, imposing hard labor upon us, we cried to the LORD (YHWH), the God of our fathers, and he heard our cry and saw our affliction, our toil and our oppression. He brought us out of Egypt with His strong hand and outstretched arm, with terrifying power, with signs and wonders (Dt 26:5-8 NAB).

To see how that last passage could be stretched out, one only needs to look at some Midrash about "with terrifying power," "signs," and "wonders."

> "With terrifying power." This refers to the revelation of the Divine Presence. We understand this from the verse, "Has God ever sought to go and take for Himself a nation out of the midst of another nation, by trials, signs, wonders, war, by a mighty hand, outstretched arm and by great awe, just as the LORD (YHWH) your God did for you, before your very eyes in Egypt" (Dt 4:34).
> "Signs." This alludes to the rod of Moses, as we are told, "Take this rod in your hand, and with it perform signs" (Ex 4:17).
> "Wonders." This refers to the miracle where the water of Egypt turned into blood, as we see from the verse, "I will show wonders in the heavens and on the earth."[11]

As you can see, the Midrash consisted of similar discussions from other passages in the Bible, as well as the matching up of words in other verses that were on the same subject. It was an excellent test of memory.

Everyone had to recite the creed of Deuteronomy 26 again at Pentecost. This was one of the many practices that connected Pentecost to Passover. At Pentecost or Shavuot, the people were obligated to bring the "first fruits" of the wheat harvest to the Temple. Only at Pentecost were they obligated to bake the sacrificial wheat into loaves of leavened bread. That was the only time such an offering of leaven was made in the Holy Temple.

After the recital of Deuteronomy 26 and its accompanying Midrash, there followed a ritual of the seder that children still much appreciate and enjoy: the dramatized recital of the names of the ten plagues. As the name of each plague was shouted or sung, everyone removed a little of the wine from his or her cup. That was done by dipping a finger or something else into the cup or by pouring small amounts of the wine onto the trays of meat in front of them. That was a fun but important lesson for the children. The second cup of wine was dedicated to the Exodus from Egypt. But when the Israelites were brought out of Egypt, Egyptians suffered and Egyptians died. Therefore, that second cup of wine could not be full. "Have we not all the one Father? Has not the one God created us?" (Mal 2:10 NAB). "Are you not like the Ethiopians to me, O men of Israel, says the Lord?" (Am 9:7 NAB). This taught the children that even though the Egyptians had made their life bitter, they should have compassion and not gloat over the Egyptians' suffering. The cup of the Exodus could not be full and their joy over their liberation had to be diminished because their enemy had suffered.

> He commences with shame
> And concludes with praise,
> He expounds from
> "A Wandering Aramean Was My Father"
> Until he completes the whole section
> (BT Pesachim 116a).

The whole tempo of the evening began to accelerate. The mood moved from the themes of genocide and slavery to salvation and liberation, praise and joy. God had brought them from servitude to freedom. At this point in the seder, there was a bridge between the reliving of the sufferings of the Hebrew people in Syria and Egypt and their own celebration of the Passover sacrifice in the freedom of Eretz Yisrael, "the land of Israel." Rabbi L. Finkelstein's research of the Passover prompted him to believe that the popular Dayyenu song originated before the first century.[12] If so, Dayyenu was sung at the Last Supper. Whether it was the Dayyenu of modern times or some similar song, it was based upon the Psalms of Ascents. This bridge between "suffering" and "praise" was sung at this point in the seder, where it served as an introduction to the first part of the

Hallel. In other words, the song led Jesus and the disciples from the depths of their sorrow to the heights of their joy.

The Dayyenu, as a Song of Ascents, *is* quite old. It begins with the phrase, "If only He had brought us out of Egypt and not brought upon them judgments — that would have been enough! (Dayyenu)." It goes on to climb the "fifteen steps" that correspond to the fifteen steps before the Nicanor Gate in the Court of the Women in the Holy Temple, where the Levites stood to sing the Hallel during the Passover sacrifice. It mounts until the phrase, "If only He brought us into the Land of Israel and not built for us his Holy Temple, — that would have been enough." Then it concludes with the words,

> How manifold are God's blessings in double and redoubled measure! He freed us from the Egyptians and brought judgment upon them; He destroyed their gods and smote their first-born; He gave us their treasure and divided the Red Sea for us; He led us through it dry-shod, and drowned our oppressor in it; He sustained us in the wilderness for forty years and fed us with manna; He gave us the Sabbath and brought us to Mount Sinai; He gave us the Torah and brought us into the Land of Israel; He built for us the Temple where we prayed *for the atonement of our sins*[13] (emphasis mine).

## Zikkaron: The Reactualization of the Event

> MISHNAH: "Therefore it is our duty to Thank, Praise, Laud, Glorify, Exalt, Honor, Bless, Extol, and Adore Him who wrought all these miracles for our (Ancestors,) and Ourselves. He brought us forth from Bondage into Freedom, from Sorrow into Joy, from Mourning into Festivity, from Darkness into Great Light, and from Servitude into Redemption!" (BT Pesachim 116b).

The Mishnah is emphatic on the subject. The Jews of the first century understood from the oral traditions that the Passover seder was not just a celebration or anniversary of something that had happened in ages past; rather, the Passover seder was a way of bringing those past events into the present. "Adore Him Who wrought all these miracles for our Fathers and Ourselves: He *brought us forth* from Bondage into Festivity!" (BT Pesachim 116b, emphasis mine). Therefore, everyone who was with Jesus at the Last Supper seder became actual participants in all of the events of the Exodus. Jesus and his disciples, like all Jews, understood the seder in that way because of the wording of the commandment found in Exodus, "On this day (Passover) you shall explain to your son, 'This is because of what the LORD (YHWH) did for *me* when *I came_out of Egypt*'" (Ex 13:8 NAB, emphasis mine). Fathers were obligated to teach their children that they were co-participants in the great miracles of the Exodus. "And this day shall be for all of you a memorial (zikkaron), and you shall celebrate it as a pilgrimage feast (chag) to YHWH throughout all of your generations as an eternal law (chukat 'olam)" (Ex 13:14). Unfortunately, we do not have the concept of and therefore a suitable English word for "zikkaron." It is more than a memorial. In a zikkaron, time collapses and everything of the past event is brought into the present moment! So much so that there is no advantage to being alive at the time of Moses, because through the zikkaron you *are* alive at the time of Moses!

Zikkaron is basic to Judaism. The commandment of Exodus 13:8-10 is one of the four that are handwritten on the parchments that are placed in the t'fellin, or phylactery. That raises the commandment to the level of a creed. Consequently, everything discussed, discoursed upon, narrated, recited, and sung about during the seder of the Last Supper was done so by all of those partaking in the Passover sacrifice in realization that the Exodus was happening to them all right at that moment!

# Hallel: The Great Psalms of Praise

MISHNAH: "How far does one recite it? Beth Shammai maintain, 'Until, "as a joyous mother of children"'" (to the end of Ps 113). While Beth Hillel say, 'Until "the flint into a fountain of waters"'" (to the end of Ps 114). (BT Pesachim 116a).

The great psalms of praise, Psalms 113 through 118, collectively called the Hallel in Hebrew, were sung by the Levites as the paschal lambs were sacrificed in the Holy Temple. Now, at the Passover supper, these same psalms were sung as the paschal lambs were eaten. Since it is not practical to sing and eat at the same time, the Hallel was divided into two parts: One part was sung just before the actual meal was eaten, and the second part was sung at the conclusion of the supper. Rabbi Hillel decreed that 113 and 114 should be placed before the meal. Since everyone knew these psalms by heart, the entire Hallel was sung in Hebrew.

In European culture, we are used to hearing the psalms sung in church as august and majestic choral pieces. That may well have been the way the Hallel was sung in the Temple. The Levites played an assortment of musical instruments and the priests apparently played rather grand musical interludes between psalms on silver trumpets. At the seder, however, the same psalms were sung to very popular melodies. People sang with great gusto to celebrate their liberation and freedom. Psalm 114, sung almost like a college fight song, was a favorite. Versions of it have come down to us today. The first verse is sung as a chorus; then couplets of verses 2-3, 4-5, 6-7 are sung as the verses. Verse 8 is sung twice as the final verse. The implication of the psalm is that "if any enemy takes on the people of Israel, the very mountains would shake, and the rivers and seas would roll back leaving the enemies destitute; while the very rocks would supply the Israelites with abundant water!" This psalm was particularly popular with the children. The younger children got up and paraded about the room, singing and clapping, as they joyously marched "out of Egypt."

Another reason this psalm was a favorite was that it meant it was finally time to eat. Even today, family members count the pages in their Haggadot to see how many remain before they can eat.

At the conclusion of the psalm, Jesus led them directly into the singing of the Formula of Redemption. Everyone lifted their wine cups in a toast and sang,

> Blessed are You, O LORD (YHWH) our God,
> King of all creation,
> Who redeemed us
> And redeemed our ancestors from Egypt,
> And brought us to this night
>> To eat therein unleavened bread and bitter herb.
> Therefore, O LORD (YHWH) our God
> And God of our Fathers,
>> Bring us to festivals
>> And other pilgrimages
>> That come towards us in peace,
> Joyful in the building of your city
> And happy as your servants
> There to partake of the sacrifices
> And from the Passover offerings
>> Whose blood is poured out
>> Against the walls of your altar.
> We shall sing to you
> A new song,
>> Before our redeemer
>> And before the deliverer of our souls.[14]
> Blessed are You, O LORD (YHWH)
> Redeemer of your people, Israel.

Then they all recited the blessing of the wine and drank the second cup.

Blessed are You, O LORD (YHWH) our God,
King of all creation
Creator of the fruit of the vine.

## Rachatz: Washing the Hands Before Touching the Matzah

The pitchers of water with the basins and towels were brought to every table again so that everyone could wash their hands before they touched the bread. As the disciples one by one extended their hands over the basin and had the water poured over them, they recited,

Blessed are You, O LORD (YHWH) our God
King of all creation,
Who has sanctified us through your commandments
And commanded us to wash our hands.

## HaMotzi: Blessing of Bread

**Special Blessing for the Matzah:** Before the supper could begin, the host blessed and shared bread with everyone at the table. This was done at every Sabbath and festival meal.

The tray with the three large sheets of watched matzot was placed again before Jesus. For other feast days, it was customary to bless one loaf of bread. For the Sabbath, it was traditional to bless two loaves in honor of the double portion of manna that fell for the Sabbaths in the wilderness (Ex 16:21-26). For the Passover seder, there were three loaves of unleavened bread to be blessed to signify the preeminence of this special feast. Jesus removed the beautiful handmade cover his mother had made and recited the customary blessing said over bread on all Sabbaths and feast days,

Blessed are You, O LORD (YHWH) our God,
King of all creation,
Who brings bread forth from the earth.

Then he recited the special blessing for the unleavened bread
of Passover,

Blessed are You, O LORD (YHWH) our God,
King of all creation,
Who has sanctified us through your commandments,
And commanded us concerning the eating of Matzah.

Jesus took the matzot, "and after he had given thanks (*hamot-zi-matzah*), broke it and said, 'This is my body, that is for you.
Do this in remembrance of me'" (1 Cor 11:24 NAB). His words
must have sounded like a thunderclap throughout the upper
room. Somewhat dazed, some disciples took the tray from him
and took the pieces of the matzot that he had broken, so that
there was a piece for each table — to be shared by its oc-
cupants — and they distributed this very special watched matzot to everyone. As each one received their piece of bread, they
sprinkled some salt on the matzah, repeated the two blessings,
and then ate the *matzah sh'murah*. Fortunately, Jesus had
prepared them for this moment, so they would not think — as
they were later accused — that he was initiating a cannibal cult.
In the setting of Passover, they soon understood most of what
Jesus meant, but it would take until Pentecost for the full
realization of his words and actions to sink in.

The first thing they understood was that Jesus was identifying himself with the paschal lambs — he was calling himself a
Passover lamb. That was readily apparent because the matzah
of Passover had already been identified completely with the
Passover sacrifices. That identification enabled the rabbis to instruct the people on how they were to continue the observance
of Passover without the sacrificed lambs after the loss of the

Temple. By instructing the disciples, "This matzah is me," Jesus clearly meant, "I am your real Passover sacrifice." All that the sacrifice of the paschal lambs in the Holy Temple meant to God's people, Israel, Jesus meant to his people, the New Israel. For that, the Twelve Apostles were to be his witnesses. We have biblical testimony that the disciples understood this point quite clearly;[15] there is the very early testimony from Paul in 1 Corinthians 5:7-9 and the later passages of John 1:29 and especially John 19:29,33-36.[16]

**Manna-Pesach-Matzah:** One reason that Jesus' Apostles and disciples understood him immediately was that he had carefully prepared them for that moment when he took bread, blessed it, broke it, and gave it to his disciples to distribute to everyone. Although the blessing, breaking, and sharing of bread at the beginning of the main course of every Sabbath and festival meal was traditional — it symbolized the unity and oneness of the family in table fellowship — Jesus evidently had developed a style that his disciples could readily recognize. The two disciples (also present at the Last Supper) on the way to Emmaus only recognized the risen Jesus in the blessing of bread (Lk 24:30,31). The four evangelists were so impressed by his style that it colored the way they wrote their Gospels.

The scribes, the rabbis, had already identified the matzah of Passover with the Passover lamb and sacrifice. The people themselves had carried that identity even further and had already identified the matzah of Passover with the manna that their ancestors had eaten in the wilderness. They had been taught that the Messiah was about to appear and save them, and that he would make his appearance during Passover. They all believed that, when the Messiah came, the whole world would be transformed and filled with a great abundance of food and that the manna once more would fall down from heaven.[17] Jesus used that popular belief to prepare them and his future disciples for his introduction of the Eucharist at the Last Supper. Jesus prepared them by walking on the water of the Sea of Galilee.[18] In so doing, he presented his credentials as the New Moses. Moses had led the people through the waters of the sea. Now Jesus had walked over the sea and was therefore equal to Moses. In Matthew, Mark, and John, the miracle of walking on the water is connected to the feeding of the five thousand and followed in Matthew and Mark by the feeding of the four thousand (although a subtle distinction is made between the two feedings). The feedings are clearly associated with Moses' feeding of the people with manna in the wilderness. John makes that association clearest by situating the feeding during Passover and by following the story with Jesus' discourse on himself as the "true bread" that comes down from heaven (Jn 6:25-55).

It is important that John records the miracles of the feedings as happening during the weeklong feast of Passover. Passover occurs during the barley harvest in Israel, so the five barley loaves are actually barley matzot. The Synoptics support this timing by noting that the bread was, indeed, barley loaves. In Jewish gematriya (numerology), the number "5" refers to the five books of Torah. Thus, Jesus is feeding the people with a new Torah. And what is Jesus' new Torah? It is both family unity and community table fellowship bound together by his love. Jesus made this point by performing the easily recognized ritual known to all Jews as the formal beginning of all Sabbath and feast day meals: He took bread, blessed it, broke it, and shared it. To that ritual, Jesus added his own rubric of first looking up to his Father in heaven. This action united God with the celebration—much as the offering of lamb's blood and the emurim made God a part of the Passover celebration. Matthew, Mark, and Luke identify the blessing Jesus said over the barley loaves as the hamotzi-matzah with the Greek verb, *eulogeo* (Mt 14:19; Mk 6:41; Lk 9:16). "Eulogeo" and "eulogia" were already well established in the Septuagint as translations of the Hebrew *barukh* ("blessed") and *b'rakhah* ("blessings").[19] Both the hamotzi and the blessing of the matzah begin with the words, "Barukh Ata" ("Blessed are You"). Then Jesus himself broke the sheets of bread and handed them over to his disciples to distribute to the assembly that was to join him in table fellowship. His actions produced an abundance of food: twelve baskets. The gematriya here is clear: this is a messianic abundance of food — enough to feed the twelve tribes of Israel! The dried fishes meant that the meal was not the main meal, which would have been a meat meal, but a collation that would tide them over until he shared with them the main or meat meal, which will be the Eucharist (Jn 6:55). The gematriya of the two fish may have signified the two Covenants, the one of Moses and the new one of Jesus. Or it might have indicated the familiar Johannine dualism that the present food was perishable but that the Christ would soon give them another food that would give them eternal life.[20]

In Matthew and Mark, there was a second feeding of four thousand. The scene is similar, except that the Gospels imply that it took place in gentile territory. Clearly, Mark and Matthew have Jesus preparing to feed the Gentiles also. The smaller size of this "gentile" feeding probably reflects the actual numbers at the time the Gospels were written: there were more Jewish Christians than Gentile Christians. Now there were seven loaves and seven baskets of leftovers. Seven, the perfect number, was also the number of lamps on the great menorah that lit the interior of the Holy Temple itself. Gematriya would suggest the Jesus is the Light of the World and that there would be complete abundance for the gentile world too. The formula is the same here: Jesus took the bread, blessed it, broke it, and gave it to his disciples to share with all of those gathered in table fellowship with him. This time, however, and in John 6:25, the Greek verb used to express the blessing is *eucharis-*

*teo* with its accompanying noun *eucharistia.*[21] It is obvious that the Evangelists wanted to unite the feeding of the multitudes with the Last Supper and with the future Lord's Supper celebrated by the Christian communities (1 Cor 11:24, *eucharistesas).*[22]

**The Ritual Grace Before the Meal:** Because regular meals and special events like the feeding of the multitudes had familiarized the disciples with how Jesus established table fellowship, they were better able to understand his intentions when he took, blessed, broke, and shared with them the "bread of affliction" that they would eat together at that Passover seder of the Last Supper.[23]

**HaMotzi: Table Fellowship and Family Unity:** Breaking bread together and sharing a meal has always been a sign of fellowship among the Jews. The Pharisees were scandalized when Jesus ate with sinners because that meant that he was in fellowship with them. Part of the purpose of the dietary laws was to prevent Jews from eating with people with whom they could not enter into fellowship.

> The distinctive feature which marked Judaism off from the surrounding cultures in the time of Jesus was the element of prayer, of "giving thanks" for *fellowship at table,* and for the provision of food. The formula known to us in modern Judaism has endured through the centuries, and has an ancient prayer as the head of the table takes a piece of bread and breaks it: "Blessed art thou, O Lord our God, ruler of the universe, thou who bringest bread from the earth." *The symbolic sharing of the bread conveyed the blessing of peace and fellowship.*[24] Similarly, at the end of the meal there was a further blessing: "Blessed be our God, he of whose bounty we have partaken, and through whose goodness we live." After a response (Amen) the one who presided over the meal took in his hand the "Cup of Blessing" and recited a further thanksgiving for God's goodness to the world, for the land itself, and for Jerusalem (both the city and

Temple). *The response "Amen" and the sharing of the cup effected a community of blessing and fellowship.* Not only was the fellowship of Jesus and his disciples so cemented and sustained, the same symbol of table fellowship provided fuel for critics who charged Jesus with sharing that fellowship with undesirable and the non-observant (emphasis mine).[25]

The concept of table fellowship among the Jews was such that it could be considered sacramental if not a sacrament; that is, it was an exterior sign of an interior grace. The common bond was expressed by everyone's affirmation of "Amen" at the end of the hamotzi and by the salting of each person's portion of bread—the same way the priests salted the animals in preparation for sacrifice. Table fellowship was so important among the first Christians that to deny fellowship meant to deny God (Rom 14:1-3; 15:1-16; Gal 2:11-21). Among the Gentiles, however, sharing a meal did not have the same meaning. Gentile etiquette was more divisive and made more distinctions along class and group lines. The purpose of a gentile meal was entertainment, even self-indulgence. For that reason, Paul had trouble with the church at Corinth, which felt no need for table fellowship as an essential part of their Eucharist (1 Cor 11:17-22).

This deeply ingrained understanding of table fellowship among the Jewish disciples of Jesus enabled them to understand that Jesus was declaring himself the head of the family of his new community through the words and actions of the hamotzi of the Passover ritual of the Last Supper. Thus, Peter could address the same group, later in that same room, as "brothers" (Acts 1:15,16,21,22).

**Matzah: The Equality of the People of God:** The three sheets of the matzah sh'murah, the traditional watched or guarded matzah of Passover, symbolized the unity and equality of the Jewish people.[26] Over time, the three special matzot that were to be blessed and shared at Passover took on names. The top loaf was named for the priests and is called kohen. The middle matzah is called levy in honor of the Levites, and the bottom one is called Yisrael ad is named for the people of Israel. All three are shared and eaten by everyone at table. They were another sign of the unity and equality of the people.

In the present liturgy of the seder, the three are broken in a special way and then shared in three different stages. At the *yachatz*, "The master of the Seder breaks in two the middle of the three wafers of Unleavened Bread on the platter, wraps up the larger half in a cloth and sets it aside for the Afikoman."[27] At the hamotzi-matzah, the master of the seder breaks into pieces the upper and remaining half of the middle matzot and distributes them.[28] Later, the bottom matzah (Yisrael) is broken and shared with everyone so that they can make the "Hillel Sandwich" to commemorate the lost Temple. Then, after the meal, the afikoman is brought back to the table, or ransomed back if stolen by the children, and becomes the "dessert" or "last thing eaten."[29] At the Last Supper, however, the afikoman was a piece of the paschal lamb, "the size of an olive," and the ritual of making and eating the Hillel Sandwich was unnecessary because the Holy Temple was still standing and the rubric of eating the paschal lamb together with the matzah and maror (bitter herb) was carried out during the meal as the normal way of eating the Passover scrifice (Ex 12:8). Jesus, therefore, probably shared all three matzot with his disciples at the hamotzi-matzah.

The Synoptics and St. Paul are in complete agreement that Jesus took the matzot, said the blessing, broke them up, and gave them to his disciples to distribute and eat together with him (Mt 26:26; Mk 14:22; Lk 22:19; 1 Cor 11:23,24).[30] In the same verses, they all agree on the basic words of Jesus on the institution of the Eucharist. These words represent an independent oral tradition of the Christian community that the

Synoptics and Paul inherited. In Greek, the words of interpretation that Jesus said over the unleavened bread were, in the Synoptics, *touto estin to soma mou* and in Paul, *touto mou estin to soma* or "This is My Body."[31] All represent an agreement on an Aramaic original. Each author, however, added his own words because it was necessary to amplify the meaning of words from Hebrew and Aramaic into Greek, as well as to express the developing understanding of Christ's words in the early liturgical language of the church.[32]

Jesus said of the bread, very simply in Aramaic, *Den bisri*, "This is my body," or, even more likely, *Ha den bisri*, "Behold, This is My Body" (to recall the invitation to Passover, which begins, "Ha lachma anya," "Behold the bread of poverty"). The Aramaic word, *bisra*, like the similar Hebrew word, *basar* means both "flesh" and "body" as well as "kindred" and "blood relation."[33] There is common agreement that Jesus did not use another word for body, *guph*, which at that time referred only to a corpse. This seems to be confirmed by John 6:51, "I am the living bread that came down from heaven; whoever eats this bread will live forever; and the bread that I will give is *my flesh* for the life of the world" (NAB, emphasis mine), which preserves a possible Johannine tradition of the words of institution.[34] Moreover, "soma" is used to translate "basar" 143 times in the Septuagint, and basar/bisra have sacrificial connotations as well because both "body" and "flesh" are terms used to describe the sacrificial offering, especially of the paschal lambs.[35] Consequently, when Jesus simply announced, "Den bisri" or "Ha den bisri," he was clearly identifying himself as the Passover sacrifice (1 Cor 5:7,8). Mark and Matthew felt secure in simply recording Jesus' words of institution as "this is my body" (Mt 26:26; Mk 14:22 NAB). But Luke and Paul felt that the sacrificial reference that Jesus made might be missed by Gentile Christians and added the sacrificial reference in the Greek, "This is my body, which will be given for you" (Lk 22:19 NAB) and "This is my body that is for you" (1 Cor 11:24 NAB).

There is further reason for Jesus to use "basar/bisra." The Hebrew idiom *basar-dam* or the Aramaic *bisra-adam*, both of which mean "flesh and blood," was the Semitic idiomatic phrase meaning "a person." The disciples understood that Jesus' words of institution meant that he was not offering them pieces of his sacrificial flesh in the pieces of bread that they received, but *that he was giving each and every one of them his whole and entire self!*

There are two more reasons to believe that Jesus built upon the Hebrew concept of "basar-dam" in his use of the Aramaic "bisra-adam" to identify himself as wholly present in the bread and as the sacrificed Paschal Lamb of the Church. Baruch M. Bokser quotes a significant passage in the Gemara of the tractate Pesachim that is taken from the Aramaic Tosefta,

> A. It is taught (TNY)
> R. [Rabbi] Yehudah ben Betira says, "When the
> Temple exists, 'joy' derives only from meat (BZMN
> SBYTHMQDS QYYM 'YM SMHH [simchah,
> 'joy'] 'L' BBSR [basar, 'flesh, of the paschal lamb']).
> "As it was said, 'You shall offer peace offerings and eat
> them, and *be happy before the LORD your God*'
> (Deut 27:7).
> "And now (when the Temple does not exist), 'joy [sim-
> chah]' derives only from the wine.
> "As is is said, 'And wine gladdens the human heart (Ps
> 104:15).'" (Bokser, *Origins of the Seder*, 46, em-
> phasis mine)

Also, the Hebrew word "biser" comes form the same root as "basar (flesh, body)" and means "to bring good news, to herald" (Alcalay, *Complete Hebrew-English Dictionary*, col. 299). Kittel asserts that the New Testament concept of "evanggelion (gospel, the good news)" comes from the rabbinical use of the verb "biser" for "proclaiming good news" and that it is not derived from some Greek source. That implies that the concept of the Good News (evanggelion) originates in Jesus' words, "Den bisri."

But as Jesus said those simple words and identified the bread as himself—"(Ha) den bisri," "(Behold) this is my body" — he shared the hamotzi-matzah with his disciples in Passover table fellowship. His words took on added meaning, therefore, *for not only was the bread his actual body, but all of those in table fellowship with him were his body also!* And that is exactly how the original Christian community understood him, for Paul not only says, "The cup of blessing that we bless, is it not a participation in the blood of Christ? The bread that we break, is it not a participation in the body of Christ?" (1 Cor 10:16 NAB), but also, "Now you are Christ's body, and individually parts of it" (1 Cor 12:27 NAB). This was no mystery to the disciples because they were already bound together in Passover table fellowship, or chavurah, a unity that...

...far from being superficial, was carried through into everyday morality...No one could join a Chavurah without sponsors, and all would have a trial period of membership to ensure that they were *ne'emanim* (trustworthy).[36]

In 1 Corinthians 10:18, Paul refers to the Passover table fellowship of the chavurah as *koinonoi tou thusiasteriou* or, "the table fellowship (sharers) of the altar" (the altar representing God).

Much has been written about the use of the Greek verb, "estin," which was used to translate Jesus' Aramaic, "Den bisri," into the Greek, "Touto estin to soma" ("This is my body"). Neither Hebrew nor Aramaic has an equivalent to "estin." In those languages there is no present tense for the verb, "to be." "Is" is simply understood. "Estin" had been understood as "is" until Berengar of Tours questioned the translation in the eleventh century. "Estin" can mean "is really, is identical with" (Lk 6:5, Mt 3:17; 13:55; 14:2), but it can also mean, "is symbolically, is spiritually" (Jn 10:8-11; 11:25; 15:1; Gal 4:24). The way "estin" is used elsewhere, particularly in the *Ego eimi* passages of John,[37] suggests a meaning closer to "is and signifies more than." Thus, Jesus is not only the "bread of life," he is also the "I Am." "The Hebrew 'Ani YHWH' in Isaiah 14:18 is translated in LXX simply as 'ego eimi.' In this use which stress unicity, a Hebrew alternate for 'Ani YHWH' is 'Ani Hu' ('I [am] He'), and the later expression is always translated in LXX as 'Ego Eime'" (Brown, *Anchor Bible* 29:536). John's translation of "Ego Eime" for Jesus' "Ani Hu" clearly identifies Jesus as The Lord.

Great care must be taken in any discussion of the Greek verb "estin" not to ignore the fact that the original Aramaic "Den Bisri" can only mean "This *is* my body." The Greek translation can say no less than that and be honest. The translator, however, can use words in the translation that add further insights to the original meaning if those insights are consistent with the original intentions of the speaker. That seems to be what has taken place here. Not only is the bread the actual body of Christ, but the disciples who are in table fellowship with him at the Passover seder of the Last Supper are equally the body of Christ (1 Cor 12:12-13,27).

Paul will call this new Chavurah shel Pesach the "Koinonia tou somatos kai aimatos Christou" (1 Cor 10:16), or "The table fellowship community of the body and blood of Christ" (E. v. Dobschutz).[38] Paul also uses the Hebrew and Aramaic idiom of "basar dam" and "bisra-adam" to mean a living person of "flesh and blood." He means that Jesus is alive in the sharing table fellowship community that is his body, and that each member of that fellowship community is of the same flesh and blood as the Lord through Holy Communion.

Jesus announced in his words of institution— "den bisri" — a way for him to continue his physical presence among his disciples. It was not to be a continuation of his physical incarnation, which severely limited where and with whom he could be. From that time on, he was to be present among them as the risen Lord in the table fellowship of the Lord's Supper.

"[Jesus] addresses the disciples, not in order to propose to them a definition of the bread which he has just broken and distributed, but to invite them to recognize in the bread shared his own body and to constitute in this way a community" among them; he thus *"inaugurates a new mode of presence among his disciples, not through some prolonged form of the incarnation, but as the risen One who will thus sustain the life"* of his own (*Prenez!*—E. Leon Dufour, 239 [slightly modified]). This meaning will become clearer in the scene in which the risen Christ appears to the disciples at Emmaus and they recognize him in the "breaking of the bread."[39] "I will not leave you orphans" (Jn 14:18 NAB). From now on, his followers would recognize Jesus as actually present in the fellowship of the sharing community (koinonia) and especially in the table fellowship of the Lord's Supper. They would recognize him in the bread of life that they shared with each other in the Eucharist of that Lord's Supper. In the words of consecration over the bread at the hamotzi-matzah of the seder, Jesus invited his followers to come, along with those disciples not present, to his messianic banquet, in the Passover table fellowship of his body and blood.

Jesus' disciples understood him from the beginning. All records attest to the fact that the first Christians believed in the real presence of Jesus in the Eucharist and that they were careful to protect the words of consecration from ridicule.[40] They also understood themselves to be a koinonia and a direct continuation of the Passover chavurah.

No one could take these words lightly. Paul warns,

"Therefore whoever eats the bread or drinks the cup of the Lord unworthily will have to answer for the body and blood of the Lord. A person should examine himself, and so eat the bread and drink the cup. For anyone who eats and drinks without discerning the body, eats and drinks judgment on himself" (1 Cor 11:27-29 NAB).

William F. Orr and James A. Walthers' comments on these verses are enlightening:

Traditional interpretations of 1 Corinthians 11 have been wrong in many particulars because they have not been read with the Jewish practice of the common meal in view. Paul's instruction begins with his chagrin, not that the Corinthians are profaning a holy rite, *but that they are fragmenting a holy society.* In the first four chapters of the epistle he demonstrated how seriously he regards schisms. With apparent resignation he accepts the inevitability of *factions* as a means of testing, *but in no way does he approve the division that results from their practice in the celebration of the Lord's Supper.*

Failure to (discern) his body is the same as failure to (discern) ourselves, and that means failure to recognize that people together in the church constitute the very presence of Christ and are to be treated appropriately. The identity of the church with the body of Christ leads Paul to attribute the physical problems of the Christians to the violation of this body. *This violation hampers and restricts the redemptive and healing nature of the fellowship wherein the poor are fed, the lonely are befriended, the sick are visited, the grieving are comforted, and sinners are forgiven.* Such a redemptive fellowship can produce both spiritual and physical health while the breaking of the fellowship may cause the converse (emphasis mine).[41]

## Pesach: The People of God Redeemed by the Lamb of God

The earliest words of the institution of the Eucharist are recorded by Paul, who said, "For I received from the Lord what I also handed on to you..." (1 Cor 11:23 NAB). The words of institution were not his own, but were those of the original community who heard Jesus speak them. The words are liturgical, yet they accurately convey their origin in the ritual of the Passover seder of the Last Supper.

"...that the Lord Jesus, on the night he was handed over, took bread" (1 Cor 11:23 NAB). The Christian community wanted to pass on information to those who would follow them. In the Jewish mind, and according to biblical reckoning, the night of the Last Supper, the morning of the trial, and the afternoon of the crucifixion and burial all constituted one and the same day. The 15th of Nisan lasted from sunset Thursday until sunset that Friday. All of those momentous events took place on the same day, which was the first day of Passover. Jewish Christians must have been frustrated when the Gentile Christians, whose day began at midnight, understood the Last Supper and the crucifixion as two events that took place on two different days. That gentile perception tended to break apart what was a single reality. The Last Supper cannot be separated from the sacrificial death of Jesus on the cross.

"The Lord Jesus...took bread, and after he had given thanks, broke it and said, 'This is my body that is for you...'" (1 Cor 11:23,24 NAB). Jesus offered thanks to God in the blessings of the hamotzi-matzah, then he took the three watched matzot from the tray before him, broke them and gave the pieces to his disciples to share with him and eat. In doing so he identified himself with the Paschal lambs. "Unless this association of the Passover lamb was made by Jesus, it is difficult to explain the promptitude with which the early Christians identified Jesus as the Christian paschal lamb." 1 Cor 5:7-8 presents us with the unleavened bread of pure self-offering because the Passover feast, the eschatological feast, has already begun, and Jesus as the lamb has already been sacrificed. We must also not overlook the fact that, in the entire sacrificial system of Judaism, the lamb was the *only animal associated with the divine act of redemption and deliverance*. Though the Greek word used for "lamb" (*arnion*) in Revelation is not the same as that used in other contexts — John 1:29,36; Acts 8:32; and 1 Pet 1:19 — it is relevant to ask whence was derived the notion of the slain lamb *if not from the Passover* and from its links with Jesus' self-designation.

Finally, our sources describe the sacrificial death of Jesus as vicarious. Mark follows Matthew in saying "poured out for the community," whereas Luke follows Paul in saying "given for the life of the world" (Jn 6:51), though this Johannine example is only marginally sacrificial. Granted that by the time of Jesus, Passover had become a *feast upon a sacrifice* and sacrificial ideas were associated with it more and more, we would search in vain in the contemporaneous literature for any notion of Passover as an expiatory sacrifice. Yet Paul uses phrases such as "died for our sins" to describe the work of Jesus (1 Cor 15:3; cf. Rm 6:10). The Johannine tradition has John the Baptizer describing Jesus as "the lamb of God that takes away the sin of the world." We must therefore, try to determine the source of this association of ideas: Jesus' table fellowship, the idea of Passover as sacrifice, or the notion of the Passion and death of Jesus as expiatory. (We now realize that they come from the priestly Passover sacrifice offered on the 15th, the same day Jesus died, which was both a holocaust and a sin offering for the atonement of sins [Nm 28:19,22].) The second has been examined already, and the Last Supper must (as we have said) be understood in the context of the other examples of table fellowship in the ministry. But the meaning of the final meal, interpreted as linking it with a sacrificial death of expiation, can only have come from *Jesus himself!* Paul's account in 1 Cor 11 is already a liturgical formula; it is older than our written Gospel accounts, and its vicarious sacrificial element is firmly established. Yet Paul insists that he received this in the tradition of the community. Our Gospel accounts of the Last Supper are in *narrative* form, and such a form by its very nature is earlier than the *liturgical* text of Paul. It is impossible — though the attempt has been made more than once — to attribute the idea of a vicarious, expiatory death to some supposed Hellenistic "savior god" myth utilized by Paul. Savior gods had never been a serious feature of Greek religion, and an attempted importation of such a motif among the predominantly Jewish members of Paul's congregations would have been an act of consummate folly.

> Finally, it should be noted that the Passover meal with its blessings over bread and cup was not only *the principal act of table fellowship in the year* but also carried *an eschatological promise of a coming age of blessings.* Attention should also be paid to the words of interpretation over bread and cup, and the participation of the disciples in eating and drinking. All of these words and acts, taken together, *are a demonstration proleptically of a share in the Age of Blessings, but also a participation in the redemptive death of Jesus* (emphasis mine).[42]

Jesus is the paschal lamb of God who takes away the sin of the world (Jn 1:29). By his sacrificial death he will give life to the people of God. By his death he will defeat the Pharaoh of Pharaohs, the prince of this world, the prince of darkness, and overpower his kingdom of selfishness and manipulation, avarice and greed, lust and loneliness, and all resulting sin and death (Jn 12:31-32). By his death he will deliver his people from the slavery in the kingdom of this world and take them into the kingdom of love of God his Father (Jn 12:32). As the Passover sacrifice of his body, his flesh is the food that nourishes the new sharing community that gathers in table fellowship around the table of the Lord and celebrates the Eucharist, which is the seder of his new paschal sacrifice (1 Cor 5:7,8). His koinonia, nourished by him, will share him with each other and care for each other in the liberty and equality of his messianic banquet (Jn 13:12-17; Mt 20:25-28). By sharing in the koinonia of the body and blood of Christ and by keeping his commandments of love, the community in table fellowship with Christ will be united in fellowship with God our Father (Jn 14:21-23). It was the blood of the paschal lambs that united the people to God and made him a member of the table fellowship of their seder.

The paschal lamb of God, Jesus, invites the whole world to join him in his Passover banquet, "ha lachma —ha den bisri" ("Behold this Bread—Behold, This is My Body") wherein he will remove their poverty and alienation of sin and death and give them eternal life (Jn 6:51-54); wherein he will remove their bondage to sin, selfishness, and mortality and unite them with their Father (Jn 1:12-13) in loving fellowship.

The symbolism of the Passover sacrifice inherent in Jesus' words could not have been lost on his Jewish disciples. In the Gospels of Matthew and Mark, which were written for Jewish Christians, the words are simply, "this is my body" (Mt 26:26; Mk 14:22 NAB). The rest is understood from the context of the Passover seder. However, they add, "Take this" and "Take this and eat it" to reflect that the invitation of "ha-lachma" was also to be understood in the sharing of the hamotzi-matzah.

## Zikkaron-Anamnesis: A Memorial Feast Through All Your Generations as an Eternal Law (Ex 12:14)

Jesus' words of institution are tied inexorably to the seder of Passover supper. He announces, "Do this in remembrance of me!" (1 Cor 11:24). His words can only be understood in the context of the Haggadah. However, Jesus did not say, "Do this in remembrance of me" but "Touto poiete eis emen anamnesin," which means "Do this as my anamnesis" (1 Cor 11:24). The Greek word "anamnesis" translates the important Hebrew word "zikkaron," which means "to reactualize," to bring the experiences of the past into the present so as to participate in them. Concerning the Passover seder, the Mishnah clearly states that "in every generation a man is bound to regard himself as though he personally had gone forth from Egypt. Because it is said, 'And thou shalt tell thy son in that day, saying: "It is because of that which the Lord did for *me* when I came forth out of Egypt"'" (BT Pesachim 116b; Ex 13:8). At the Passover supper, all of the events of the Exodus are brought into the present so that each individual, in fellowship at the supper, actually becomes a participant in all of those events. Time collapses; participants do not remember the Exodus, they reactualize it! They participate in the events of the Exodus. The Chag HaPesach is the zikkaron that the People of God are to observe as an eternal law (Ex 12:14). "W' hayah hayom hazeh alkhem l'ZIKARON w' hagotem oto Chag laYHWH l'dorateykhem chuqat 'olam t' chaguhu!" "It is God the Father's Zikkaron for Israel, His People!"

But now, wholly within the context of the Passover seder, Jesus announces that the Eucharist is to be his anamnesis-zikkaron! That means that when Christ commanded us to "Do this as my anamnesis," we are not supposed to remember what he did at the Last Supper; we are commanded to actually share the Last Supper with him. What Passover is to the Exodus, the Eucharist is to the Last Supper!

The events of the Pascha of Christ are brought into the present where we all become participants in these events. At Holy Communion each one of us is actually present there in the upper room sharing in the table fellowship of the chavurah of Passover with Jesus and all his disciples.

## Maggid: "The Retelling of the Exodus Events"

As he cites the account of the institution, Paul adds a sentence: "For as often as you eat this bread and drink the cup, you proclaim the Lord's death until he comes" (1 Cor 11:26). Because of the preceding "for," "you proclaim" must be understood as indicative, as is generally accepted; the verb (*kataggellein*) means, "to proclaim" and designates the "proclamation, announcement of a completed event," whereby the general usage suggests a proclamation in words. Paul therefore establishes that in Corinth at every Eucharist ("as often as") the death of the Lord is proclaimed. An indication of how this "proclamation of the death of Jesus" was carried out is gained when one observes that in Symmachus (Ps 39[40]:6), "kataggellein" represents the Hebrew *higgid* ["narrate," hence "Haggadah"]. (The correspondence of these two verbs was noted by G.H. Box, "The Jewish Antecedents of the Eucharist," *The Journal of Theological Studies* 3 [1901-2] Oxford, 365 n.I.)[43]

An early Christian Haggadah celebrated the paschal death of Jesus. Paul insisted that Christians proclaim the saving paschal death of Jesus in the same manner as the Passover Haggadah proclaims the sacrifice of the paschal lambs. In the beginning, the whole Christian community did just that as the *koinonia tou somatos kai aimatos christou!*

It should come as no surprise that there was a Christian Haggadah. The theme of the victorious lamb was inherent in Judaism and was celebrated in the traditional Haggadah of Passover. The victory of the paschal lambs was manifested in the requirement that seder participants recline on dining couches as free men and women and temper the bitterness of their suffering with the liberating sweetness of the charoset. When Jesus identified himself as the paschal lamb at the Last Supper, he became for Christian Jews the focal point of their future Passover seder celebrations. The lamb was Jesus. The matzot was Jesus. The maror was his suffering and death, and the sweet charoset was his victory over betrayal and death. The whole

Haggadah became a celebration of his victory over the alienation of this world, over sin, and over death. Eusebius records
that in the Middle East, where the influence of the Apostles was
greatest, the death and resurrection (pascha) of Christ was
celebrated on the first day of the Jewish Passover.[44]

However, Christians could not wait for a once-a-year
celebration. Almost immediately, they developed a simplified
Haggadah for use at the weekly gathering of the koinonia,
where they broke bread together at the common meal (Acts
2:42-47; 1 Cor 10:16-17). As the thanksgiving prayers after the
common meal, the Eucharist evolved as a simplified Haggadah
of the Pascha of Christ. The necessary candles were lit. The
necessary instructions on the meaning of the seder of the
Eucharist were given. Psalms and hymns were sung. Hands
were washed before the bread was blessed, broken, and shared
by everyone in table fellowship. The Cup of Blessing, which
may have been the same kiddush cup that blessed the common
meal, was then blessed and shared by everyone. And they called
it the agape or "love feast."

## Shulchan Orekh: "The Passover Meal"

At long last, everyone could join in the paschal feast. The
wine cups were refilled, but this time informally because the
wine was simply the beverage taken with their meal. During
the meal itself — that is, between the Cup of the Maggid and the
Cup of Blessing — individuals could have their cups refilled as
often as they wanted. Along with the platters of roasted paschal
lambs and chaggigot, extra trays of homemade matzah were
placed among the bowls of bitter herb, charoset, mustard, and
salt.

Leaning their heads upon their left hands, each person picked up leaves of lettuce or broke off pieces of unleavened bread
and used these to gather up portions of the roasted lamb to eat.

They often did this with lettuce and matzah together, as did Hillel. They would frequently dip these "sandwiches" into the various condiments. Not unusual would be sandwiches made of matzah, lamb, and bitter herb (Ex 12:8). Children, of course, preferred extra portions of the sweet charoset scooped up with their morsels. Some of the little ones vehemently avoided the maror after the first obligatory taste of its bitterness. Needless to say, they wanted to know why they had to eat the maror at all, and that opened up some more of the necessary discussions of the supper.

Somewhere at the beginning of supper, portions of the paschal lamb were removed from the trays and wrapped in a special cloth. These portions were set aside for the afikoman, which would be eaten at the conclusion of the meal proper. Since the afikoman was an obligation, the tradition of hiding it from the children might have already been established as another way of getting them to ask more questions. Before the Cup of Blessing could be poured after the meal, the master of the seder had to pay the children a ransom price to buy the afikoman back.

MISHNAH: "Rabbi Gamaliel used to say: 'Whoever does not make mention of these three things on Passover does not discharge his duty. And these are they: 'Pesach' — The Passover Offering, 'Matzah' — Unleavened Bread, and 'Maror' — Bitter Herb.

"'Pesach' — The Passover Offering is sacrificed because the Omnipresent Passed Over the houses of our Fathers in Egypt, as it is said, 'Then you shall say: This is the Passover Sacrifice of the LORD (YHWH) who passed over the houses of the Israelites in Egypt; When He struck down the Egyptians, He spared our houses' (Ex 12:27).

"'Matzah' — The Unleavened Bread is eaten because our Fathers were Redeemed (Yatzah) from Egypt, as it is said, 'And they baked Unleavened Cakes [matzah] of the dough which they brought forth out of Egypt' (Ex 12:39).

"'Maror' — The Bitter Herb is eaten because the Egyptians Embittered the lives of our Fathers in Egypt, as it is said, 'And they made their lives Bitter'" (Ex 1:14; BT Pesachim 116b).

As the supper progressed, the paterfamilias, Jesus, and all of the parents were obligated to continue instructing each other and the children on the significance of the seder, even though this had already been done during the maggid. During the supper itself, however, all of the instructions would be accompanied by "visual aids." The unleavened bread, roasted lamb, and bitter herb were on the tables in front of them to be eaten while their importance was explained further. Now, not only was the sense of hearing involved in learning about Passover; sight, sound, taste, touch, and smell were included as well.

While simple instructions were enough for the smaller children, the older children and the adults received a much more intense indoctrination. Actually, questions were answered with more questions. Individuals were encouraged to create their own midrash on the "text" of the Haggadah and the significance of the objects before them on the tables. Quotations upon quotations would be pulled from numerous verses of the Torah and the Haftora of the Prophets and Writings, which were the other two sections of the Hebrew Scriptures.[45] The Hebrew Bible is approached in much the same that Christians approach their New Testament. In the Greek Scriptures, the four Gospels form the core and are supported by Acts, Letters, and Revelation. In the Hebrew Bible, Torah forms the core and is supported or embellished by the books of the Prophets and the Writings. Typically, a quotation from the Bible was preceded by the phrase, "as it is said," because they all had the Bible memorized. The quotation would then be followed by elucidations based upon Hebrew and Aramaic word association and gematriya, such as: "If God struck Egypt with His finger and that resulted in Ten Plagues, then, if God struck Pharaoh at the

Red Sea with His hand, then at the sea the Egyptians suffered Fifty Plagues!" (Haggadah shel Pesach).

Jesus used the same visual aids — the lamb, the matzah, the bitter herb — to instruct his disciples about who he was and what he was doing for them. But this was not new information. Raymond E. Brown, commenting on John 6:35-50, notes some evidence that Jesus had already related Passover to himself in Sabbath sermons near Passover time, probably at the synagogue in Capernaum.[46] Aileen Guilding observes the striking similarity between verses in John and the readings heard in the Sabbath services around Passover. In the first century, it took three years to complete the reading of the Torah in the synagogues. In the first year, Genesis 1-8 were read on the Sabbaths around Passover; in the second year, Exodus 6-16; and in the third year, Numbers 6-14.

> Genesis 3:3 repeats God's warning from 2:17: "You shall not eat of the fruit of this tree...lest you die." This may be contrasted with John 6:50: "This is the Bread that comes down from heaven that a man may eat it *and never die.*"
> Genesis 3:22 has God's decision to drive man out of the garden "...lest he put forth his hand and take also of the tree of life and eat and live forever." This may be contrasted with the invitation to eat the Bread of Life of which John 6:51 says, "If anyone eats this Bread, he will live forever."
> Genesis 3:24: "So he drove man out." In John 6:37: "Anyone who comes to Me I will never drive out" (emphasis mine).[47]

Of course, John 6 is based primarily upon Exodus 12, but it appears that Jesus used Genesis 3 as well. So, it may very well be that Jesus used the whole three-year cycle of the Torah in the synagogue to prepare his disciples for his final teaching on the night of the Last Supper.

Sometime during the supper, Jesus must have picked up some of the unleavened bread, and just as he had done with the watched matzot at the lachma anya, he announced:

"I am the bread of life; whoever comes to me will never hunger, and whoever believes in me will never thirst. But I told you that altough you have seen [me], you do not believe. Everything that the Father gives me will come to me, and I will not reject anyone who comes to me, because I came down from heaven not to do my own will but the will of the one who sent me. And this is the will of the one who sent me, that I should not lose anything of what he gave me, but that I should raise it [on] the last day. For this is the will of my Father, that everyone who sees the Son and believes in him may have eternal life, and I shall raise him up [on] the last day" (Jn 6:35-40 NAB).

These words bring to fruition the opening verses of Deuteronomy 8:

Be careful to observe all the commandments I enjoin on you today, that you may live and increase, and may enter in and possess the land which the LORD (YHWH) promised on oath to your Fathers. Remember how for forty years now the LORD (YHWH), your God, has directed all your journeying in the desert, so as to test you by affliction and find out whether or not it was your intention to keep his commandments. He therefore let you be afflicted with hunger, and then fed you with manna, a food unknown to you and your fathers, in order to show you that not by bread alone does man live, but by every word that comes forth from the mouth of the LORD (YHWH) (Dt 8:1-3 NAB).

Jesus is the Word, the Word of God made flesh, who is empowered to make all of those who accept him the children of God (Jn 1:1- 16).

No one can come to me unless the Father who sent me draw him, and I will raise him on the last day. It is written in the prophets: 'They shall all be taught by God.' Everyone who listens to my Father and learns from him comes to me. Not that anyone has seen the Father except the one who is from God; he has seen the Father. Amen, amen, I say to you, whoever believes has eternal life. I am the bread of life. Your ancestors ate the manna in the desert, but they died; this is the bread that comes down from heaven so that one may eat it and not die. I am the living bread that came down from heaven; whoever eats this bread will live forever; and the bread that I will give is my flesh for the life of the world" (Jn 6:44-51 NAB).

Then Jesus lifted up a portion of the paschal lamb for all to see and continued the discourse,

> Amen, amen, I say to you, unless you eat the flesh of the Son of Man and drink his blood, you do not have life within you. Whoever eats my flesh and drinks my blood has eternal life, and I will raise him on the last day. For my flesh is true food, and my blood is true drink. Whoever eats my flesh and drinks my blood remains in me and I in him. Just as the living Father sent me and I have life because of the Father, so also the one who feeds on me will have life because of me. This is the bread that came down from heaven. Unlike your ancestors who ate and still died, whoever eats this bread will live forever (Jn 6:53-58 NAB).

Jesus lowered the lamb and matzah to the table again, then pointed to the maror, the bitter herb, and repeated a familiar prophecy, "The Son of Man is to be handed over to men and they will kill him, and three days after his death he will rise" (Mk 9:31 NAB).

> The hour has come for the Son of Man to be glorified. Amen, amen, I say to you, unless a grain of wheat falls to the ground and dies, it remains just a grain of wheat; but if it dies, it produces much fruit. Whoever loves his life loses it, and whoever hates his life in this world will preserve it for eternal life. Whoever serves me must follow me, and where I am, there also will my servant be. The Father will honor whoever serves me.

> I am troubled now. Yet what should I say? "Father, save me from this hour"? But it was for this purpose that I came to this hour. Father, glorify your name....Now is the time of judgment on this world; now the ruler of this world will be driven out. And when I am lifted up from the earth, I will draw everyone to myself (Jn 12:23-28,31-32 NAB).

The rubric of lifting up these items of food from the table as they are explained during the seder is still preserved to this day. Either the item itself, or the seder plate containing them is lifted up for all to see, so as to involve everyone's attention.

If you do not explain the following, you do not fulfill your Passover obligation:

Pesach — The Paschal Lamb
Matzah — The Unleavened Bread
Maror — The Bitter Herb (BT Pesachim 116a).


## Tzafun: "The Hidden Things"

When, at long last, the meal was over and everyone was completely satisfied, the tables were cleared of all the trays. The leftover meat was gathered and placed in a container to be burned the following morning (Ex 12:10). Some of the disciples went for the trays of the afikoman that had been set aside and hidden. Most of them had been discovered by the older children and rehidden. As the adults tried to find out which ones had taken the afikoman, there was much comedy. After the facade of innocence was broken down and the culprits identified, spirited negotiations began, the older children encouraging the younger to hold out for a better price. At last, the parties agreed on an appropriate ransom, and the children lead the adults to where their hiding places were. The afikoman was finally brought to the tables and the seder continued.

Everyone received a small piece of the roasted paschal lamb, "the size of an olive." A short blessing was said, and then everyone ate their portion of the afikoman. Today, in Sephardic and Oriental Jewish homes, that blessing is said as a "remembrance of the Passover sacrifice, eaten after one is sated." This is the dessert of the Passover supper. After the afikoman, no other food was eaten. Only the final two cups of wine prescribed by the ritual of the seder could be drunk. After them, only water could be taken for the rest of the night.[48]

## Barekh: "The Blessing After the Meal"

MISHNAH: "They filled the third cup for him. He then recites Grace after Meals. Over the fourth cup he concluded the Hallel, and recites the 'Grace of Song.' Between these cups, (the second and third) he may drink if he wishes. Between the third and the fourth he may not drink" (BT Pesachim 117b).

The large goblet that had served as the kiddush cup shared at the beginning of the Last Supper was again brought to Jesus' table. The disciples filled it for him. This third cup of the seder, called the Cup of Blessing or *kos shel b'rakhah* (1 Cor 10:16), was the occasion for a thanksgiving blessing that the Greek-speaking Jews called eucharistia.

Jesus lifted up the Cup of Blessing and said,

My friends, let us say the blessing.

They responded,

May the name of the LORD (YHWH) be blessed from now on and throughout all eternity.

Jesus said,

With your permission,
Let us bless our God,
of whose bounty we all have eaten!

The rest of the thanksgiving grace was said in unison,

Blessed are You, O LORD (YHWH) our God
King of all creation,
Who feeds the whole world in his goodness
    with grace and love
    and with compassion.
He gives bread to all flesh.
Because his love is everlasting,
    and his great goodness is constant
We have never lacked food,
and may we never lack food ever and forever,
for his great name's sake.
Because He feeds and supports all
    and is the benefactor of all
    preparing food for all
    the people He has created,
Blessed are You, O LORD (YHWH) who gives food to
    all!


We thank You, O LORD (YHWH) our God,
because you have endowed to our ancestors
    this good land, desirable and broad
and because, OLORD (YHWH) our God,
    You have brought us forth from the land of Egypt,
    and redeemed us from the house of slavery,
and because of your covenant which we
    have sealed in our flesh,
and because of your Torah,
    which You have taught us,
and because of your Laws,
    which You have made known to us,
and for the life, grace and love
    You have given to us,
and for the food we eat,
    with which You nourish and support us,
Always, every day, at all times, and every hour.

For all this, O LORD (YHWH) our God,
   We thank you,
   and bless You.
May the blessing of your name
be in the mouth of all living things
   Always, everywhere, and forever.
As it is written,
"But when you have eaten your fill
you must bless the LORD (YHWH) your God
for the good country He has given you" (Dt 8:10).
Blessed are You, O LORD (YHWH)
for the land and for the food.


Our God, and God of our Fathers
May there rise and come to you
   and come unto You
   to be seen and to be pardoned by You
   to be heard and to be numbered by You
   and remembered by You,
Our memorial and our recollection
   A memorial of our fathers
   and a memorial of the messiah
   The son of David your servant[49]
A memorial of Jerusalem
   Your holy city
and a memorial of all your people
   the house of Israel.
As a memorial before You,
   for rescue and for good
   for grace and for love
   for compassion and for life and for peace,
Be this day —
   The Feast of Unleavened Bread!


Remember us, O LORD (YHWH) our God, for good
and recollect us for a blessing
and save us so that we may live!
With the word of salvation and compassion
   Spare us and be gracious to us,
   have compassion for us
   and save us,

Because you are our eyes,
and because You are a gracious king over us
    and You are merciful.


Blessed are you, O LORD (YHWH), our God,
King of all creation.
The God of our fathers,
Our king, our mighty one, our creator,
Our redeemer, our maker, our holy one,
    the holy one of Jacob,
Our shepherd, the shepherd of Israel,
The good king who does good to all,
Who every day and daily,
    is good, and does good, and will do good to us,
Who has favored us, Who favors us,
    and who will favor us forever.
For the grace and love,
    for the compassion and relief
    for the deliverance and success,
    for the blessing and salvation
    for comfort, support and maintenance
    for compassion and for life, peace and all good,
and from all good may we never be lacking!


O merciful one,
Bless my father and my teacher,
and bless the master of this house.
Bless my mother and my teacher,
and bless the mistress of this house,
    and all who dwell in the household,
    their offspring
    and all of their possessions.
Bless us,
    our wives and our children
    and all that we possess.
Bless us,
    and all who have gathered here
    around these tables,
In the same way that you blessed our fathers,
    Abraham, Isaac, and Jacob,

each one and all together
with their own special blessing,
In the same way
Bless us all together
and bless each one of us individually
Each with our own complete blessing!

And to all of this
Let us all say,
AMEN![50]

Jesus picked up the Cup of Blessing again, and everyone said,

Blessed are You, O LORD (YHWH) our God,
King of all creation,
Creator of the fruit of the vine.

Then Jesus drank from the cup and passed it to his disciples, who took it to each table where it was shared by everyone. Various thanksgiving psalms may have been sung while the Cup of Blessing was passed.

Scholars generally believe that it was over this third cup, the Cup of Blessing, that Jesus pronounced the words of consecration, "This cup is the new covenant in my blood" (1 Cor 11:25 NAB). I, however, do not agree. The words of consecration do not seem to fit here. The Passover supper is the zikkaron/anamnesis of the Exodus, not of the reception of the Covenant at Sinai (Z'man Natan Toratenu, "The Time We Received Our Torah"), which is referred to by the "blood of the Covenant" (Ex 24:8). Both Luke and Paul state that it was *after supper* when Jesus took the cup and said, "This cup is the new covenant in my blood, which will be shed for you" (Lk 22:20 NAB). And Paul records Jesus' extremely significant words, "Do this, for as often as you drink from it, it is My Anamnesis" (1 Cor 11:25, translation mine). Pentecost is the zikkaron/anamnesis of receiving the Covenant (Dt 5:2-4; 26:16-19).

At the risk of belaboring a fine point, the Kos shel B'rakhah, the Cup of Blessing, is an integral part of the Passover supper, as is the fourth and final cup. The supper is not concluded until the fourth cup is consumed (BT Pesachim 99b and 108b). It is a mistake to relate the cup that Jesus consecrated to the conclusion of the actual eating of the Supper. Instead, consider the relationship of that cup to the *religious obligations that must be met in order to fulfill all of the requirements of the Passover seder supper.* In this light none of the four cups required by the ritual of the Passover seder could have been used. None could be drunk "after supper" since they were all a religious requirement of the supper. I maintain that the cup used was the fifth cup, a cup that was not a part of the obligations of the Passover supper, but a cup that was poured to satisfy a legal dispute over the significance of the wording of the Fourth Promise found in Exodus 6:7.

> Mishnah: They filled the third cup for him. He then recites grace after meals. Over the fourth (cup) he concludes the Hallel, and recites the Grace of Song (BT Pesachim 117b).

The Cup of Blessing was an obligation of the Passover supper. It was part of the Grace after the meal (Birkat HaMazon); as such it was a necessary part of the supper because it confirmed the table fellowship of the evening.

> "The distinctive feature which marked Judaism off from the surrounding cultures in the time of Jesus was the element of prayer, of 'giving thanks' *for fellowship at table,* and for the provision of food. The formula known to us in modern Judaism has endured through the centuries, and has an ancient prayer as the head of the table takes a piece of bread and breaks it: 'Blessed art thou, O Lord our God, ruler of the universe, thou who bringest bread from the earth.' *The symbolic sharing of the bread conveyed the blessing of Peace and Fellowship.* Similarly, at the end

of the meal there was a further blessing: 'Blessed be our God, he of whose bounty we have partaken, and through whose goodness we live.' After a response the one who presided over the meal took in his hand the *Cup of Blessing* and recited a further thanksgiving for God's goodness to the world, for the land itself, and for Jerusalem (both the city and the Temple). *The response 'Amen' and the sharing of the cup effected a Community of Blessing and of Fellowship!* The importance of all this in the ministry of Jesus is obvious" (Mann, "Mark," *The Anchor Bible* 27, 572).

It is important to realize, on the other hand, that the Passover supper shared the Kiddush (the blessing of the wine and sanctification of the Holy Day), the HaMotzi (the blessing, breaking, and sharing of bread at the beginning of all Feast Day meals), and the Kos shel B'rakhah (the Cup of Blessing said with the Grace after all festival suppers) with all Sabbath and festival suppers. Because of this, the first Christian communities did not wait for an annual celebration of the Lord's Supper/Eucharist. Instead, they adopted the Saturday evening havdalah supper as their weekly communal meal and weekly Eucharist. For Jewish Christians, the havdalah did not so much end the Sabbath; rather, it began the "first day" of the week (Yom Rishon), which was the day Christ rose from the dead and the day the Holy Spirit descended upon the church. Christians quite naturally took over this already important meal and made it a community pot luck where they shared the food that they brought to the table fellowship. The shared supper was renamed "agape" or "love feast." At the conclusion of the havdalah/agape supper, the Cup of Blessing was blessed as the Eucharist Cup of the community's weekly Lord's supper, followed by the special blessing said over the loaf of bread that would become the Body of Christ (1 Cor 10:16-17). Consequently, the Birkat HaMazon (Eucharistia), the thanksgiving blessing for the shared meal of the havdalah/agape, became the model for the Eucharistic prayers, and the Cup of Blessing of the havdalah/agape became known as the Eucharistic cup (1 Cor 10:16).

## The Hallel: "The Great Psalms of Praise"

Again, those disciples who had served the others as wine stewards mixed water with the last of the wine and filled everyone's cup for the fourth and last time. They also filled the great cup that was shared for the "Cup of Blessing." Traditionally, this fifth cup was filled but not drunk from. The reason for the fifth cup was confusion over Exodus 6:7. The previous three promises of God to Israel that gave rise to the first three cups were straightforward.. "I will free you...," "I...will deliver you...," and "I will rescue you...." (Ex 6:6 NAB). But the fourth promise contained two clauses, "I will take you as my own people," and "you shall have me as your God" (Ex 6:7 NAB). Some rabbis taught that the two phrases were meant only to make the fourth promise more emphatic, and therefore, only four cups are necessary for Passover. Other rabbis, however, felt the two clauses differed enough to imply two promises. If so, then five cups should be drunk at the seder. The controversy was never resolved. So, it was decreed that a fifth cup be poured, but no one should drink from it. It was hoped that when the prophet Elijah came, he would resolve the problem; thus, the fifth cup became known as the "Cup of Elijah."[51]

Actually, you might say there are two blessings after the supper of Passover. The first, said over the Cup of Blessing, was very much like the blessing said after every Sabbath and festival meal. For Passover, however, the second part of the Hallel was recited or sung in thanksgiving and praise to the all-loving and compassionate God. The Hallel must be sung before and after the paschal lambs were eaten because they were also sung as the lambs were sacrificed.

Also, the first blessing was said over a single cup that everyone shared. Now, the second blessing was sung over each one's individual cup. The difference emphasizes a predominate theme that weaves throughout the entire seder. The whole group has obligations to meet and blessings to receive. But then, each individual has those same obligations to meet and those same blessings to receive. That theme may be wrapped up in a paraphrase of the closing lines of the grace after the meal, "Bless us as you blessed our ancestors, Abraham, Isaac and Jacob, whom you blessed together, and whom you blessed each one with his own complete and special blessing. Bless us altogether, and bless each one of us with our own complete and special blessing, and to this let us all say, Amen!"

> MISHNAH: "If some of them fell asleep, they may eat when they wake up; If all of them fell asleep they must not eat. (In the latter case they have all ceased to think about the Paschal Lamb; when they awake it is as though they would eat in two different places, sleep breaking the continuity of action and place, and thus it is forbidden.) Rabbi Jose said: If they fell into a light sleep, they may eat; if they fell fast asleep, they must not eat" (BT Pesachim 120b; Mt 26:40-46).

It may be that Jesus had everyone stand up to sing the second half of the Hallel. Sitting through a complete seder tends to cause most people to get a little groggy. Reclining on couches for the same amount of time is even more sleep inducing (Lk 22:45-46). Having them stand and sing would give everyone a lift.

They sang Psalms 115 through 118, the great psalms of praise, from which we get our word "Halleluyah," which means "praise to the Lord." Of all these psalms, 118 was considered the most important. Verses 19 through 29 were thought of as referring to the coming Messiah, and because of that, they were sung in an antiphonal way. As master of the seder, Jesus sang each verse first and then everyone responded by singing it a second time. When a Christian, such as myself, discovers this ancient Jewish tradition for the first time, it is a wholly overpowering experience. I am almost certain that the disciples had a similar powerful experience:

JESUS:
Open to me the gates of justice;
I will enter them and give thanks to the LORD (YHWH)
This gate is the LORD'S
    the just shall enter it.
I will give thanks to you, for you have answered me
    and have been my savior.

ALL:
I will give thanks to you, for you have answered me
    and have been my saviour.

JESUS:
The stone which the builders rejected has become the
    cornerstone.
By the LORD (YHWH) has this been done;
    it is wonderful in our eyes.

ALL:
The stone which the builders rejected has become the
    cornerstone.
By the LORD (YHWH) has this been done;
    it is wonderful in our eyes.

JESUS:
This is the day the LORD (YHWH) has made;
    let us be glad and rejoice in it.

ALL:
This is the day the LORD (YHWH) has made;
    let us be glad and rejoice in it.

JESUS:
[I beseech you, LORD, — Salvation Now!
   (ana Adonay — hoshi'ah na!)]

ALL:
[I beseech you, LORD, — salvation now!]

JESUS:
[I beseech You, Lord, — success now!
   (ana Adonay — hatzlichah na!)]

ALL:
[I beseech You, Lord, — success now!]

JESUS:
Blessed is he who comes in the name of the LORD
   (YHWH)
We bless you from the house of the LORD (YHWH).

ALL:
Blessed is he who comes in the name of the LORD
   (YHWH)
We bless you from the house of the LORD (YHWH).

JESUS:
The LORD (YHWH) is God, and he has given us light.
Join in procession with leafy boughs up to the horns of
   the altar.

ALL:
The LORD (YHWH) is God and he has given us light.
Join in procession with leafy boughs up to the horns of
   the altar.

JESUS:
You are my God, and I give thanks to you;
   O my God, I extol you.

ALL:

You are my God, and I give thanks to you;
O my God, I extol you.


JESUS:

Give thanks to the LORD (YHWH) for he is good;
for *his everlasting love* [chesed] endures forever!


ALL:

Give thanks to the LORD (YHWH) for he is good;
for *his everlasting love* [chesed] endures forever![52]
(Ps 118:19-29, translation and emphasis mine).

MISHNAH: "Over the fourth cup He concludes the Hallel, and recites the 'Grace of Song.' What is 'The Grace of Song?' Rab Judah said; 'They shall praise Thee, O Lord, our God'; while Rabbi Jochanan said, 'The Breath of all living.' Our Rabbis taught: At the fourth He concludes the Hallel and recites the Great Hallel....Others say: 'The Lord is my shepherd, I shall not want.' What comprises the Great Hallel? Rab Judah said: From 'O Give Thanks,' (beginning of Psalm 136) until, 'The rivers of Babylon' (Psalm 137). While Rabbi Jochanan said: From 'A Song of Ascents,' (Psalms 120 to 134) until 'The Rivers of Babylon.' Rabbi Acha ben Jacob said: From, 'for the Lord hath chosen Jacob unto himself,' (Psalm 134) until 'The Rivers of Babylon.' And why is it called the Great Hallel? —said Rabbi Jochanan: 'Because the Holy One, Blessed be He, sits in the heights of the universe and distributes food to all creatures' (BT Pesachim 117b-118a).

To those unfamiliar with the celebration of Passover, the long and involved conclusion to the Hallel may seem unnecessary. But to all of those who love the seder, the lengthy grace of blessing is only natural. When you love something, you want to prolong the conclusion as long as possible. Like the Sabbath, which Jews personify as "Queen Sabbath," the seder was not easy to part company with. The disciples held the final embrace of the Grace of Song as long as possible—and for their love and intense reluctance at parting, the heavenly Father would reward them abundantly through his son Jesus, the Messiah of Israel.

## The Grace of Song

**Y'haleluka**—**"You Shall Be Praised"**: The hymn, "You Shall Be Praised," followed the Hallel very naturally. The name for the hymn in Hebrew, "Y'halelukha," comes from the word "hallel" and means literally "The great songs of praise shall be sung before you."

> You shall be praised, O LORD (YHWH) our God
> by all of your works and by your righteous ones,
> the just, who do your will,
> and all of your people, the house of Israel,
> breaking out in joyous song.
>
> We shall thank and bless, laud and glorify,
> exalt and respect, sanctify and give sovereignty,
> to your name, O our King!
>
> Because it is good to render our thanksgiving to you.
> It is fitting to sing praises to your name.
> From all eternity and throughout all eternity
> You are God! (Haggadah shel Pesach),

A number of favorite psalms followed. Psalm 23, "The Lord is My Shepherd," was a fitting reminder of the magnificent procession of the men to the Temple with the paschal lambs borne upon their shoulders. Psalms 120 to 134 were the Psalms of Ascents that the men sang on their way to the Passover sacrifice, and Psalm 136 recounted all of the Passover themes and, "Because the Holy One, Blessed be He, sits in the heights of the universe and distributes food to all creatures" (BT Pesachim 118a).

**Nishmat — "The Breath of Every Living Thing"**: The final hymn of the Grace of Song was the richly beautiful "Breath of Every Living Thing." Over the centuries much was added to it, but it has never lost its essential radiance.

The breath of every living thing
Blesses your name,
O LORD (YHWH) our God,
And the spirit of all flesh
Glorify and exalt
Your memory.
Our king for ever,
From all eternity and through out all eternity
You are King!

Without you
We would not have a king to save us
Nor a savior to redeem us
Nor a lifesaver to support us,
Nor a compassionate One
       at the times of our distress and oppression.

We have no king but you,
O God of all first things
       and all last things,
God of all humanity,
Lord of all generations,
Who is praised in numerous songs of praise,
Who conducts his creation with eternal love (chesed)
And all humanity with compassion.

The LORD (YHWH) never slumbers and never sleeps
It is He who arouses the sleepers
And awakens the slumberers and heals the mute.
It is He who sets free the imprisoned
And supports the falling

And raises up the bowed down.

We are thankful to You alone!
If our mouths were filled with song like the sea
And our tongues of exultation
      like the multitude of waves,
Our lips of praise
      like the space of the firmament,
Our hands spread out
      like the eagles of heaven,
Our feet light
      like the swift hind
We could not give sufficient thanks to You,
O LORD (YHWH) our God,
And God of our Fathers,
And to bless your name
for one of a thousand times a thousand,
      or a vast magnitude,
      or myriads of occasions,
For the good You have done at times
To our forefathers and our people.

From Egypt You ransomed us
O LORD (YHWH) our God,
And from the house of slavery You redeemed us.
In famine You provided for us,
And in abundance You nourished us,
From the sword You saved us,
And from the plague You delivered us,
And from the raging sickness You lifted us up.
Up until now You have helped us
      through your compassion.
May your eternal love [chesed] never desert us,
And may You never abandon us
O LORD (YHWH) our God for ever.

Therefore,
The limbs You have distributed to us
And the spirit and breath
You blew into our nostrils
And the tongue You put into our mouths,

They shall all thank you and bless you
  Praise You and glorify You,
  Exalt You and reverence You and sanctify You,
Enthroned be your name, O our king,
Every mouth gives thanks to You
And every tongue shall swear to You,
Every knee shall kneel to You
Every height brought low before You,
Every heart shall be in awe of You
And all our inward parts and organs
  Shall sing praise to your name.
As it is written,
  "All my being shall say,
  'O Lord, who is like You'" (Ps 35:10).


Who can be compared to You,
And who is equal to You,
Who can be esteemed as You.
The God who is great,
The mighty one,
The terrible God on high,
Creator of heaven and earth.


May You be praised, glorified, and magnified,
Blessed is your Holy Name.
As it was said by David,
  "Bless the Lord, O my soul,
  And all my being,
  Bless His Holy Name" (Ps 103:1).
O God,
In the strength of your power,
  Great in glory is your name.
Mighty for ever,
Awesome in your amazing acts.
O King
Who sits upon an exalted and lofty throne!
Blessed are You, O LORD (YHWH),
  God and King,
  Great in praises
  God of thanksgiving
  Lord of constant wonders,

Acclaimed in song and Psalm.
King, God, Life of all existence!

Everyone returned to their couches and reclined again. Then they all lifted their cups and said the blessing before drinking the Cup of the Hallel, the fourth and last required cup of wine.

Blessed are You, O LORD (YHWH), our God,
King of all creation,
Creator of the fruit of the vine
(Haggadah shel Pesach).

## Nirtzah: "May Our Observance Be Acceptable"

Jesus and the disciples now recited together the concluding thanksgiving prayer.

Blessed are You, O LORD (YHWH) our God,
King of all creation,
For the vine,
    And the fruit of the Vine.
For the produce of the fields,
For the land,
    Which is pleasant,
    Spacious and good,
Which You willed and endowed
    To our Ancestors
    To eat of its fruit
    And to be surfeited from its goodness.
May we also be worthy of its fruitfulness
And be surfeited of its goodness,
And may You be blessed
Over its holiness and purity.

We shall rejoice in this day
The pilgrimage feast of unleavened bread,

Because You, O LORD (YHWH), our God,
Are the benefactor of all.
We thank You,
    For the land,
    And for the fruit of the vine.
Blessed are You, O LORD (YHWH) our God,
    For the land,
    And for the fruit of the vine. Amen.
(Haggadah shel Pesach).

"Concluded is the Passover" (*chasal sidur pesach*). All of its laws and customs had been observed. The disciples prayed that they would be privileged to observe Passover again with Jesus in the coming years. For the rest of the night, the men intended to gather even more closely about their Rabbi Y'shu'a and dig more deeply into the nuances of this seder, especially of the maggid. The women would play Passover games and sing traditional songs with the younger children until they fell asleep. And then the dining couches would be converted into beds for them all.

## Kos Shel Eliyahu: "The Cup of Elijah"

But instead of letting his followers settle into the traditional after-seder activities, Jesus sent a jolt throughout the upper room. He picked up the great cup that had been filled as the "fifth cup," the Cup of Elijah, and announced to them all, "This cup is the new covenant in my blood. Do this, as often as you drink it, in remembrance of me" (1 Cor 11:25 NAB).[53] The realization swept over the room that Jesus was, at that moment, establishing the kingdom of God on earth![54] In the Jewish experience, Passover prepared Jews to become the people of God, but it was at Mount Sinai that God actually made them his people. It was the Covenant that made the escaped slaves (*avedim*) into a holy nation and a kingdom of priests (*b'nai chorim*) (Ex 19:6).[55]

These words did not fit into the context of Passover. This was a Pentecost pronouncement. The earlier words over the bread ("This is my body") initiated the anamnesis of his pascha (Passover seder, death and resurrection). However, these words over the wine initiated an anamnesis of a new Pentecost — when the Messiah would return in the power of the Holy Spirit, fully as Lord, coming down from heaven with a New Covenant that, when accepted, would make his people into a new nation of the children of God! A new nation, not organized as a political unit, but organized as a living and loving family, the family of God.

From Jesus' words, "This is the new covenant in my blood," the disciples knew that they would not receive and share the cup of the Covenant until Jesus had explained the New Covenant to them, as Moses had done when he had bound them in the Covenant with God at Sinai. They all, men and women, must have gathered around Jesus to hear his words of instruction, just as all of the Israelites had gathered before Moses at the foot of the mountain to hear the words of instruction from God.

> Moses came and told the people all of the commandments (divrey YHWH — "Commanding Words of YHWH"[56] and all of the judgments. The people replied with one voice and said, "All of the commandments [*ha-dvarim*] which the LORD (YHWH) has spoken [diber] to us we will do!" And Moses wrote down [*yiktov*] all the commanding words of the Lord (divrey YHWH). He then rose early in the morning and built an altar below the mountain and (set up) twelve memorial pillars [*matzebah*] to represent the twelve tribes of Israel. He sent young men of the children of Israel and they offered up burnt offerings and sacrificed bullocks as peace offerings to the Lord (which would then be shared in a sacrificial banquet with the people). Moses took half of the blood (of the sacrifices) and put it into basins, and half of the blood he threw on the altar. He took the book of the Covenant and read it in the hearing of the people, and they said,

"All that the LORD (YHWH) has spoken [diber] we will do!" And Moses took the blood and threw it onto the people. He said, "Behold the blood of the covenant which the LORD (YHWH) has made with you, concerning all of these commandments (hadvarim).

Moses went up (the mountain) with Aaron, Nadab, Abihu, and the seventy elders of Israel. They saw the God of Israel. Under his feet it was as a pavement of sapphire, like the heavens for clearness. To the nobles of the sons of Israel, he did not stretch out his hand (and destroy them). *And they saw God, and they ate and they drank (in fellowship)* (Ex 24:3-11, translation, notes, and emphasis mine).

All were familiar with these words. They were from the Torah, the Book of Shmot (Exodus) and described the formula of institution of the divine Covenant.[57] They were heard every year in the synagogues at Shavuot (Pentecost) as the whole people reaffirmed the Sinai Covenant with God. They were equally familiar with Moses' words to them at Horeb, the mountain of Sinai, on the anniversary of their first receiving the Covenant,

And Moses called to all of Israel, "Hear O Israel! (sh'ma yisra'el!) All of the laws and judgments which I speak into your ears today. Learn them and be careful to do them! The LORD (YHWH) made a covenant with us at Horeb.[58] *Not with our Fathers did the LORD (YHWH) make this Covenant, but with us, even us, with all of these here today, with all of us who are alive!* Face to face the LORD (YHWH) spoke with you on the mount out of the midst of the fire. At that time, I stood between the LORD (YHWH) and you to declare to *you* the commanding word of the LORD (YHWH), because you were afraid to face the fire and did not go up into the mountain" (Dt 5:1-5, translation and emphasis mine).[59]

The disciples understood that Shavuot/Pentecost was the zikkaron/anamnesis of the Sinai experience just as Passover was the zikkaron/anamnesis of the Exodus. And they put Jesus' words into this context. Moreover, they knew the formula for the institution of a divine Covenant and they heard how Jesus, in his words after the supper, faithfully followed this formula.[60]

### The Preamble:

Jesus said to him, "I am the way and the truth and the life. No one comes to the Father except through me. If you know me, then you will also know my Father. From now on you do know him and have seen him. Whoever has seen me has seen the Father. How can you say, 'Show us the Father'? Do you not believe that I am in the Father and the Father is in me?" (Jn 14:6-7,9-10 NAB).

### The Prologue:

So when he had washed their feet [and] put his garments back on and reclined at table again, he said to them, "Do you realize what I have done for you? You call me 'teacher' and 'master,' and rightly so, for indeed I am. If I, therefore, the master and teacher, have washed your feet, you ought to wash one another's feet. I have given you a model to follow, so that as I have done for you, you should also do" (Jn 13:12-15 NAB).

### The Stipulations:

"I give you a new commandment:[61] love one another. As I have loved you, so you also should love one another. This is how all will know that you are my disciples, if you have love for one another" (Jn 13:34-35 NAB).

From that time, the disciples had to show that they were authentic followers of Jesus Christ by the love (agape) they showed each other. For the religious Jew, there are ten fundamental commandments, but for the authentic Christian there are eleven commandments — and the eleventh is the most important. "This is how all will know that you are my disciples, if you have love (agape) for one another" (Jn 13:35 NAB).

## The Public Reading:

"As the Father loves me, so I also love you. Remain in my love. If you keep my commandments, you will reamin in my love, just as I have kept my Father's commandments and remain in his love.

"I have told you this so that my joy might be in you and your joy might be complete. This is my commandment: love one another as I love you. No one has greater love than this, to lay down one's life for one's friends" (Jn 15:9-13 NAB).

"For as often as you eat this bread and drink the cup, you proclaim [kataggellete] the death of the Lord until he comes" (1 Cor 11:26 NAB).[62]

## The Witnesses:

During the supper the Twelve Apostles, whom Jesus had placed nearest to him so that they could hear all of his words, began arguing about which of them was the most important. Jesus rebuked them, "For who is greater: the one seated at table or the one who serves? Is it not the one seated at table? I am among you as the one who serves" (Lk 22:27 NAB). But then he went on and said why the Twelve were so important to him. "...you may eat and drink at my table in my kingdom; and you will sit on thrones judging the twelve tribes of Israel" (Lk 22:30 NAB).

The Twelve Apostles are the twelve witnesses to the institution of the Eucharist and the Lord's Supper, and they are also the required twelve witnesses to the institution of the New Covenant. They stood in place of the twelve memorial stone pillars (matzevah)[63] that stood as witnesses for the twelve tribes of Israel as Moses instituted the Sinai Covenant.

Judas was no longer present. He had left early in the evening. That reduced the number of official witnesses to eleven and thus would have invalidated that witnessing. But Matthias was present among the disciples with Jesus at the Last Supper (Acts 1:15-17, 21-26), and therefore the required twelve witnesses to the New Covenant were all present. From among the 120 male disciples, who were also witnesses (Ex 24:4), Matthias was elected to be one of the twelve official witnesses (Acts 1:21-26). The necessary number of twelve witnesses remained important until Pentecost when the infant church, filled with the power of the Holy Spirit, ratified the New Covenant of love. Then, the company of twelve official witnesses changed into the company of ambassadors (or apostles) of the risen Lord. The number of apostles expanded after Pentecost and far exceeded the number twelve.

### Formula of Blessings and Curses:

If you love me, you will obey my commandments. And I will ask the Father, and he will give you another Advocate (Paraclete[64]) to be with you always, the Spirit of truth, which the world cannot accept, because it neither sees nor knows it. But you know it, because it remains with you, and will be in you (Jn 14:15-17 NAB).

Whoever has my commandments and observes them is the one who loves me. And whoever loves me will be loved by my Father, and I will love him and reveal myself to him.

Whoever loves me will keep my word, and my Father will love him, and we will come to him and make our dwelling with him. (Jn 14:21,23 NAB).

I am the the vine, you are the branches. Whoever remains in me and I in him will bear much fruit, because without me you can do nothing. Anyone who does not remain in me will be thrown out like a branch and wither; people will gather them and throw them into a fire and they will be burned (Jn 15:5-6 NAB).

## The Covenant Is Sealed in Blood:

Then he took a cup, gave thanks, and gave it to them, saying, "Drink from it, all of you, for this is my blood of the covenant, which will be shed on behalf of many for the forgiveness of sins" (Mt 26:27,28 NAB).

"Since the life of a living body is in its blood, I have made you put it on the altar, so that atonement may thereby be made for your own lives, because it is the blood, as the seat of life, that makes atonement. That is why I have told the Israelites: No one among you, not even a resident alien, may partake of blood. Since the life of every living body is its blood, I have told the Israelites: You shall not partake of the blood of any meat. Since the life of every living body is its blood, anyone who partakes of it shall be cut off" (Lv 17:11,12,14 NAB).

The Apostles and disciples must have been taken aback, at first, when Jesus asked them to drink his blood. They had spent their entire lives and had gone to great lengths to fulfill the commandment not to "partake of the blood of any meat" (Lv 17:14 NAB).

But they also understood that the blood of the Covenant was the seal that glued all parties of a Covenant into a new relationship and that Covenant fellowship was committed to the fulfillment of the commandments or activating conditions of the Covenant. At Sinai, Moses poured half of the blood of the Covenant onto the sides of the altar, which represented the presence of God there, and half the blood on the new people after they had sworn to uphold all the commandments. It bonded the people together into a new nation under the kingship of God. The disciples understood this use of blood, but they could not as easily understand why they would seal this New Covenant by drinking the blood of Jesus from a common cup.

Either Jesus reminded them, or they soon recalled, that Jesus' intentions were put forth in that powerful and majestic prophecy,

> Behold,
> The days are coming.
> The LORD (YHWH) says,
> When I will cut a new covenant,
> With the House of Israel and with the House of Judah.
> Not like the covenant that I cut with their ancestors
> In the day that I took them by their hand,
> To bring them out of the land of Egypt,
> Because they broke my covenant!
> Even though I was a husband to them!
> The LORD (YHWH) says,
> This is the Covenant that I will cut with the
> House of Israel,
> After those days,
> Says the LORD (YHWH),
> I will put My Torah in their innards,
> And I will write it upon their hearts.
> For them, I will be God,
> And they will be a people to me.
> And each man will not teach his neighbor,
> Nor teach his brother,
> Saying, "Know the LORD (YHWH)!"
> Because they shall all know Me
> From the least of them
> Even to their greatest.
> Says the LORD (YHWH),
> "I will forgive their iniquity
> And I will not remember their sins any more!"
> (Jer 31:30-33; Heb 8:8-12, translation mine).

To paraphrase the prophecy, God promised to make a New Covenant with them. He promised to enshrine his New

Covenant within them, to make them his temple (1 Cor 3:16), and to write his new commandment upon the tablet of their hearts. The Covenant of Sinai was an external Covenant of ordinances and laws and, therefore, the blood of the Covenant was splashed upon them. The conditions of that Covenant, the Ten Commandments, were carved upon tablets of stone and enshrined in the Ark of the Covenant, which stood in Solomon's Temple. But the New Covenant was a Covenant of love (agape), which was to be enshrined within each one of them, and the commandment of agape-love was to be engraved upon the living tablet of their hearts. This New Covenant of agape-love was an interior and intimate Covenant, and, therefore, the blood of the New Covenant was to be drunk, internalized, to seal all parties into the New Covenant fellowship.

The Apostles and disciples understood Jesus within the context of the Israelite understanding of Covenant initiation and ratification. To become partners in a Covenant relationship meant that all of the conditions and commitments of that Covenant must be accepted by all parties before ratification. Moses read the law and commandments of the Sinai Covenant to all of the people, and when they swore to accept all of the conditions of the Sinai Covenant and to obey all of its laws and commandments, *then* Moses sealed the people to God in the Covenant relationship of the king and nation of Israel.

In the same way, everyone had to wait until Jesus had instructed them on the conditions of the New Covenant before they could drink from the cup. When all of the disciples clearly understood Jesus and accepted the New Covenant and swore to be faithful to it, then Jesus passed the cup to everyone. As the disciples accepted the cup, they accepted the New Covenant of agape-love, and as they drank from it, they ratified within themselves the new commandment: *agapate allelous — Love one another.*

## Nefesh Ha-basar: "The Life of the Flesh"

> Since the life of a living body [nefesh ha-basar] is in its blood,
> I have made you put it on the altar, so that atonement may thereby
> be made for your own lives [nafishtekhem], because it is the
> blood, as the seat of life that makes atonement (Lv 17:11 NAB).

This quotation from Leviticus has a direct bearing on a complete understanding of the Eucharist. It is particularly significant that the word for life throughout this verse is "nefesh" and not the usual *chai.* "Nefesh" is translated as "soul, life, spirit, mind, breath, respiration, person, human being, creature." The verb "nefesh" means "to animate, breath life into, enliven, to be animated." Jesus used the word "basar/bisra" to identify his body, which is present in the Host and all those in Passover table fellowship with him. It should follow, then, that the life of the body of Christ is in his blood, which is the blood of the New Covenant.

The Eucharist is the heart of the body of Christ. But that heart can only be effective if it nourishes and animates the body of Christ with the blood of Christ. If the individual cells (disciples) of his body (the church) are not nourished and animated with his agape-love, then they languish and die.

The breath of the body of Christ is the Holy Spirit (ruach ha-kodesh). But, as the verse from Leviticus states, the breath of the body is tied to the blood. Nefesh is an animated and breathing body. Therefore, without agape-love in each and every vein, the Holy Spirit can do little to animate the body of Christ!

At Holy Communion then, if we, the body of Christ, the church, nourish ourselves only with the flesh of Jesus, then we are incomplete and ill-suited to continue his ministry to each other and the world. We must also accept the New Covenant and take the chalice of his blood. When we accept the consecrated chalice, we accept "the new covenant in my blood" (1 Cor 11:25). We accept his Covenant of agape-love. When we drink from his cup we seal ourselves to him and each other. We enshrine the new commandment within our hearts, "Love one another. As I have loved you, so you also should love one another" (Jn 13:34 NAB).

Animated with his blood and love and his spirit of compassion, we the body of Christ can truly minister to the whole world and prove to everyone that Jesus lives! By sealing ourselves to each other in service, caring, and agape-love, we enter into the kingdom of God.

*This is how all will know you for my disciples,*
if you have love for one another (Jn 13:35 NAB).
The Covenant Banquet (Exodus 24:9-11 & 24:5)
"Do this, whenever you drink The Cup, as My
   Anamnesis"
Every time, then, you eat This Bread,
and drink This Cup,
you Proclaim the Pascha-Death of the Lord
until He Comes!
(1 Cor 11:25,26, translation mine).

At the HaMotzi of the seder, when Jesus first announced over the bread, "This is My Body, Do this as My Anamnesis" (1 Cor 11:24), he established the present and future Lord's Supper as a Passover table fellowship, a Passover chavurah. The disciples clearly understood that Jesus had formed them into a community of service to each other, koinonia. Just as each member of a body is responsible for the health and well-being of every other member, or else all suffer (isn't cancer a runaway cell doing its own thing?), so is each member of the body of Christ responsible for the health and well-being of every other member (1 Cor 10:16-17; 12:12-27).

But Jesus had distinctly added another whole dimension to the table fellowship of the Lord's Supper. All future Eucharists are to be Covenant fellowship banquets as well. At all Covenant banquets, all parties to the Covenant swear brotherhood to each other and pledge themselves wholly to fulfilling all of the conditions, or commandments, of that Covenant. If they are faithful to the Covenant brotherhood and carry out all of the commandments, then they will continue to receive all of the blessings of the Covenant relationship. Through his new commandment, Jesus commissioned all of his disciples to continue his ministering presence to the whole world! *Through their love and care for everyone, they would be able to show very clearly to the whole world that he, Jesus, is alive!* (Jn 13:35; Gal 2:20).

Jesus is incarnate love (1 Jn 4:16), and the true body of Christ continues to minister that love, caring, compassion, and service of the Risen Lord!

Whenever we receive the chalice of the blood of Christ, the blood of the New Covenant, the consecrated chalice changes our Eucharist into the Covenant banquet of Christ and unites us to the Lord Jesus in a special way. We must be aware of what that new relationship is. "If you keep my commandments, *you will remain in my love,* just as I have kept my Father's commandments and remain in his love. *I have told you this so that my joy might be in you and your joy might be complete"* (Jn 15:10,11 NAB, emphasis mine). The Covenant relationship with Christ is much more than the brotherhood fellowship of the Sinai Covenant. We, the Church, are the bride of Christ. For just as the Father married Israel at Sinai in the blood of the Covenant shared there, Christ — the Lamb of God — married the Church in the sharing of the blood of the New Covenant (Rv 12:1-6). The bride and bridegroom have become two in one flesh, the body of the bridegroom, Christ (1 Cor 10:17; 12:12-27), and share the one Spirit with him (Eph 4:4) in the Covenant banquet of the Eucharist. That is why we should always respond to the Eucharist as "blessed are those who have been called to the wedding feast of the Lamb" (Rv 19:9 NAB). As we share in the joy and love of the Lamb of God (Jn 15:11-13), all of us who joined together in Baptism as the bride of Christ should greet each other with the warm embrace of peace (1 Pt 5:14) and a holy kiss (1 Cor 16:20; 2 Cor 13:12).

> Every time, then, you eat this bread and drink this cup, you proclaim the death of the Lord until he comes! This means that whoever eats the bread or drinks the cup of the Lord unworthily [without the commitment to love] sins against the body (the community) and the blood (the New Covenant) of the Lord. People should examine themselves first (are they selfish or selfless, loving or indifferent), only then should they eat of the bread and drink of the cup. They who eat and drink without recognizing the body of Christ eat and drink a judgment on themselves. That is why many among you are sick and infirm, and why so many are dying. If we were to examine ourselves, we would not be falling under judgment in this way; but since it is the Lord who judges us, he chastens us to keep us from being condemned with the rest of the world. Therefore, my brothers and sisters, when we assemble for the Lords supper, *let us wait upon one another* (1 Cor 11:26-33, paraphrase and emphasis mine).

St. Paul tells us that if we do everything else right, but we do it all without agape-love, then we have done everything wrong! (1 Cor 13:1 3). We have become flippant about our agape-love and marriage relationship with Christ and his whole church.

> If I speak in human and angelic tongues, but do not have love, I am a resounding gong or clashing cymbal. And if I have the gift of prophecy and comprehend all mysteries and all knowledge; if I have all faith so as to move mountains but do not have love, I am nothing. If I give away everything I own, and if I hand my body over so that I may boast, but do not have love, I gain nothing.
>
> So faith, hope, and love [agape] remain, these three; and the greatest of these is love (1 Cor 13:1-3,13 NAB; Mt 7:21- 23; 25:34-40, 41-45).

> "Come, then! Let us be on our way" (Jn 14:31, translation mine).

The time had come for Jesus to leave the warm, loving, companionship of the table fellowship of his Last Supper. He had established his continuing presence among his disciples. He had committed them to the serving table fellowship (koinonia/chavurah) of his Pascha. He had sealed them into the kingdom of God his Father and assigned and dedicated them to continue his ministry to the world. But now the hour had come for him to prepare for his death.

Taking just the men with him, he left the upper room and walked the short distance down from Mount Zion to the Kedron Valley and the Garden of Gethsemane. He had some last things to confide to those with him, and particularly, to prepare them for the horror that they were about to experience.

> Behold, the hour is coming and has arrived when each of you will be scattered to his own home and you will leave me alone (Jn 16:32 NAB).

Jesus knew it would be hard for them to understand what the Kingdom of God was all about. They had no models to go by — Jesus was turning religion upside down — and there would continuously be the temptation to turn it "right side up" and conform to what they did understand. But Jesus did not want great temples erected in his honor. He wanted people for his holy places where "he chooses to dwell" (Jn 14:23). "Are you not aware that You are the Temple of God, and that the Spirit of God dwells in you?" (1 Cor 3:16). He would soon vividly demonstrate that fact during the Feast of Pentecost. The Holy Spirit would appear as that same fiery cloud that covered Mount Sinai when God spoke to Moses and the children of Israel; that same cloud of fire that covered the meeting tent and tabernacle where the Ark of the Covenant rested (Ex 40:34-38); that same cloud that filled the Holy of Holies of Solomon's Temple to manifest God's presence (1 Kgs 8:10-13). On Pentecost, that cloud of fire, manifesting God's presence among his people, would break apart and enter each one in the upper room, thereby making each one of them his temple and dwelling place (Acts 2:3,4).

Part of the great agony that Jesus would suffer was the realization that not all of his followers were able to understand him. Agape-love and forgiveness, compassion and service were too difficult for them to grasp. "But how narrow is the gate that leads to Life, how rough the road, and how few there are who find it!" (Mt 7:12-14). Too many were seduced into "giving greater honor and Glory to God" in much more spectacular and satisfying ways. But Jesus will rebuke them because that way was not his way (Mt 7:15-23).

But to the very end, he reached out to all of them and all of us with his great forgiveness and love,

Father, the hour has come. Give glory to your son, so that your son may glorify you, just as you gave him authority over all people, so that he may give eternal life to all you gave him. Now this is eternal life, that they should know you, the only true God, and the one whom you sent, Jesus Christ. I glorified you on earth by accomplishing the work that you gave me to do. Now glorify me, Father, with you, with the glory that I had with you before the world began.

I revealed your name to those whom you gave me out of the world. They belonged to you, and you gave them to me, and they have kept your word. Now they know that everything you gave me is from you, because the words you gave to me I have given to them, and they accepted them and truly understood that I came from you, and they have believed that you sent me. I pray for them. I do not pray for the world but for the ones you have given me, because they are yours, and everything of mine is yours and everything of yours is mine, and I have been glorified in them. And now I will no longer be in the world, but they are in the world, while I am coming to you. Holy Father, keep them in your name that you have given me, so that they may be one just as we are. When I was with them I protected them in your name that you gave me, and I guarded them, and none of them was lost except the son of destruction, in order that the scripture might be fulfilled. But now I am coming to you. I speak this in the world so that they may share my joy completely. I gave them your word, and the world hated them, because they do not belong to the world any more than I belong to the world. I do not ask that you take them out of the world but that you keep them from the evil one. They do not belong to the world any more than I belong to the world. Consecrate them in the truth. Your word is truth. As you sent me into the world, so I sent them into the world. And I consecrate myself for them, so that they also may be consecrated in truth.

I pray not only for them, but also for those who will believe in me through their word, so *that they may all be one, as you,. Father, are in me and I in you, that they also may be in us,* that the world may believe that you sent me. And I have given them the glory you gave me, *so that they may be one, as we are one, I in them and you in me, that they may be brought to perfection as one, that the world may know that you sent me, and that you Joved them even as you loved me* (Jn 17:1-23 NAB, emphasis mine).

## NOTES

1. Although they spoke Aramaic, traditional prayers were recited in Hebrew, which was the religious and liturgical language. Hebrew, which is not that different from Aramaic, was easy to learn. Even today, most families recite the important prayers of the Haggadah in Hebrew.

2. The phrase, *melekh ha'olam*, is difficult to translate accurately into English. In Biblical Hebrew it usually meant, "forever, ever, everlasting, evermore, perpetual, old, ancient," and "world" (R. L. Harris, G. L. Archer, B. K. Waltke, *Theological Wordbook of the Old Testament* [Chicago: Moody Press, 1631a). Under Greek influence, this all-encompassing word took on much added meaning, such as, "world, universe, space existence," as well as "eternity" (Alcalay, *The Complete Hebrew-English Dictionary,* col.1866.) In other words, "olam" refers to the whole of "time" and "space." The popular translation today is "universe," but since astronomers have found other universes, I prefer the translation, "all creation," encompassing all of the space/time continuum.

3. Ephraim and Mannasseh were the sons of Joseph born in Egypt. Joseph's father, Israel, accepted the two grandsons as his own sons and gave them the parental blessing (Gn 48:1-20). Ephraim and Man-

nasseh divided the inheritance of Joseph and became known as the Twin Tribes. The tribes of Ephraim and Manasseh prospered among the tribes of Israel and became quite famous.

4. The Passover laws recorded in the Mishnah refer to the pater-familias, or leader of the seder, as "He."

5. In Israel, the season for harvesting and pressing the grapes is September/October when the New Year, Rosh HaShanah, and the Feast of Tabernacles, Sukkot are celebrated. In one part of each vineyard, there was a cistern dug and plastered to make it waterproof. The harvested grapes were placed in the cistern and crushed. Fermentation began very quickly and lasted several days or weeks. When the bubbling and agitation stopped and the liquid calmed, the juice was drawn off the leavings of grapeskins and stems and funneled into the new wineskins, which were then placed in cool caves for preservation. That was the only way that grape juice could be preserved for the rest of the year. Only fermented grape juice or wine was available for Passover, which arrives in the following spring. It has only been since the nineteenth century, with the discovery of pasteurization, refrigeration, and inhibiting chemicals, that plain, unfermented grape juice has been available for the whole year.

6. The Greek is much more emphatic here, "With desire I desired to eat this Passover with you...that never in any way will I eat of it until when it is fulfilled" (my translation).

7. Jeremias, *The Eucharistic Words of Jesus*, 207-218. Jeremias gravely misunderstands Jesus' words here. Jeremias believes that Jesus fasted at the Last Supper, which does not make sense in light of Luke 22:15 and John 13:18. It would be an awkward table fellowship if the host abstained. Also, Jeremias believes that the Kingdom of God does not appear until the Parousia, which makes no sense in light of such parables as the mustard seed (Lk 13:18,19) and the yeast (Lk 13:20,21). The Kingdom of God, beginning with Jesus, makes its appearance on earth on the following Pentecost, with the coming of the Holy Spirit.

8. Bread is always blessed, shared, and served at the main course.

9. This invitation to Passover, the ha lachma!, stirred in the Jewish people an intense hope for freedom from Roman domination, "Now we are enslaved!" But the next line confirmed the hope of seeing the Messiah and his deliverance, "Next year, may we all be free!"

10. The Hebrew of Deuteronomy 26:5 ordinarily reads, "Arami oved avi," which means, "My father was a wandering Aramean." But in memory of the persecution under Antiochus IV Epiphanes, the

vowels of "oved" were changed to "avid," which means "perish, be exterminated" (Brown, Driver, *Hebrew and English Lexicon*, [Oxford at the Clarendon Press, 1968], 1. This changed the reading to "Arami avad avi," which means "The Aramean (Syrian) [intended] my father be exterminated." It was upon this second understanding of Deuteronomy 26:5 that the Midrash was based at the Passover supper.

11. Silverman, *Passover Haggadah*, 20.

12. L. Finkelstein, "The Oldest Midrash: Pre-Rabbinic Ideals and Teachings in the Passover Haggadah," *Harvard Theological Review* 31 (1938): 291ff; "Pre-Maccabean Documents in the Passover Haggadah," *Harvard Theological Review* 35 (1942): 291ff; 36 (1943): 1ff.

13. Silverman, *Passover Haggadah*, 25.

14. I have given in to the usual translation of "nefesh" as "soul." A better translation might be "living soul." "Nefesh" is another of those all-encompassing words meaning, "*soul*, life, spirit, *mind*, *breath*, respiration, *person*, *(living) creature*, self, *body*," (from Alcalay, *The Complete Hebrew-English Dictionary*, col. 1669.) "Soul" is incomplete compared to "nefesh," which encompasses the whole, living, breathing person or being.

15. "Unless this association of the Passover Lamb was made by Jesus, it is difficult to explain the promptitude with which the early Christians identified Jesus as the Christian Paschal Lamb. 1 Cor 5:7-8 presents us with the unleavened bread of pure self-offering because the Passover feast, the eschatalogical feast, has already begun, and Jesus as The Lamb has already been sacrificed" (Mann, "Mark," *The Anchor Bible* 27:575).

16. It is unfortunate that so much is lost in translation here. Those verses covering the Eucharist should have pages of notes attached to them. No wonder there is so much dispute over them. I remember how, in my Protestant youth, I loved to argue with my Catholic friends about whether Jesus was really present in the Eucharist. At that time, I was taught to vehemently deny it. I was so impressed by the strong Catholic conviction of the Real Presence that in my first year of college I felt compelled to study the source of that conviction. By nineteen I was myself a Catholic and by twenty a Franciscan brother. I had been exposed to some of those notes that had not been in my King James and that are not, for that matter, in other translations either.

17. "We have evidence in later Jewish documents of a popular expectation that in the final day God would again provide manna—an expectation connected with the hopes of a second Exodus. The second-century A.D. apocryphon II Bar xxix 8 says: 'The treasury of Manna shall again descend from on high, and they will eat of it in those years.' The Midrash Mekilta on Exod xvi 25 says: 'You will not find it [manna] in this age, but you shall find it in the age that is coming.' The Midrash Rabbah on Eccles i 9 says: 'As the first redeemer caused manna to descend, as it is stated, "Because I shall cause to rain bread from heaven for you" (Exod xvi 4), so will the latter redeemer cause manna to descend'" (Brown, "John (1-12)," The Anchor Bible 29:265).

18. Mt 14:22-32; Mk 6:45-52; Jn 6:16-21. Luke modifies the miracle, which the Gentiles would not understand, by having Jesus calm a storm (Lk 8:22-25).

19. Kittel, Theological Dictionary of the New Testament 2:755ff.

20. Brown, "John (1-12)," The Anchor Bible 29:272.

21. Kittel, Theological Dictionary 9:407ff., esp. 411-415.

22. Brown, "John (1-12)," The Anchor Bible 29:290. See also Daube, Ziener, Gartner, Kilmartin and the association of the Jewish Passover Haggadah and a Christian Haggadah.

23. Jeremias, The Eucharistic Words of Jesus, 108a ff.

24. John 14:27; 15:14-15.

25. Mann, "Mark," The Anchor Bible 27:572.

26. Silverman, Passover Haggadah, 6.

27. Glatzer, The Passover Haggadah, 7-9.

28. Ibid., 54-55.

29. Ibid., 56-57.

30. "All of this is impressive unanimity, not the least in that both the stylized liturgical formulations of Paul and the narrative forms of the synoptists carry us back to a tradition belonging to the earliest days of the community. The tradition then, as it has come to us in our sources, belongs to the time of Jesus himself" (Mann, "Mark," The Anchor Bible 27:573).

31. Jeremias, Eucharistic Words of Jesus, 164ff.

32. Jeremias, "The Developement of a Christian Liturgical Language," Eucharistic Words of Jesus, 111ff.

33. Alcalay, The Complete Hebrew-English Dictionary, 300.

34. Jeremias, "The Semitic Equivalent of Soma (Body)," Eucharistic Words of Jesus, 198-201.

35. Ibid., 220-225.

36. Raphael, *A Feast of History,* 81.

37. Brown, "John (1-12)," *The Anchor Bible* 29:533-538.

38. Kittel, *Theological Dictionary,* 3:804-809, n. 805.

39. Fitzmyer, "Luke (10-24)," *The Anchor Bible* 28a:1392.

40. Jeremias, *Eucharistic Words of Jesus,* 125.

41. Orr and Walther, "1 Corinthians," comment on "divisions existing at the Supper," *The Anchor Bible* 32:269,274.

42. Mann, "Mark," *The Anchor Bible,* 575, 576.

43. Jeremias, *The Eucharistic Words of Jesus,* 106.

44. Eusebius, *The History of the Church,* 230-231.

45. The Hebrew Bible is called the Tanakh after the first three letters ("T," "N," "Kh") of its principle parts: Torah (the Five Books of Moses), Navi'im (The Prophets), and Ketuvim (The Writings). Christians mistakenly refer to the Hebrew Bible as The Old Testament, basing that title on a translation of "diatheke" as "testament" instead of a more accurate "covenant."

46. Brown, "John (1-13)," *The Anchor Bible* 29:278-279.

47. Ibid., 279.

48. Glatzer, *The Passover Haggadah,* 57.

49. This passage demonstrates that not only is the seder the memorial/zikkaron/anamnesis of past events but of future events also, especially the coming Age of the Messiah.

50. "The grace at the seder is not different from that which follows all meals, except that on this occasion the diners are enjoined to drink the cup of wine otherwise optional. The main part of the grace contains four benedictions, the first three very ancient known long before the destruction of the Temple, the fourth a supplement by the sages of Jabneh after the Bar Kokhba rebellion (Berakhot 48b). The first benediction expresses thanks for the food, and the second thanks for the land of Israel; the third is a petition for the restoration to Him 'who is good and does good.' Over the centuries there have been numerous additions" (Glatzer, *The Passover Haggadah,* 58-59).

51. "The Haggadah opens with the words: 'Let all who are hungry come and eat.' Among the awaited guests is the prophet Elijah who, according to tradition, never died, but was carried up to heaven. The life of no other character in Jewish history is so surrounded with a halo of mystery and wonder as is that of Elijah. In Jewish legend, the ubiquitous Elijah is the champion of the oppressed; he brings hope, cheer, and relief to the downtrodden; and he performs miracles of rescue and deliverance. It is Elijah who can explain all difficult passages in the Bible and Talmud, and will settle all future controversies. The

prophet Malachi says of him, 'He will turn the hearts of parents to their children, and the hearts of children to their parents.' Elijah is the harbinger of good tidings of joy and peace. His name is especially associated with the coming of the Messiah, whose advent he is expected to announce" (Silverman, *Passover Haggadah*, 43).

52. Glatzer, 75; Silverman, 52-53; Raphael, 71.

53. Scholars have reconstructed Jesus' words over the Cup as *kasa den (hu) geyama chadatet'a bidmi* ("This Cup [is] the new covenant of my blood"). However, I believe that Jesus would have used the Hebrew word for "covenant" instead of the Aramaic. In Hebrew Aramaic, important words such as "Torah" or "Pesach" remained in Hebrew just as in Yiddish and English many words, such as "kosher" and "mazel tov," remain in Hebrew. Thus, Jesus' actual words would have been *kasa den b'rit chadatet'a bidmi*.

54. The "kingdom of God" and "kingdom of heaven" are one and the same. Some scholars make a distinction between the two, but they do not seem to understand Jewish sensibilities. Religious Jews go to great lengths to protect the Holy Name. "YHWH" is never to be pronounced, except by the high priest who pronounced it three times on the Day of Atonement, at which everyone in his hearing was to prostrate themselves in awe. Whenever the tetragrammaton, "YWHW," appears written in the Bible or other religious writings, what is said is "adonai" or "the Lord." Many very devout Jews find even "adonai" to be risky and say instead "ha-shem" ("the name") and sometimes a combination of the two, such as "ado-shem." Even the English word "God" troubles some and is often written or printed as "G_d" and pronounced as "Lord," "adonai," or "ha-shem." In the same manner, the Gospels sometimes substituted "kingdom of heaven" for "kingdom of God," which sounded disrespectful to pious ears.

55. "Beginning with the day after the sabbath, the day on which you bring the wave-offering sheaf, you shall count seven full weeks, and then on the day after the seventh week, the fiftieth day (*pentecoste*), you shall present the new cereal offering to the LORD" (Lv 23:15-16 NAB). Beginning on the first day of the week after the Sabbath of Passover, the priests offered a wave- offering sheaf before the Lord every day for seven full weeks and then, on the fiftieth day, the feast of Pentecost was celebrated. In Hebrew, the feast is called "Shavuot" or "the Feast of Weeks." At the time of Christ, Jews celebrated two Pentecosts. In the Temple in Jerusalem, Pentecost was known as the "chag ha-bikurim" or the "Feast of the First Fruits (of

the wheat harvest)" as well as "chag ha-shavuot" or the "Feast of the Weeks." Unique to the Temple feast was the offering of two leavened loaves of bread on the altar, which was the only time leavened bread was used in Temple worship (Lv 23:17). Throughout the rest of the world, as well as in the synagogues of Jerusalem, rabbis led their congregations in the celebration of another Pentecost known as "z'man matan toratenu" or "The Time We Received our Torah." This celebration was a memorial of the time when, three months after the Exodus, the people stood before the Lord at Mount Sinai and received the Covenant from God. Frequently, these two separate Pentecosts did not fall on the same day. The Temple priests counted their fifty days, called the "omer," from the first day after the Sabbath (Saturday) of Passover. But the rabbis considered the first day of Passover a "Sabbath" as well and began their fifty-day count from the day after the first day of Passover.

56. There is some confusion here among translators on the intent and meaning of the Hebrew. In Hebrew, there are three words for "word." "Dabar" means "spoken word, commanding word, accomplishing word, something." "The Word of God" is always "dabar YHWH" or *dabar elohim.* *Milah* also means "word" and is much the same as our English word. One looks up "milah" in a *milon* (dictionary). A third word is *katav,* which means "written word" or "inscription." Katav is what is written down, such as the third section of the Hebrew scriptures, which is called the *ketuvim.* In this passage of Exodus, both "dabar" and "katav" are used and each have their distinct meaning which some translators ignore. In Hebrew, the Ten Commandments are sometimes called *aseret ha-dibrot,* "the ten words."

57. For a fuller explanation of the Jewish concept of covenant, see *The Jerome Biblical Commentary,* 3:44-68, 77:74-98.

58. The Hebrew idiom *karat b'rit* means "to make a covenant" or "to cut a covenant." In the time of Abraham, two parties signified a covenant between them by splitting in half a sacrificed animal and walking between the halves. The parties pledged, symbolically, that if they broke the covenant, their fate would be to be split asunder just like the sacrifices.

59. Immediately following is a reaffirmation of the Ten Commandments (Dt 5:6-21). For other references to the Covenant renewal ceremony, see Jos 8:30-35 and Jos 24:16-28.

60. Brown et al., *The Jerome Biblical Commentary,* 3:44; G.E. Mendenhall, *Law and Covenant in Israel and the Ancient Near East,* (Pittsburgh, 1955). "Here we shall merely indicate the essential

characteristics of the suzerainty treaty relevant to the text of Exodus: The Preamble, which identifies the great king (Ex 20:2), the Historical Prologue (I-Thou address) (Ex 20:2), which summarizes the benefits bestowed upon the vassal in the past by the great kind, The Stipulations (in particular, the prohibition of any treaties with other nations) (Ex 20:3-17 and Dt 5:6-21), The Public Reading (Ex 24:4-7), The List of Gods as Witnesses (Ex 24:4; Jos 8:30-35), and the Formula of Curses and Blessings" (Ex 23:20-33; Dt 11:26-32; 27:14-26; 28:1-48; Jos 8:30-35; Brown et al., *Jerome Biblical Commentary,* 3:44). To these characteristics of the suzerainty treaty that they shared with other nations, such as the Hittites, the Israelites added the covenant banquet that established the fraternal partnership of all parties (Ex 24:5, 9-11) and the sealing with blood that made them all blood brothers (Ex 24:8).

61. For the Christian, there are eleven commandments and the eleventh is the supreme commandment (Jn 13:34,35).

62. "Just as the Passover celebration commemorated the deliverance of Israel from Egyptian bondage (Ex 12:14), so the Eucharist commemorates the deliverance brought about by Christ. The Eucharist is the proclamation (kataggellete) of the Lord's redemptive death that the church makes until his coming, when there will no longer be need of his sacramental presence" (Brown et al., *Jerome Biblical Commentary,* 51:71).

63. "Some light has been shed, not clearly enough on the interesting term 'matzebah,' 'pillar,' by archeological discoveries. It has an apparent primary reference to cultic objects....Many matzebot have been found in Palestinian excavations. While the famous ones at Hazor (BA 19,22) and at Byblos are clearly monumental and cultic, other standing stones were for a time wrongly identified....In Ex 24:4 Moses, besides the altar he built, erected twelve stones (pillars) representing the Twelve Tribes of Israel....In Ex 24:24 the expansion upon the Decalogue—near the conclusion of the so-called Book of the Covenant—*calls for action; Israel must not bow down to other gods, but break down their images.* (ASV and RSV, "pillars," with a margin "obelisks in the former)" (Harris, R. Laird, editor; Archer, Gleason L., Jr., and Walkte, Bruce K., associate editors, *Theological Wordbook of the Old Testament* 1 (Moody Press, 1980): 592 [italics mine]).

64. Brown, "John (13-21)," *The Anchor Bible* 29a, app. 5, 1136-1137. Analysis of the title *parakletos:*    (a) Parakletos as a passive form from par/kalein in its elementary sense ("to call alongside"), meaning "one called alongside to help," thus an advocate (OL, *ad-*

*vocatus*) or defense attorney. Some point to the role of the Holy Spirit as a defender of the disciples when they are put on trial (Mt 10:20; Acts 6:10).    (b) Parakletos in an active sense, reflecting parakalein in its meaning "to intercede, entreat, appeal to," thus an intercessor, a mediator, a spokesman. This is clearly the meaning in 1 John 2:1....Related to this interpretation is the suggested meaning of Parakletos as "helper, friend."    (c) Parakletos in an active sense reflecting paraklein in the meaning "to comfort," thus a comforter or consoler....The element of consolation is confined to the context, for example 16:6-7, which prefaces a Paraclete passage.    (d) Parakletos as related to paraklesis, the noun used to describe the exhortation and encouragement found in the preaching of the apostolic witnesses (1 Th 3:2; Rm 12:8; Hb 13:22; Acts 13:15).

# SEVEN

# *The School of Jesus*

Jesus never wrote a single word of his teaching on a scroll or in a book. Nor is there any record of his commissioning any of his disciples to write down his teaching. It was years after his death that the converted Paul began to write letters of correction and exhortation to the churches he founded. But the Epistles did not presume to contain the whole of Christ's teaching; they presume, in fact, that the teaching has already been received. It was approximately thirty years after the crucifixion that the twofold crisis of Peter's death and the Jewish War urged and inspired the evangelists to put the teachings of Jesus in writing. According to Papias, Mark, a companion of Peter, wrote his Gospel based upon what he had learned form the Apostle. Matthew compiled a Mishnah (written collection of oral teachings) in Aramaic, which Papias called the Sayings (Eusebius; *The History of the Church* 152). To the modern mind, this seems extraordinary, but it was the normal way of teaching in the first-century Jewish world. The great rabbis had their disciples memorize all their teachings and sayings.

The Bible was hand lettered on parchment scrolls, which severely limited the available copies. Only the wealthy could afford their own copy. Yet the law required that every Jewish male be able to read the Bible and to quote extensively from the Torah. Every Jewish boy learned to read Hebrew in synagogue school and, by the age of thirteen, demonstrated his skills before the congregation, thereby making his bar mitzvah.[1] But the sacred scrolls from which he read were kept in the Ark of the Torah. The scrolls of the Prophets and of the Writings were kept in the synagogue library. Therefore, the boys had to memorize the scrolls. In the Hebrew schools, the rabbi quoted the verses and the students repeated them, over and over again, until they learned them by heart.

The oral law and oral tradition, obviously, were passed on strictly by word of mouth (until it was written down and became the Talmud). The students of the various rabbis learned their masters' teaching entirely by rote. Before the destruction of the Temple, it was not lawful for any part of the oral law to be written down. All of it had to be committed to memory. "Rabbi so and so says," and "the school of rabbi so and so said," was the formula used in teaching the oral traditions. This is one reason why Jesus made other rabbis so angry. His formula was different: "You have heard it said, but I say to you..." This was a break in tradition and suggested that he was setting himself above the oral traditions.

Within that context, Jesus set up his own school—the Beyt Y'shu'a (House of Jesus). He picked twelve of his disciples to be his constant companions (Mk 3:14). These were the students who would commit to memory his every word. Those who were most adept at memorizing were called tana (memorizers).[2] Evidently, Peter, James, and John were the primary tana'im[3] of Jesus' school. Their responsibility was to insure that the others learned everything correctly and forgot nothing. As his popularity grew, Jesus added another seventy-two to his school (Lk 10:1). These also learned from him and then preached his word throughout the countryside. By the time of the Last Supper, the Beyt Y'shu'a had grown to 120 men (Acts 1:15). In typical rabbinical fashion, these disciples were organized into twelve groups of ten each. A group of ten men, known as a minyan, was the necessary quorum to make up a synagogue. Therefore, each of the Apostles was responsible for his own minyan, which he was to teach as he was taught by Jesus. He gave Simon, whom he renamed Peter (the Rock), the responsibility of heading the whole school. Peter was the chief tana to whom was entrusted the whole oral teaching of Jesus. The Twelve Apostles became the teaching elders of Jesus' school (Mt 16:18-19).

The memorization of Jesus' instructions and parables was not a wholly passive system of learning. The tradition of a yeshiva, a school headed by a rabbi, is to pair off all the students. One from each pair is to take the "pro" of every discussion, and the other is to take the "con." By quoting Scripture and the sayings of the rabbis, especially their own master, they were to debate until a synthesis was arrived upon. If their conclusion was accepted by their rabbi, they would receive his approval. If not, the rabbi would challenge the pair with more quotes and sayings and they would continue their debate until they came to the conclusion that their master had intended or found acceptable. Constant repetition, constant challenges and argument, constant discussion and debate was a marvelous method of learning. The words of Jesus were burned into the disciples' minds. When scriptural scholars refer to the oral tradition of the church that preceded the writing of the Gospels, they are not referring to weak hearsay evidence or popularized storytelling. They are referring to a highly structured, refined, and formalized technique that passed on information with extraordinary accuracy. The teachings of Jesus were well preserved in the tradition of the tana'im.

If the Jewish nation of the first century had survived, the Beyt Y'shu'a would have survived with it and the body of teaching left to us by Jesus would have remained primarily oral. What little that might have been written down would have been commentary to clarify points of that oral teaching — much as the letters of St. Paul were commentary on the oral traditions of Jesus. But the Jewish nation of the first century did not survive. In the year 66 C.E., the Jewish people broke into open revolt against Rome. Emperor Nero sent Vespasian and his son, Titus, to suppress the Jews. About the same time, Nero began the persecution of the Christians in Rome. Peter, a Jew, was crucified, but Paul, a Roman citizen, was beheaded. Both Jews and Christians reacted to the destruction of the Jewish nation in the same way. They gathered together their surviving tana'im and set down in writing all they had memorized. For the Jews, that was the Mishnah, the oldest part of the Talmud. For the Christians, that was Mark's Gospel and Matthew's original document, the so-called Sayings of Jesus. Then followed the other Gospels. The Sayings of Jesus are recorded and preserved in the Gospels of Matthew, Mark, and Luke. The school of John, one of the first three of Jesus' tana'im, records even more in the fourth Gospel. But the Gospels, like the Mishnah, were the result of an overwhelming crisis: the destruction of the Jewish nation and the culture that had nurtured the tradition of the tana'im.

As Gentiles, we might ask why the Jews and Jewish Christians would have preferred oral to written traditions. The answer is that Jews considered written teaching — with the exception of the Torah — to be impersonal and dead. Oral teaching, on the other hand, was vibrant and alive. A recital of a tana was like hearing a recording of their master's voice.

# Ha-Chavurah Ha-Chesed

The Beyt Y'shu'a was also a chavurah, a Passover society organized into a table fellowship. Originally, the chavurot may have been organized simply to insure that individuals had a place reserved for them in the crowded observance of the Passover sacrifice and seder in Jerusalem. As it evolved, the Passover chavurah became a year-round fellowship in which each member was committed to the well-being of all members. They preferred to conduct all their business within the chavurah. They knew that every member of their fellowship was a faithful observer of the mosaic law. They met frequently to celebrate the Sabbaths and holy days. When they traveled together to Jerusalem for Passover, they traveled as an extended family and thought of each other as brothers and sisters.

By the time of the Last Supper, the Beyt Y'shu'a was a well-established chavurah; all of the 120 men, with their wives and children, were one family. At the Last Supper, Jesus elevated his chavurah to a covenant fellowship. At Pentecost, that Passover chavurah and covenant fellowship began to think of itself as a family bound together by the flesh and blood of Jesus. They were children of the same Father. As the body of Christ, they were more intimately united to each other than to their own flesh and blood. Their chavurah had become the family of God.

The first Christians[4] naturally organized themselves into extended family units. What seem to be radical communes in the Book of Acts are actually Jewish extended families. When there was a household complex large enough to hold them all, they moved in together. When this was not possible, they lived as close together as they could so that they could share table fellowship frequently. As an extended family unit, they shared all their possessions, incomes, and products of their labors (Acts 2:42- 47).

They probably continued to call their groups a chavurah, but they had to express their new relationship as well. The new Covenant of agape love was expressed with the Hebrew word for covenant love: chesed. The Christian chavurah became the chavurah ha-chesed. Paul expresses the chavurah ha-chesed in Greek as the koinonia, "the sharing table fellowship of the Lord's supper and the Lord's ministry."[5] "The cup of blessing which we bless, is it not a fellowship-sharing (koinonia) of the blood of Christ? The bread which we break, is it not a fellow-ship-sharing [koinonia] of the body of Christ?" (1 Cor 10:16, translation mine).

The chavurah ha-chesed prayed together. "Every day they devoted themselves to meeting together in the temple area and to *breaking bread* [ha-motzi] *in theirhomes"* (Acts 2:46 NAB). That simple verse says volumes when placed in its proper context of first-century Judaism and Jewish Christianity. Every day, they shared in the morning and evening sacrifices in the Temple. There was also a large synagogue in the Royal Stoa where they could attend the Sabbath and daily services. Christians continued to attend the synagogue until the end of the first century, when they were formally evicted. Since Christians were indistinguishable from Jews at that time, the eviction was accomplished by the addition of three blessings that were an affront to Christian belief to the traditional eighteen benedictions of the synagogue service. But that proved to be a minor annoyance. The Jewish Christians had their own rabbis and they could assemble their own synagogues. Jesus had organized them into study groups of ten and twelve members each, and those were legal synagogues.

## The Sabbath Observance

That they "broke bread" together suggests that the Jewish Christians spent their Sabbaths and their Lord's Suppers together. The sabbath meal is and always has been a family institution. Whether the sabbath meal was a simple meal of the poor or an elaborate supper of the affluent, it was a joyous celebration of God's love for his people and his creation. All the family members looked forward to breaking bread together in their fathers' houses. For the Christian community, there was the added dimension of gathering together in their Father's house.

Just before sunset on Friday, the women lit the sabbath lamps. These lamps were designed with an added reserve of oil attached to the back so they would stay lit from sunset Friday until well past sunset Saturday.[6] Nobody worked on the Sabbath; the lamps even had to be lit before sunset. Food had to be cooked on Friday. Most of the food could be eaten cold, but hot casseroles were kept in ovens where the heat was banked to last until the casserole was removed. One such casserole, cholent, is still popular among both Sephardic and Ashkenazic Jews, which shows its great antiquity. Cholents of rice, beans, meat, chicken, hard-cooked eggs, vegetables, and spices steeped in a pot were common fare in the first century.

The traditional blessing of the sabbath lights is,

> Blessed are You, O LORD (YHWH) our God,
> King of all creation
> Who has sanctified us with your commandments
> And commanded us to light the sabbath lights.

The father of the family began the sabbath meal with a reading from Genesis:

> Evening came, and morning followed — the sixth day.
> Thus the heavens and earth and all their array were completed.
> Since on the seventh day God was finished with the work he had been doing, he rested on the seventh day from all the work he had undertaken. So God blessed the seventh day and made it holy, be-

casue on it he rested from all the work he had done in creation
(Gn 1:31; 2:1-3 NAB).

Then the paterfamilias lifted up the large kiddush cup and
blessed it.

> Blessed are You, O LORD (YHWH) our God
> King of all creation,
> Creator of the fruit of the vine.

Everyone responded with "Amen" and then shared from the
kiddush cup.
The paterfamilias continued, either reciting or singing,

> Blessed are You, O LORD (YHWH) our God,
> King of all creation,
> Who has sanctified us with your commandments
> And who is pleased with us.
> Out of love and favor, He has given to us
> His Holy Sabbaths as our inheritance
>     A memorial of creation,
> The day is foremost of the holy convocations
>     recalling the Exodus from Egypt.
> You have chosen us and sanctified us
> from out of all nations.
> You sanctified the Sabbath
> and out of love and favor
> You have given it to us
> as our inheritance.
> Blessed are You, O LORD (YHWH)
> Who sanctifies the Sabbath.

For the sabbath meal, two loaves of bread were blessed and
shared. They symbolized the extra portion of manna that the
Israelites gathered on Friday mornings in order to have enough
for Friday and the Sabbath (Ex 16:21-26). The sabbath loaves,
now called *challah*, were made with flour, eggs, sugar (or
honey), a leavening agent (now yeast), and salt; but instead of

milk and butter, water and vegetable oil were used as the liquid and shortening so that the challah could be eaten at a meat meal. Nowadays, the challah is braided into dark golden loaves. Archeological evidence suggests that the sabbath challah of the first century was made into round loaves with deep crosses cut into the top. The Christian mother cut I and X into the loaves, which represented Iesous Xristos (Jesus Christ). The Jewish mother cut the simple X, which represented the ancient form of the last letter of the Hebrew alphabet, "taw," which means "good" and "the sign of the LORD (YHWH)."

While the wine was blessed and shared and the Kiddush recited, the two sabbath loaves were covered with a special embroidered cloth. After the kiddush, the father of the family uncovered the challah and recited,

> Blessed are You, O LORD (YHWH) our God
> King of all creation
> Who brings forth bread from the earth.

He tore apart one loaf, or cut it into portions, and shared the sabbath bread with everyone at table. The sharing of the kiddush cup and sabbath loaf represented the unity of the whole family. This unity was reaffirmed at the conclusion of the sabbath meal when everyone recited the long grace and received the Kos shel B'rakhah or Cup of Blessing.

The Christian Sabbath and Jewish Sabbath remained substantially identical throughout the first and well into the second century. In fact, the idea of a Christian as opposed to a Jewish Sabbath would not have made any sense at the time. There was God's commandment to celebrate the Sabbath, period (Ex 20:8-11).[7] If you loved and served God, you observed his Sabbath.

## The Havdalah—Agape

On the other hand, the Havdalah, the ritual supper that concludes the Sabbath — for which there is no commandment — became something uniquely Christian. For Jews, the Havdalah was and is simply the closing of the Sabbath. For the Christians, it was the beginning of the first day of the week, "which they eventually called the Lord's Day. It became the primary supper of the Christian community.

In the first century, a sabbath meal centered on God the Father and was already a centuries-old tradition. The Havdalah, on the other hand, was still in the formative stages, according to evidence in the Talmud. It was a simple matter for the Christian community to take it over, make it their own, and make it Christ-centered.

The community that gathered on Friday evening as the people of God gathered again on Saturday evening as the body of Christ. If they did not all live under the same roof, they gathered at the home of their bishop.

The first Christian communities continued to organize themselves along the same lines as Jesus had organized his original school. He had been the Good Shepherd and guardian of his flock (1 Pt 5:24). He had been assisted by the Twelve elders. It was only natural that the Apostles organized every Christian community under the care of a pastor (shepherd) who was also the bishop (*episkopos,* which means "guardian, overseer, protector, patron) (Kittel, *Theological Dictionary of the New Testament* 2 608-620). The bishop, in turn, was assisted by a number of elders or presbyters, who may have been the fathers of the individual families. But Jesus had transformed his school into a real family, the family of God. Through baptism, each individual became a child of God, and through the Eucharist everyone shared the same flesh and blood and became a single family of brothers and sisters. Therefore, each bishop was the

actual paterfamilia of the community over which he had juris-
diction.

The Havdalah was the highlight of everyone's week as they
gathered in the home of their paterfamilia, the pastor, and
bishop, who was the head of their household. They called the
Havdalah the "agape" or "love feast" because they were all
sharing in Christ's love.

With the sabbath lamps still burning, the bishop began the
Havdalah-Agape by reciting the opening verses of the Torah,

> In the beginning, when God created the heavens and the earth,
> the earth was a formless wasteland, and darkness covered the
> abyss, [and the spirit of God hovered over the waters].
>     Then God said, "Let there be light," and there was light. God
> saw how good the light was. God then separated the light from
> the darkness. God called the light "day," and the darkness he
> called "night." Thus evening came, and morning followed — the
> first day (Gn 1:1-5 NAB, bracket insert is my translation of
> *W'Ruach Elohim m'rachefet 'al p'ney ha-mayim*).

The opening lines of John's Gospel show how much impact
this reading had on the Christian community. In the original
Hebrew, the word used here for "God" is "Elohim." Because
this word is in the masculine inclusive plural, the Christians
could see the action of the Holy Trinity in creation. God spoke
his Word, and his Word, the Son, went forth, accomplishing the
Father's will. "Then God said, 'Let there be light,' and there
was light" (Gn 1:3 NAB). "All things came to be through him,
and without him nothing came to be" (Jn 1:3 NAB). The Holy
Spirit was also present. She (in Hebrew, the Spirit is feminine)
is bringing to birth the will of the Father in union with the Son.
In the second verse, the verb used to describe the action of the
Holy Spirit in creation is *m'rachefet (et* is the feminine ending),
which is the same verb used in Deuteronomy 32:11 (*rachef*:
hovering) to describe the action of eagles in relation to their
young. The Father creates through the Son, and the Holy Spirit

nurtures that creation into life as a mother eagle guards and nurtures her young.[8]

The bishop began the recital of the blessing over the wine for the Havdalah, which the church had inherited from Judaism and was more elaborate than that for the Sabbath. First the kiddush cup was filled to overflowing to symbolize the overflowing blessings of God.[9]

> Blessed are You, O LORD (YHWH) our God,
> King of all creation
> Creator of the fruit of the vine.

The bishop shared the kiddush cup with everyone, and the cup returned to him so that he could fill it again for the Cup of Blessing or Eucharistic Cup (1 Cor 10:16).

Then he blessed a small container filled with fragrant spices, such as cinnamon and cloves, and passed the container to everyone so that they could smell "how sweet is the Lord."[10]

> Blessed are You, O LORD (YHWH), our God
> King of all creation,
> Creator of various species of spices.

A special lamp was now lit. It became the Light of Christ that would be featured in future Pascha (Easter) celebrations. The special lamp that was used for the celebration of the Havdalah had several wicks because the phrase in the blessing, *m'orey. ha-esh* (Lights of Fire), is plural. For Christians, it was natural to use three wicks. Whoever gave the blessing folded their fingers back into their palms and then cupped their hands around the flames so that the light shone off their fingernails while their fingers cast a shadow onto the palms of their hands. This made the distinction ("havdalah" means "distinction") between "light and darkness."[11]

Blessed are You, O LORD (YHWH), our God,
King of all creation,
Creator of the lights of fire.

A few centuries later, when candles replaced oil lamps, the
three-wicked havdalah-agape lamp was replaced by a very
large candle that became the modern paschal (Easter) candle.
In Judaism a twisted candle of several wicks, usually four,
replaced the havdalah lamp.
The recital concluded with,

Blessed are You, O LORD (YHWH), our God,
King of all creation,
Who makes the distinction
between the holy and the secular
between light and darkness
between Israel and the Nations
between the seventh day
and the six work days.
Blessed are You, O LORD (YHWH)
Who distinguishes between
the sacred and the profane.

It is easy to see how the Havdalah-Agape could inspire the
first Christian communities. We have only to compare this Kiddush with the opening lines of John's Gospel, which, I believe,
were inspired by it.

In the beginning was the Word,
the Word was with God,
and the Word was God.
He was in the beginning with God.
All things came to be through him,
and without him nothing came to be.
What came to be through him was life,
and this life was the light of the human race;
the light shines in the darkness,
and the darkness has not overcome it.

He was in the world,
   and the world came to be through him,
   but the world did not know him.
He came to what was his own,
   but his own people did not accept him.

And the Word became flesh
   and made his dwelling among us,
   and we saw his glory,
   the glory as of the Father's only Son,
   full of grace and truth.

From his fullness we have all received, grace in place of grace, because while the law was given through Moses, grace and truth came through Jesus Christ. No one has ever seen God. The only Son, God, who is at the Father' side, has revealed him (Jn 1:1-5, 10-11, 14, 16-18 NAB).

At the conclusion of the blessing, the bishop uncovered the bread to be blessed for the supper. Since the Havdalah-Agape was also an anamnesis-zikkaron of the Last Supper, I believe that three loaves were blessed. They were a reminder of the three sheets of the watched matzot that Jesus blessed at the Last Supper and of the three persons in the Holy Trinity. Two of these loaves were broken and shared as the hamotzi of the agape-supper. The third loaf was set aside with the Cup of Blessings for the Eucharist at the conclusion of their supper.

The Havdalah-Agape was not only a time for sharing food and fellowship. It was also a time for learning. Jesus' sayings were repeated and commented upon. His parables were retold and incidents from his life recounted. In later years, the letters of Paul and the other Apostles were read. In the beginning, each fellowship had its own tana, who had been trained by one of the Apostles, by the community in Jerusalem, or by a representative of one of these. It was his responsibility to insure that everything retold and recounted was exactly correct. He himself was called upon for much of the recitation. Important, also, were the annual letters from the bishop of Jerusalem computing the exact date for the Passover observance each year.

At the conclusion of their supper, as the tables were cleared and prepared for the Eucharist, everyone joined in singing. Isaiah 12 was popular, but the most common songs were the Psalms of the Hallel, especially Psalms 116 and 118. The phrases, "The cup of salvation I will take up" and "My vows to the Lord I will pay in the presence of all his people," had special importance to them, as did the closing verses of Psalm 118.

Originally, the grace after the meal, the Eucharist, began with the traditional,

> My Friends, let us say the blessing for our food,
>
> May the name of the Lord be blessed
> from this time forth and forever.
>
> With your permission,
> Let us bless our God,
>     of whose bounty we have eaten.
>
> Blessed be God,
>     of whose bounty we have eaten,
>     and through whose goodness we live.
>
> Blessed is He and blessed is his name!

Within the lengthy eucharistic prayers, the body of Christ shared the body and blood of Jesus. The one was nourished and animated by the other.

## The Seder of the Exodus and the Pascha of Christ

When the new moon of spring was sighted by the priests from the pinnacle of the Temple, they blew the silver trumpets to announce the beginning of Nisan, the month of Passover. The bishop of the Jerusalem community sent letters to all of the Christian communities throughout the world, notifying them of the exact date on which to celebrate the seder that year. Pesach became both the seder of the Exodus and a celebration of the great Passover of Christ. Passover was the most important celebration of the whole Judeo-Christian calendar. The Aramaic word for Passover, "pascha," passed easily into Greek and became the Greek word for the weeklong feast.[12]

> Clear out the old yeast [chametz], so that you may become a fresh batch of dough, inasmuch as you are unleavened. For our paschal lamb, Christ, has been sacrificed. Therefore let us celebrate the feast, not with the old yeast, the yeast of malice and wickedness, but with the unleavened bread [matzah] of sincerity and truth (1 Cor 5:7-8 NAB).

As long as the Jerusalem community was the official church, the Christian observance of Passover was identical with the Jewish. The ceremony was exactly the same, but for the Christian, Christ became the central focus of the ritual. The seder became a reliving of the Last Supper, death, burial, and resurrection of Jesus. Every movement and comment Jesus made on the evening of the Last Supper was reenacted and repeated. Every event of that momentous week was reenacted, symbolically, during the supper. The paschal lamb was Christ. The matzot was Christ. The chavurah was Christ. The maggid was centered on Christ. And the wine was the covenant blood of Christ. Every action of the seder revealed the presence of Christ and recalled all of the activities of that eventful week from Palm Sunday until the resurrection. This reactualization of the Last Supper in each succeeding Passover seder influenced the observance of the weekly Eucharist so much that the weekly Eucharist of the Havdalah-Agape became a miniature seder.

But Jesus had warned, "When you see the desolating abomination standing where he should not (let the reader understand), then those in Judea must flee to the mountains" (Mk 13:14 NAB). That is, when the Romans profaned the Temple, the Jews should flee Jerusalem. The Romans did just that in 66 C.E. The emperor Nero allowed pagan sacrifices in public at Caesaria Maritima, the political capital of Judea. The people protested to the procurator, Gessius Florus, who ignored them and then robbed the Temple treasury of 17 talents for his own use. The Jewish people protested, rioted, and were slaughtered (Brown et al., *Jerome Biblical Commentary*, 75:157). That was the last straw.

The whole nation rose in rebellion against Rome. Inspired by the victory of the Maccabees, the Jews were sure of final triumph even though they were vastly outnumbered by the armies of the Empire. But Jesus had warned his disciples that there would be no victory this time, only a horrible defeat such as the world had not seen before or after. Of the Temple, he said: "There will not be one stone left upon another that will not be thrown down" (Mk 13:2 NAB). The Christian historian Eusebius records that the Jerusalem church fled to Pella in Trans Jordan for safety and remained there until after the war. They returned after the war to a Jerusalem in ruins. Its former inhabitants were either dead or carried off into slavery.

When the Christian community returned to Jerusalem, they were met by Jews from surrounding villages who had survived. They set about to restore what they could, but all they could do was establish a small and poor village in the ruins of a once majestic city. Their meager efforts were under the constant observation of a large garrison of pagan Roman soldiers that had created a fortress out of the towers of Herod's ruined palace.

## Jerusalem Destroyed

The Romans began their seige of Jerusalem during the Passover pilgrimage. The city was packed with pilgrims who had come up to observe the feast, as well as with refugees from the defeated north. The seige began in the normal fashion with earth and stoneworks thrown up around the city so that it was entirely cut off from the outside world. Jews who saw the futility of the defense tried to escape. At first, some were successful, but then the Romans began to worry that such a rich and beautiful city must support rich inhabitants who would hide their wealth by swallowing their jewels before leaving. The Roman soldiers began slitting bellies of the escapees to see if that might be a possibility. Then the general decided to use psychological warfare against the city to shock it into surrender. The Romans had stripped the surrounding hills of trees so that they could build their great war machines. On them they planted a new forest of crosses upon which the escapees were crucified in full view of all of the inhabitants.

Seeing hundreds of their people die slowly and in agony only made the defenders more determined. The horror only dried up the hemorrhage of people trying to escape. But those shut up in the city faced a greater horror. The city did not unite. Instead it became a battleground for religious fanatics who thought those who practiced Judaism the "wrong way" were worse enemies than the Romans. Zealots and all of their various subgroups spilled each others' blood in an orgy of religious fratricide and civil war.

A crowded city under siege soon faced starvation. There was plenty of water but not enough food and no possibility of getting more. To make matters worse, the factional fighting prevented an orderly conservation of resources. Bands of Jewish soldiers searched the city for forage. They tortured anyone who did not look sufficiently starved to reveal where they were hiding supplies. They broke into any house with a locked door. No one could cook because the aroma signaled to the marauding bands that there was food in the house. One band of marauders smelled roasting meat and broke into the house only to find a driven and demented woman who had gorged herself on the roasted carcass of her own infant. She defiantly demanded that her tormenters share the feast with her because it was they who had driven her to that madness. That time, the soldiers withdrew.

Mercifully, the Romans at last breached the outer walls. House-to-house fighting began as the defenders withdrew to the inner and older city walls. Small fires started; some of them were put out by the rivulets of blood that spilled down alleys where the slaughter was fiercest. As the inner walls were breached, the defenders took up their positions on the walls and roofs of Temple courts. The Roman general, Titus, had hoped to spare the magnificent Temple. But the defenders had turned the Temple into an enormous fortress, and the Romans would have to destroy it.

Because it was built upon a mount of near-solid rock, it took fierce assaults to overcome it. Breaching the gates in the outer walls of the Court of the Gentiles only spurred the defenders to greater resistance. There was hand-to-hand combat within the Temple courts. Defenders on top of the porticoes pelted the Romans below with missiles. The Court of the Women and the Courts of the Men and of the Priests became the inner sanctuary of the impromptu fortress. As the Romans began to breach the gates of the inner stronghold, the Temple caught fire. The defenders did nothing to stop the spreading fire, but the Romans rushed the sanctuary and stripped it of the Golden Menorah, the Altar of Shew Bread and the Altar of Incense. They salvaged whatever other vessels and instruments they could. Even the sight of the sanctuary in flames did not stun the zealous Jews into surrender. Death, *kadush ha-shem* (sanctifying the Holy Name) was preferable to capture and slavery.

Later, when Titus stood in the ruins of the Temple he had wanted to spare, his anger became uncontrollable. He called for his engineers and ordered them to dismantle the Temple complex. Every stone that stood upon another stone was pushed over the sides of the Temple Mount. All the gold, the silver, and the bronze were melted down for booty. When the engineers finished, nothing remained except the retaining walls that supported the sides of the Temple Mount.

Even after the Temple fell, the battles continued in the lower parts of the city, south of the Temple ruins. In the final orgy of slaughter, a fire broke out and spread across the city. What had not been broken down in battle was now offered up to the consuming flames. Jerusalem had been sacrificed to religious fanaticism and now was consumed in a holocaust.

The Romans rounded up the survivors, who were divided into three groups. Those who could still make a good appearance were sent to Rome for the victory parade. Those who were still strong were shackled together and taken off to slavery. Those who were too weak or sickly to be useful were killed. Those who died were the fortunate ones. Those who lived never again saw the Torah scrolls or heard the rabbis read from them. They never again ate kosher food. They never again observed the Sabbaths and Holy Days, and they never again celebrated the Passover. They were permitted to live, but their lives were that of the living dead, cut off from the people of Israel. They were unclean, never to be washed clean again.

## Out of the Ashes

Slowly and painfully, Jerusalem stirred back to life out of her ashes. Jews who had lost land and property elsewhere took up residence in the Holy City. Within the ruins, a meager village stirred to life.

As soon as it was safe, the Christian community returned from Pella. It had no reason to stay there. Jerusalem was the sight of the Last Supper, the crucifixion, and the empty tomb. They needed to restore these holy places and take care of them. Jerusalem was home; Pella was not.

As they rebuilt, their political position changed. There was no priestly Sanhedrin to persecute them. Their fellow Jews now accepted them as fellow countrymen and allies. They had all suffered and lost equally. The Holy Temple was gone (Acts 2:46). The priesthood was abolished because there were no more sacrifices. Many priests now became Christians. Of all the branches and divisions of Judaism, only the Pharisees and Christians survived. Even though they agreed to disagree over whether the Rabbi Y'shu'a was the Messiah or not, as fraternal survivors of the national calamity, they set about to rebuild together. The Jerusalem church quickly regained its authority, not only because of its location, but also because many of its bishops were relatives of Jesus and members of his family.

The rabbis, meanwhile, set up a school at Yavneh, near modern Tel Aviv, where they gathered the surviving tana'im. Now it was their duty to set down all of the oral law and traditions in writing. During this period of reconstruction, the bishops of Jerusalem and the rabbis of Yavneh cooperated in the reconstruction of Judaism without the Temple. Their differences were no greater than those that had existed previously between the Sadducees and the Pharisees.

Among the many casualties of the war was Passover itself. No longer could there be paschal lambs (the first Passover sacrifice) or the pesach of the priests (the second Passover sacrifice). The small village rebuilt in the ruins could not accommodate the pilgrimages of the past. Life was meager, and there was nothing left over for any guests. From then on, Passover became strictly a family affair celebrated in the home.

Reconstructed, Passover was a sad affair at first. It took some time before new traditions replaced those that had been lost. At that time, Christian and Jewish Passover were still identical. They were survivors of cataclysmic, national calamity, and they worked hard together to restore what they could out of the ashes and debris. But because of the nature of the feast, Christians found it easier to restore a sense of joy sooner to their celebration of the feast.

## The Christian Haggadah for Passover

In the first few years of restoration, Passover was primarily a feast of national identity and unity in the face of the loss. As the seder strengthened the hopes of the people, however, it reasserted itself as the zikkaron of the Exodus and, for the Christians, the anamnesis of the Last Supper. After only a few years, the symbols of sorrow became, instead, symbols of joy.

The Christian Passover seder was celebrated by the whole community in the house of their bishop. The bishop was the father figure of the community, and the whole community was one family, the family of God.

**The Seder Table:** Historians pay little attention to a Passover celebration that occurred during the Second Temple period: the Passover celebrated by those who could not make the pilgrimage to Jerusalem. Such celebration had no paschal lamb because paschal lambs could only be sacrificed in the Temple, but they did include symbolic items placed on the seder tables as reminders of those lambs. Families who had made the pilgrimage to Jerusalem would keep the tray that held the paschal lamb as a memento of their supper. Naturally, they would use this tray at their home Passover for holding a item, usually a lamb bone, that represented the paschal lamb shared in the Holy City.

After the destruction of the Temple, the families in the Diaspora began to put a roasted egg on the tray, next to the lamb bone. The egg represented their mourning for their loss of the Temple. A cooked egg was the traditional symbol of mourning and was presented to the grieving family after a funeral. An egg is unique in that the longer it is cooked the harder it becomes. This represented the strengthening of character in adversity. So the people grieved over the loss of the Temple but hoped to see it rebuilt "speedily in our day!" (Haggadah shel Pesach).

Because the vast majority of Christian families were Jews, they too had their Passover trays. For that matter, many of the gentile families who kept Passover had their own special trays. The majority of gentile converts to Christianity came from the "Fearers of God" associated with the synagogues. As Josephus noted, many Gentiles made the Passover pilgrimage to Jerusalem. They could not offer the Passover sacrifice themselves, but according to the Talmud, they could commission someone to make the sacrifice for them, and if they submitted to the laws of levitical purity and circumcision, they could join in observing Passover (BT Pesachim 89b; Ex 12:48).

From the end of the first century until the mid-second century, the roasted egg stood beside the lamb bone on the Passover trays of Christian families. Until the failure of the Bar Kochba revolt in 132 to 135, Christians and Jews prayed for the rebuilding of the Temple. The last hope died as Emperor Hadrian built his pagan Roman city, Aelia Capitolina, over the ruins of Jerusalem. Then, Christians began to look upon the roasted egg in a new way. Even though they loved the Temple, they no longer felt a theological need for it. Christ's one, perfect sacrifice had replaced all of those of the Temple priesthood (Heb 7:26-28). And the body of Christ was the new Temple where God had established his dwelling place (1 Cor 3:16). The cooked egg became a symbol of Christ's resurrection instead of a symbol of mourning. They reasoned that, just as the living chick cannot be restrained by the stony shell when it hatches, Christ could not be restrained by the stone of his tomb when he rose from the dead. Slowly, but inevitably, brownish roasted eggs of mourning became the brightly colored eggs celebrating the resurrection. In the ancient Greek church, the custom arose of smashing red-colored eggs while shouting, "Christ is risen! He is risen indeed!"

Another custom developed. The condiments that had surrounded the paschal lamb on the tray—lettuce leaves, bitter herb, charoset—were now added to the tray with the lamb bone and the roasted egg.

As time went on, more and more families appeared who had never had a chance to make a Passover pilgrimage and acquire a special tray. They placed smaller versions of those trays on their Passover tables, and these evolved into the seder plates with which we adorn our Passover tables today.

The families of the Diaspora used the unleavened bread to represent the paschal lamb. This was easy to do because the Feast of Unleavened Bread (chag ha-matzot) and the Feast of Passover (chag ha-pesach) had become one and the same. This custom, which may have been frowned upon during the Temple period, was a gold mine for the rabbis who wrestled with the question of how to continue the Passover celebration without the paschal lambs. In the Talmud, they reasoned that the triumvirate of paschal lamb-unleavened bread-bitter herb could be sustained with the remaining two parts. A Hebrew play on words, *yatzah* (to go forth) and matzah (unleavened bread) allowed them to transfer the theme of liberation from the slain lambs to the matzah of Passover. The bitter herb, which had been looked upon as merely the obligatory condiment of the paschal supper, became the primary symbol of the bitterness of slavery, suffering, and oppression.

By the end of the second century, the seder table as we know it today had come into being.

**The Christian Passover Kiddush — Blessing the Wine and the Day:** The mingling of water and wine for the Kiddush of Passover became a symbol of the arrival of the Messianic Age. Jesus' first miracle was at the wedding feast at Cana in Galilee (Jn 2:1-11). There he changed the "living" water[13] (stored in stone jars for use in the numerous rites of purification) into excellent wine — 120 gallons of it! They were familiar with the characterization of the coming days of the Messiah as a wedding and a banquet (Is 54:5-8; 62:4-5), which Jesus drew upon to describe the Kingdom of God as a wedding banquet (Mt 22:1-14; Lk 14:16-24). The prophets had foretold that there would be an abundance of wine "in the later days" (Am 9:13-14; Hos 14:8; Jer 31:12). Special importance must be given to the Jewish apocryphon, 2 Baruch 29:5, which gives a fantastic portrait of the Messianic Age when the earth would give a 10,000-fold yield of its fruit. Each vine would have 1,000 branches; each branch would hold 1,000 bunches of 1,000 grapes. And each grape would produce 120 gallons of wine! (Brown, "John (1-12)," *The Anchor Bible* 29: 105).

The concept of the now-dawning Messianic Age as a wedding banquet was easy for the first generations of Christians to understand and accept. Every community was a chavurah gathered in the table fellowship of the Lord's Supper. Every Eucharist was transformed into a covenant banquet as each one shared the Cup of Blessing, wherein the "blood of the grape" (Gn 49:11; Dt 32:14) had become the Blood of the Covenant (Ex 24:8; 1 Cor 11:25), "and the blood of his son Jesus cleanses us from all sin" (1 Jn 1:7). If the Sinai Covenant could be understood as the marriage of God to his bride, Israel, then the Christians could sing in fraternal fellowship at the covenant banquet of the New Covenant, the Eucharist, "Blessed are those who have been called to the wedding feast of the Lamb" (Rv 19:9 NAB).

In the Johannine account of the marriage banquet at Cana, when the waiter in charge proclaims to the bridegroom, "What you have done is keep the choice wine until now" (Jn 2:10), may be equally understood as a proclamation of the arrival of the Messianic Age (Brown, "John (1-12)" *Anchor Bible* 29:105). Also, from the earliest days, Christians have understood Jesus' unusual address to his mother as "Woman" was intended to identify her as the new Eve (Gn 3:15) and as the symbol of the church as described in Rev 12:1-17 (Brown, "John (1-12)" *Anchor Bible* 29:108). Consequently, her remark, "They have no more wine" (Jn 2:3) has been understood as a reference to the insufficiency of the Jewish rites of purification, which had to be repeated perpetually (Brown, "John (1-12)" *Anchor Bible* 29:105). The reference would be to the fact that stone jars there contained only 120 gallons of water, which would not be enough to fill a mikveh requiring 170 gallons of "living water." That was not enough to cleanse "all his flesh" by covering the whole body (BT Pesachim 109a).

There was no rejection of the Jewish rite of purification, but only a reference to the fact that those who perform those rites must do so again and again. What that should be compared with is Jesus' statement to the Samaritan woman at Jacob's well, "Everyone who drinks this water will be thirsty again. But whoever drinks the water I shall give will never thirst" (Jn 4:13,14 NAB). Link that to his statement on the last day of the Feast of Tabernacles (Sukkot),

> "Let anyone who thirsts come to me and drink. Whoever believes in me, as scripture says: 'Rivers of *living water* will flow from within him.'" He said this in reference to the Spirit that those who came to believe in him were to receive. There was, of course, no Spirit yet, because Jesus had not yet been glorified (Jn 7:37- 39 NAB, emphasis mine).

At the time of his glorification, just before he handed the Spirit over to his church, Jesus once again addresses his mother as "Woman" (Jn 19:26). Jesus' ministry began with the changing of water into messianic wine, and it ended when he sucked the wine-soaked sponge that had been offered him. "When Jesus had taken the wine, he said, 'It is finished.' And bowing his head, *he handed over his spirit"* (Jn 19:30 NAB, emphasis mine). His addressing his mother as "Woman" at Cana and the cross, and the fact that wine is important in the beginning and end of his ministry, combine to suggest that Mary's declaration that they have no wine is a proclamation that the people have not yet received the Holy Spirit.

From these two symbols, the Christians saw the special wine blessed for Passover as a sign that they had accepted the Gospel and were living in the Messianic Age. By adding the water to this wine, they proclaimed the pouring out of the Holy Spirit upon God's people as prophesied in Isaiah 44:1-5.

**Shehecheyyanu—He Who Gives Life To Us:** Along with their Jewish relatives and neighbors, Christians added the Shehecheyyanu to the kiddush of their Passovers. This prayer began as the priestly benediction said over the infant son when his parents brought him to the Temple for the sacrificial offering of the firstborn. After the destruction of the Temple, there was no longer any atonement through blood poured out upon the altar. The rabbis replaced the atoning blood of the paschal sacrifices of the priests with the blood shed in the circumcisions of the firstborn, and for that reason, added the Shehecheyyanu to the Kiddush. Christians accepted the rabbinical reasoning, but to them the prayer represented the blood of the firstborn son of God instead of the blood of all firstborn sons.

The term, "firstborn son of God," had a specific meaning to first-century Jews. The expression, "child of God," meant a good and virtuous person. "Son of God" meant much the same thing but was usually reserved for a virtuous Jewish king. As

Messiah, Jesus was king of the Jews and merited the "Son of God" title. But Christians also saw Jesus as the "firstborn son of God." In Yiddish, there is a saying that there is no greater curse than being a firstborn. The reason for this belief was that the firstborn had no choices in life. He had to follow in the profession of his father. If he refused to do so, the father had to say kaddesh (prayers for the dead) for him and regard him as dead. If the father was a carpenter, then the firstborn son was a carpenter also. In first-century Israel, being a carpenter meant more than making furniture and farm implements; it meant constructing houses and barns and digging cisterns as well. When the father retired or died, the eldest son took over the family business. When the father was absent from home or business, the firstborn son assumed all of his responsibilities. If the father sent the eldest son to conduct business for him, those who received the son considered him the same as the father. When the son attained the age of thirty — the retirement age in an era when the life expectancy was thirty-five years — he could devote his time to the study of Torah and become a rabbi. However, he first had to turn the family business over to *his* firstborn, or if childless, to the eldest son of his brother in the family trade. That is what famous rabbis such as Hillel and Akiva did.

What is important to remember is, "Like father, like son!" If you have seen the firstborn son, you have seen the father.

> Philip said to him, "Master, show us the Father, and that will be enough for us." Jesus said to him, "Have I been with you for so long a time and you still do not know me, Philip? Whoever has seen me has seen the Father" (Jn 14:8-9 NAB).

Thus was the concept that Jesus was the "firstborn son of God," not merely the "son of God," that led Christians to identify him with the Father.

**Ur'hatz: The First Washing of Hands:** The first washing of hands became a perpetual memorial of Jesus' washing his disciples' feet at the Last Supper (Jn 13:1-17). In John's community at Ephesus, it is recorded that the washing of feet was an important part of a reconciliation ritual. If the relationship between two individuals was strained or broken, then one would ask the other for permission to wash the other's feet and thereby seek reconciliation. By the other's acceptance of that humble act it meant that their relationship had been restored in Christ. "If you understand this, blessed are you if you do it" (Jn 13:17 NAB).

**Karpas—Eating the Greenstuff:** With no lamb to roast, there were no longer any roasted giblets and innards to serve at the first course of the seder. All that remained was the greenstuff that was eaten with them. So the karpas became the eating of greenstuff: lettuce, parsley, celery, chervil, and such.

The symbolism of dipping the karpas into salt water remained the same. It represented the tears wept in Egypt and now the tears wept over the destruction of the Temple, the Holy City, and the nation. No longer were Jews able to say openly Eretz Yisrael (The Land of Israel) because the Romans had decreed that their land be called "Palestina."

To that Christians added the anguish of their remembrance of Christ's betrayal by Judas. "The one who ate my food has raised his heel against me" (Jn 13:18 NAB). Quoting Psalm 41:10 did not necessarily mean that Judas actually broke bread with Jesus that evening, but merely that he shared some of the meal with him. "Breaking bread together" was synonymous with sharing a meal together. Jesus dipped a small bit of food into a dish and gave it to Judas (Jn 13:26). That implies that it was at the karpas when Jesus confronted Judas with his treachery. It was customary for a host at a banquet to pick out some choice bit of food and give it to an honored guest. In doing so, Jesus showed Judas that he still loved him. Judas had been in table fellowship with Jesus and the other disciples for years. He was one of the elders. He was one of the "brothers" of their Passover chavurah, and as a brother he had become a traitor to his teacher and master. Since the Eucharist was the anamnesis of the Last Supper, the "tears" of the karpas also became those of grief over the betrayal by our brother Judas, because, in spite of what he had done, Judas remained in perpetual table fellowship with his brother disciples.

**Yachatz — Breaking the Middle Matzah:** After the destruction of the Temple, the displaying of the matzot was moved up to this point. It served as a reminder that the Passover supper itself had been served at this time. Now the matzot had to take on all of the symbolism of the paschal lamb. For Jews, these two symbols came together out of necessity. For Christians, the two symbols flowed gently together in Christ. They saw Jesus as the Lamb (Jn 1:29) and as the Bread (Jn 6:35).

The Christians also renamed the obligatory three sheets (loaves) of matzot. For Jews they remained Kohen (Priest), Levy (Levite), and Yisrael (People of God). For Jewish-Christians, the three obvious names were Father, Son, and Holy Spirit. Christians took the Son (the middle loaf), broke it, wrapped it in a white cloth to represent a shroud, and "buried" it in a hiding place to be brought back for the afikoman — as a dramatization of Jesus' death, burial, and resurrection. Some people, such as the Jews for Jesus, believe that Christians started the custom of using the middle loaf as the afikoman. There does not seem to be any reason for non-Christians to inaugurate such a tradition. Whoever started it, the tradition began early because both Christians and Jews shared it. The Jewish variation was merely to wrap and set aside just the larger half of the middle matzah for their afikoman, which for them would be "the last thing eaten" to replace the final morsel of the paschal lamb. For Christians, the afikoman was Holy Communion.

**Maggid — Retelling of the Events of the Exodus:** The host or bishop continued the custom of uncovering and holding up the Passover matzot for all to see and forcibly announcing the invitation to Passover,

> Behold the bread of poverty
> Which our ancestors ate in the land of Egypt!
>
> All who are hungry — come and eat!
> All who are in need — share our Passover supper!
>
> We are here now,
> Next year in the land of Israel!
>
> We are slaves now,
> Next year may we all live in freedom!

The bread of poverty was covered again, and the second cup of wine was poured out for everyone. Then the children were called up to ask the Four Questions. But with the paschal lamb gone, the question about roasted and cooked meat had to be changed to, "On all other nights, we eat either seated or reclined. Why on this night do we recline to eat?" Even at times when people were too poor to have dining couches, or none were available, they continued the custom by leaning onto their left hands while drinking their wine as a memorial of the first-century custom.

The first part of the maggid (retelling) was too deeply ingrained in the Passover tradition to change. Besides, it was too well grounded in Scripture for anyone to even want to change it. Even Christian children had to be initiated into the great Exodus experience because, without it, they could not completely understand the experience of the Passover of Christ (1 Cor 5:7,8). So parents introduced the maggid with an animated discussion of the Wise Son, the Wicked Son (as defiant), the

Simple Son (immature), and the Son Too Young to Ask Questions (Haggadah shel Pesach). The purpose, of course, was to encourage their children to be like the Wise Son and want to learn all of the customs, traditions, and laws of the seder.

Because of the children, such traditions as the recitation of the ten plagues and the Dayennu litany were preserved. These are "fun" things that children, Jewish or Christian, love to sing and do. But after the Dayyenu in a Christian home, the subject turned to Jesus.

*Pesach, Matzah, Maror:* When it came time to explain the meaning of the paschal lamb, unleavened bread, and bitter herb, the Christian father explained to everyone at his table how each one of these also represented Christ. Jesus is the Lamb of God (Jn 1:29); Jesus is the True Heavenly Bread that came down from heaven (Jn 6:32-58); and Jesus died on the cross in a single perfect sacrifice that atoned for all of our sins (Hb 10:10-18).

*B'khol Dor Va-dor:* Then the bishop, the father of the family, explained that just as the family's observance of the Passover seder is the zikkaron of the Exodus experience, the Lord's Supper is the anamnesis of the Last Supper, crucifixion, and resurrection of Jesus. When families celebrate the seder, they become participants in all of the events of the Exodus. When they celebrate the Eucharist with the extended family of their Christian community, they are present with Jesus at the Last Supper (1 Cor 11:24-25). They share with him in his death by virtue of their baptism (Rm 6:3-4), and, by sharing in his death, they also share in his resurrection (Rm 6:6-11).

At the conclusion of that explanation, the whole community, as a family, would break into singing the first part of the Hillel, Psalms 113 and 114.

**Rachatz:** Now the family washed their hands again as they prepared to share the matzot. For this washing they said the traditional blessing,

Blessed are You, O LORD (YHWH) our God,
King of all creation,
Who has sanctified us by the observance of your com-
mandments,
And commanded us to wash our hands.

**Motzi — Matzah:** The bishop, as the father of the family, now broke the upper matzah into portions for each person at the individual family tables so that each person could have two pieces. In Jewish homes, the father broke the upper matzah and the remaining half of the middle one for his family. When each person received their pieces, they sprinkled some salt on one of them, recalling how the bodies of the animals brought for sacrifice were salted before they were offered on the altar or roasted for the communion sacrifice. After salting the matzah,[14] they all recited the double blessing. First they said the ha-motzi, blessing the bread, and then they said the special blessing concerning the commandment to eat unleavened bread during the seven days of Passover.

**Maror:** Now they all scooped up some of the bitter herb with their second piece of matzah, and then dipped all of that into the bowls of charoset to cut the sharpness of the maror. They recited the blessing for the bitter herb, and then ate it.

Blessed are You, O LORD (YHWH) our God
King of all creation
Who has sanctified us through the observance of your
commandments,
And commanded us to eat the bitter herb.

**Korekh — Binding Together:** While the Temple was still standing, the famous Rabbi Hillel was known to have wrapped pieces of the paschal lamb, with some lettuce and bitter herb, in the matzah and made a sandwich (BT Pesachim 115a). The later rabbis who wrote down the oral law and traditions in the Talmud decreed that at this place in the seder, beginning with the ha-motzi, everyone should say the blessing over the un-leavened bread, then eat it. Then say the blessing over the bitter herb, and then eat that. Immediately following those two obligations, they should make a sandwich of lettuce, bitter herb, and the matzah, and then eat it without saying a blessing. This would be a memorial of the Passover as it was observed while the Temple stood and the Passover sacrifice was still offered (BT Pesachim 115a).

In the early years after the destruction of the Temple, Christians probably made the Hillel Sandwich at their seders also. As with the roasted egg, however, the significance changed. The first generations who knew the Temple longed to see it rebuilt. Perhaps the next generation, who had heard lavish descriptions of it, desired to see it as well. But the next generations of Christians did not consider the Temple as important. They thought of themselves as the Temple of God and of Christ as the one perfect sacrifice. There was no need for a rebuilt Temple or for the restoration of the elaborate sacrifices. If the custom of the Hillel Sandwich continued in the Christian families and communities, it was as a memorial of how the paschal lamb was eaten at the Last Supper.

Jewish families and communities, on the other hand, never stopped longing for the Holy Temple. And they continued to petition God to, "In the greatest haste, rebuild your Holy Temple, speedily before our very eyes!" (Haggadah shel Pesach).

## Shulchan 'Orekh: The Passover Meal

In the days of the Temple, the roasted paschal lamb was the the piece de la resistance while the matzah, maror, charoset, green herbs, and lettuce were the required accoutrements of the supper. After the Temple, a meal had to be inserted into the ritual that broke from the past. Not only was it a meal without lamb, it was a meal with nothing roasted over an open flame. The food had to be boiled or "seethed" within pots or pans that cooked the food indirectly.[15] The rabbis decreed, however, that there should be two "meats" served at this meal to help remember the two Passover sacrifices. They represented the paschal lamb and the chaggigah served at the seder supper in the days of the Temple. "Rabbi Joseph said: 'Two kinds of meat are necessary, one in memory of the Passover-offering and the second in memory of the chaggigah.' Rabina said: 'Even a bone and its broth'" (BT Pesachim 114b).

It was not easy to divorce the seder from the Passover lamb. The adjustment of the ritual to a new seder without a pilgrimage to Jerusalem was made simpler by the fact that the Jews of the Diaspora had celebrated Passover in their homes when they did not go on pilgrimage to Jerusalem. Naturally, their seders were observed without a paschal lamb, but they did serve a roast lamb as a substitute for the chaggigah they would have eaten if they had been in Jerusalem. For most families, Passover meant lamb, even if that lamb were not a paschal lamb.

It took the rabbis many years to convince the Jewish people to abandon roast lamb at Passover altogether. Many still insisted that their lamb was just a substitute for the chaggigah and not the Pesach. But the rabbis would not allow it. The people might become complacent and evolve a Passover seder that did not need the Temple and its sacrifices. So all lamb, even a substitute for the chaggigah, was omitted from the seder. Not only was the lamb deleted but any meat roasted over an open flame as the paschal lamb had been.

Christian communities also adjusted their Passovers to these new conditions, but they probably continued to serve roast lamb as a substitute for the chaggigah. Roast lamb remained the centerpiece of the paschal (Easter) meal among the Armenians, the Eastern Rites, and the Greeks. Records show that Christians still celebrated Passover in the second century

(Eusebius, *The History of the Church*, 229-233). The churches in the East and West continued to argue over whether Pascha should begin on "the day on which the Jews had been commanded to sacrifice the lamb" or on the Lord's Day (Sunday) after the first day of Passover. The argument was not resolved until the Council of Nicaea (325 C.E.). "At that time, under pressure from the emperor, the church in Rome began to introduce new customs in the observance of Passover to replace the ancient Jewish traditions" (Samuele Bacchiocchi, *How It Came About: From Saturday to Sunday* [Pontifical Gregorian University Press, 1977], excerpted in *Biblical Archaeology Review* 4, no. 3 [September/October]: 32-39).

In the years that the rabbis were establishing the law that no lamb must be served at Passover, Judaism and Christianity began to draw apart. The weight of the rabbinical decrees decreased for Christians over that whole period. Judaism was under the authority of the rabbis at the schools, first in Yavneh and later in the Galilee. In their place was the authority of the Bishop of the Jerusalem church. He sent the Passover letters to all the Christian communities establishing the date of the Passover observance for them each year.

But Christians still had the paschal lamb, which was Jesus Christ, the Lamb of God (Jn 1:29), who had been offered up in one perfect sacrifice (1 Cor 5:7,8; Heb 10:10-12), and of whose "flesh" they all shared (Jn 6:53-58; 1 Cor 10:16,17). A roast lamb was a natural chaggigah, a festival offering, to complement their sharing the "flesh" of the paschal Lamb of God. Christian communities followed the custom of poor communities during the days of the Temple, who dined on other roast meats for the Passover supper because they could only afford to register for enough paschal lamb to supply each one of their group a piece "the size of an olive" (BT Pesachim 89a). That small piece of paschal lamb was served as their afikoman, or last thing eaten. The afikoman of the Christian seder was the

Eucharist. Consequently, each of them received a piece of the Lamb of God "the size of an olive" as they shared Holy Communion at the conclusion of their seder.

> The cup of blessing that we bless, is it not a participation [koinonia] in the blood of Christ? The bread that we break, is it not a participation [koinonia] in the body of Christ? Because the loaf of bread is one, we, though many, are one body, for we all partake of the one loaf (1 Cor 5:16,17 NAB).

The Passover seders of the Christian communities and families actually continued just as true to all of the authentic traditions, laws, and customs of Passover as did those of the Jewish communities and families, although each interpreted them in their own way.

## Tzafun: Revealing the Hidden

The tables were cleared so that the service could continue. One of the adults looked for the afikoman in the spot where it had been reserved, but it was not there. Hilarity followed as everyone tried to find out who stole it. It was one of the children, of course, and some hard bargaining ensued. The children held out to the very last, but in the end they accepted some reward and returned the afikoman so that the seder could continue.

That little ceremony continued in both Jewish and Jewish-Christian homes. But the significance of finding the afikoman was different. For Jews, it was necessary to have the afikoman returned in order to properly conclude the service. For Christians, however, this little ceremony represented the resurrection. The breaking, wrapping, and "burying" the middle matzah in the matzah cover at the yachatz represented the death and burial of Jesus. The search for the afikoman depicted the morning when the women went to the tomb to complete the burial of Jesus and they could not find him. He was not there!

They were consumed with confusion and panic until it was announced to them that he had risen. After they had proclaimed the resurrection to the other disciples, Jesus revealed himself to them and consoled them with his presence.

After the "resurrection" of the afikoman, it was placed in a place of honor on the seder table where it remained until it became the Eucharist for the community or family.

## Barekh: The Blessings After The Meal

The blessings after the meal of the Passover supper are very ancient and are mentioned in the Talmud. There have been some additions, such as those made by the Rabbis Akiva and Tarfon in the second century, but they remain essentially the same today as they were in the first century.

Christians should be as familiar with these magnificent blessings as are their elder brothers and sisters in the faith. These prayers are known in Hebrew as Birkat Ha-mazon (Blessing after the Meal),[16] but Greek-speaking Jews knew them as Eucharistia. These prayers are a mutual inheritance for both Jews and Christians. They are an integral part of the seder, but they became, for Christians, a model for the eucharistic prayers of the Christian Havdalah-Agape.

## Hallel: The Conclusion of The Hallel

The Blessings after the Meal flowed naturally into the recital or singing of the remainder of the Hallel. Psalm 118 was of particular importance to the Christian communities and was especially popular. The closing verses, which by tradition were repeated, seemed to be a vivid description of Jesus' entry into Jerusalem,

This gate is the LORD's (YHWH),
The just shall enter it.
I will give thanks to you, for you have answered me.
and have been my savior.
The stone which the builders rejected
has become the cornerstone.
By the LORD has this been done;
it is wonderful in our eyes.

This is the day the LORD has made;
let us be glad and rejoice in it.
O LORD, grant salvation!
O LORD, grant prosperity!

Blessed is he who comes in the name of the LORD;
we bless you from the house of the LORD.
The LORD is God, and he has given us light.
Join in procession with leafy boughs
up to the horns of the altar.

You are my God, and I give thanks to you;
O my God, I will extol you.
Give thanks to the LORD, for he is good;
for his kindness endures forever. (Ps 118.20-29)

The Hallel was concluded with the recital of Psalm 136 and
the Nishmat, "The Breath of All the Living."

## Nirtzah: The Acceptable Offering

"Now the seder is concluded." All of its laws, customs, and
traditions had been observed (Haggadah shel Pesach).

For the apostolic Christian communities and families, the real
afikoman of Passover had yet to be shared by everyone. They
had not yet blessed, broken, shared, and eaten the flesh of the
true Passover sacrifice, the Lamb of God. The *nirtzah* of the
Christian Passover seder was the afikoman of the Eucharist or

Holy Communion. The Cup of Elijah was blessed and shared as the Cup of Blessing and the matzah, set aside for the afikoman, became the body of Christ (1 Cor 5:16,17).

Now that Passover is being widely revived by Christian families everywhere, it is seldom possible to conclude the seder with the Eucharist. Another spreading custom, the agape, suits the conclusion of a Christian seder very well. The agape is the simple sharing of bread and wine (or beverage) as a sign of the fellowship of sharing love. The sharing of the afikoman and Cup of Elijah are perfect symbols of table fellowship and fraternal love.

In the section on the Havdalah-Agape, it was stated that since bread and wine were used for Holy Communion, and since they were items that were common to all Sabbath, Havdalah, and festival meals, the Christian communities were able to gather every week for the table fellowship of the Eucharist. The after-supper Eucharist (grace) of the Havdalah-Agape gave the Cup of Blessing its name as the Eucharist Cup. However, as the annual Passover seder supper was the most complete reliving and reactualization of the Last Supper, the weekly Lord's Supper retained many of the symbols of the Passover seder.

Even today, if one looks closely at the Liturgy of the Eucharist as celebrated in Catholic, Episcopalian, Lutheran, Eastern Orthodox, and many other churches, some of the elements of the seder can still be seen as present. A linen tablecloth covers the altar, or table of the Lord. At least two candles are lit for the ceremony. Bread and wine are offered, and the bread in many churches is still unleavened, made according to the laws of the Passover matzah. In other churches, such as the Eastern Orthodox, the bread is a special, large loaf of leavened bread made in the tradition of the ancient Havdalah-Agape. Water is still added to wine, although no one remembers that it was originally done to make the wine kosher. Before the consecration, the hands are washed as was done before the Ha-

Motzi of the seder. The bread is blessed, broken, and shared in a ritual that can be traced back in an unbroken line to the Ha-Motzi-Matzah of the seder of the Last Supper. In fact, since the Eucharist is the anamnesis of the Last Supper, everyone who shares in the table and covenant fellowship of the Lord's Supper is actually present with the other disciples and Jesus at the Last Supper.

## The Jewish Church, The Forgotten Church

The original Christian church was Jewish, and thoroughly so. Only two branches of Judaism survived the Jewish War of 66-70 C.E.: the Pharisees' sect and the Jewish sect of the apocalyptic Nazarenes, whose primary revelation was that their founding rabbi was the long-expected Messiah of Israel and the firstborn son of God. Most Pharisees sincerely doubted the Nazarenes' (Christians') messianic claims because they could see no signs that the world had entered into the paradise of the Messianic Age. The world was in flames. Death and the awful weight of pagan oppression was everywhere. The Land of Israel — Eretz Yisrael — was in ghastly ruins. However, many Pharisees converted to the new Jewish sect, as did a great number of Essenes, Sadducees, and Samaritans. There was a significant number of gentile converts as well, but these were predominantly from the "fearers of God," who were those Gentiles that worshiped in the synagogues and were already familiar with Judaism. The vast majority of Christians, however, remained converted Jews well into the third century. The number of Gentiles was too small, and not yet inclined, to create a separate and distinct gentile church. The only alternative to Judaism was pagan superstition and moral debauchery (1 Cor 10:19- 22).

Judaism was the cradle in which Christianity was nurtured, the source to which it was uniquely indebted. It left a deep imprint, as is gererally agreed, on the church's *liturgy and ministry, and an even deeper one on its teaching....* Yet, in spite of the early rupture between Christians and Jews, it would be a grave error to dismiss it as a negligible force in our period. Until the middle of the second century, *when Hellenistic ideas began to come to the fore,* Christian theology was taking shape in predominantly Judaistic molds, and the categories of thought used by almost all Christian writers before the Apologists were largely Jewish. *This explains why the teaching of the Apostolic Fathers, for example, while not strictly unorthodox, often strikes a strange note when judged by later standards.* And it is certain that this "Judeo-Christian" theology continued to exercise a *powerful influence well beyond the second century"* (Kelly, *Early Christian Doctrines,* 17, emphasis mine).

For the first two centuries, the church remained within Judaism, and the differences between the Pharisees and Nazarenes at that time was probably no greater than Orthodox and Reform Judaism today.

A whole page is missing, however, from the history of the Christian church; that is the fact that the community of the Jerusalem church returned to the Holy City soon after the end of the Jewish War. Recent archaelogy uncovered both Jewish and Christian tombs from that period (Brown et al., *Jerome Biblical Commentary,* 701, section 75:165). Moreover, the list of Jewish bishops who governed the Jerusalem church until the year 135 C.E. still exists (Eusebius, *The History of the Church,* 415). As long as it existed, the Jerusalem church was the supreme authority over all the churches because it was Jesus' own church and because many of the bishops were sons and grandsons of James and Jude, who were Jesus' brothers, "humanly speaking" (Eusebius, *The History of the Church,* 126,127). In the mind of the Jewish-Christian church of that period, the bishop and elders of the Jerusalem church were the Beyt Din HaGadol (Sanhedrin) for all of Christianity. They were the primary keepers of all of the teachings of the Lord Jesus, whether written or still oral.

When St. Paul realized that some of the Mosaic Law did not apply in the New Covenant, he went to the Jerusalem church for the Apostles' and elders' decision on the matter, and they issued the confirming decree (Acts 15:1-20). What Paul realized was that some of the Commandments of the Torah and their supporting laws were the expressions of the divine will to keep the Jewish people, the people of God, separate and distinct from all other nations and people of the world (Ex 19:5,6). The New Covenant did not nullify or replace the Sinai Covenant (Mt 5:17-20); in fact, what was new was that this Covenant was for all the rest of the nations and people of the world, the Gentiles (Mt 28:18-20; Rm 11:16-18). The Covenant of circumcision and the dietary laws that kept the Jewish people serarate from the rest of the world no longer applied to the New Covenant relationship of love, which sought the assimilation of all humanity into a worldwide brotherhood with Christ under the universal fatherhood of God. The Ten Commandments, nevertheless, remain as valid today in both synagogues and churches as they were when God revealed them to Israel at Mt. Sinai.

The Apostolic church, the original Jewish church, was very charismatic. Every community was acutely aware that Jesus was alive and present in their midst everyday. Everyone was filled with the Holy Spirit, who guided every individual and community action. The bishop and elders of every community were responsible for feeding, housing, and clothing the community in their care; this left the community free to feed the hungry, clothe the naked, house the homeless, heal the sick, and visit the shut-ins and those in prison (Mt 25:31-40). When a problem arose in the Jerusalem church over the proper distribution of food, the Apostles created the office of deacon ("one who serves at table") to insure that everyone had enough to eat

(Acts 6:1-7). What the first Christians brought to the ancient world was active love, a ministry of caring and compassionate service to others. No one was an untouchable or an outsider. No one was too poor or too insignificant to warrant their love and care. They proclaimed that there was only one God, who was the Father of all, and everyone could enter into the fullness of being a child of God by repenting (changing the direction of their lives, turning their mind and hearts from sin toward God, *metanoina*) and being "born again" through the waters of baptism. After baptism, they were admitted into full table fellowship of the family of God, where there was no distinction between Jew or Gentile, slave or freeman, male or female because "all are one in Christ Jesus!" (Gal 3:28). The love of Christ, his forgiveness won for all humanity, and his acceptance of everyone was a fire that burned white-hot and spread rapidly to the ends of the known earth.

Unique about the Jewish church was their understanding of the Covenant. They knew how fundamental their New Covenant relationship was with God (1 Cor 11:25-33). They understood that the first law governing their lives was the new commandment of Jesus, "I give you a new commandment: love one another. As I have loved you, so you also should love one another. *This is how all will know that you are my disciples, if you have love for one another*" (Jn 13:34,35 NAB, emphasis mine). But the Passover table fellowship of the Eucharist and the extended family communities — in New Covenant relationship with God—was a concept of church that was not to last. The forces of history were about to overwhelm the original church and change it completely.

# The "Liberation of Jerusalem" and "Redemption of Israel"

*(This section uses as reference Brown et al,* Jerome Biblical Commentary, *701-2, section 75:165-171.)*

Forces were gathering that would bring the period of the Apostolic church to an end and change the Christian church substantially and fundamentally. In spite of the destruction of the Temple and the loss of the nation, the Jewish people did not lose hope of seeing the Temple rebuilt and the nation restored. It had happened once before, and, by analyzing the demolition of the first Temple by the Babylonians and the exile, they figured there would be a new Temple and a renewed nation in about seventy years. In the meantime, all Jews and Jewish Christians were forced to continue paying the Temple tax, now called the "fiscus Iudaicus," but the tax went for the upkeep of the pagan temple of Jupiter Capitolinus in Rome.

Unfortunately, the people grew impatient. Instead of waiting for God to rebuild his Temple and liberate his people in his own time, the people took matters into their own hands. Toward the end of Emperor Trajan's reign, the Jewish people began to fight for their rights. Fierce revolts broke out in the years 115 and 116 C.E. in Cyrene and Egypt in North Africa, on the island of Cyprus, and in the far east in Mesopotamia. The revolt in North Africa was almost a full-scale war. These uprisings had a great impact upon the Roman Empire. Previous to the first revolt in 66-70 C.E., the people of the empire respected the Jews because of their high moral values, their learning, and their regard for human life. But these revolts, rebellions, and wars changed their sentiments: The Roman world became anti-Jewish.

Then, despite their constant prayers, instead of getting another benevolent Cyrus the Great to rule over them, Emperor Publius Aelius Hadrianus took the reins of the empire in 117 C.E. He ruled as emperor until 138 C.E. Around 130 C.E.,

Hadrian had an imperial edict issued that prohibited the circumcision rite, which resulted in disaster. The Jewish people gathered around General Simeon Ben Kosibah, and he led them in a final war of liberation, which broke out in 132 C.E. Simeon was supported as the proper leader of Israel by the priest, Eleazar. But he drew most of his support from the famous Rabbi Akiva, who suggested that Simeon might be the real Messiah. It may have been Akiva who renamed him Bar Kokhba, or Son of the Star (of David), which was a messianic title. He went down in the pages of history under that name, Simon Bar Kokhba.

In the beginning, the Roman governor of Palestine, Teneius Rufus, was helpless in resisting Bar Kokhba's attacks. The legate of Syria, Publius Marcellus, sent him military help, but it was too little and the Romans were forced to retreat. Bar Kokhba retook Jerusalem and much of Judea. He cleared off all of the pagan shrines on the Temple Mount, and the priests built a new altar of sacrifice, restoring the offerings, and made plans for building the new Temple. Bar Kokhba set up a provisional government and issued coins stamped "Liberation of Jerusalem" and "Redemption of Israel." It all was so marvelous that the people could hardly believe their eyes. All their hopes and prayers, it seemed, had not been in vain. Jerusalem was liberated and the nation was redeemed.

The vision, however, was all too short-lived. Emperor Hadrian recalled his general, Sextus Julius Severus, from his campaigns in Britain and sent him to recover Palestine. Severus quickly recaptured the country. Bar Kokhba and the people fled to strongholds and desert caves for refuge. There were caves in the valleys of Murabba'at, Hever, and Se'elim where families hid with their belongings, Bible scrolls, and family archives. But these caves became deathtraps when they were discovered by the Romans. The general sealed off the areas and starved the people into submission. Some of Bar Kokhba's military officers who had fled to the caves in the valley of Hever had taken letters with them from their commanding general, and these were recovered in recent archaeological excavations. After Jerusalem had been recaptured by Severus, Bar Kokhba and his army made their last stand at Beth-ter, about six miles southwest of Jerusalem. It seemed that it was all over when Beth-ter fell and the war ended in 135 C.E., but a much more disastrous calamity was about to befall both Christians and Jews.

Emperor Hadrian reasoned that so long as Jerusalem existed, even in ruins, it would be a source of hope for the Jewish people to rally around and incite them to rebel against the empire. Therefore, Jerusalem must cease to exist. Hadrian brought in great machines to completely dismantle what was left of the Holy City. Much of the debris was thrown into the Tyropoeon Valley, and it filled much of the space between the western hill and the Temple Mount. Over the ruins the emperor built a completely new Greco-Roman city and named it after himself, Aelia Capitolina. Upon the Temple Mount, a large pagan temple was built and dedicated to Olympian Jupiter. Over the site of Golgotha and the empty tomb, a temple of the love goddess Venus with her priestess prostitutes was constructed. The unholy had covered up the truly holy.

Then, to confirm his intentions, Hadrian decreed that no Jew could go anywhere near Jerusalem. No-one circumcised was allowed within viewing distance of the new city (Eusebius, *The History of the Church*, 157). That meant that all Jews and all Jewish Christians were permanently evicted from Jerusalem and the holy places. The Jerusalem church ceased to exist. Only a small community of Gentile Christians remained there, but they had to be secretive about their activities, and they had no authority over the other churches. All authority, consequently, passed from Jerusalem to Rome, the capital of the worldwide empire where both Peter and Paul had been martyred.

This final catastrophe drove a wedge between Judaism and Christianity (Brown et al., *Jerome Biblical Commentary*, 702, section 75:171). It introduced the final stage of the original Jewish church while the stream of Jewish converts dried up. The Christian church was inevitably to become a gentile church.

## The Gentile Church Centered in Rome

At that same time, a whole body of Roman literature appeared that condemned the Jews (Adversos Iudaeos). "Following the Roman lead, Christians developed a 'Christian' theology of separation from and contempt for the Jews. Characteristic Jewish customs such as circumcision and Sabbath keeping were castigated" (Samuele Bacchiocchi, *How It Came About: From Saturday to Sunday*, excerpted in *Biblical Archaeology Review* 4, no. 3 [September/October 1978]: 34). The Christians' contempt for the Jews and Jewish customs proved to be a great disaster. It created a void in the Christian church that would soon demand to be filled. The Jewish holy days and traditions were abandoned (except for Passover and Pentecost) and replaced by popular pagan festivals and superstitions.

In this void, Roman arrogance put great pressure on the church. The Romans felt that the true God and Savior of the world could not possibly be a Jewish Messiah. Iesus Christus must really be the incarnation of the sun god Apollo. Apollo was the most popular god of the Roman pantheon since the time of Augustus Caesar. Succeeding emperors, especially Elagabalus and Aurelian, established Apollo as the chief protector of the emperors. They established the cult of Sol Invictus (Invincible Sun) as the chief imperial cult of Rome. Too many Roman Christians accepted the belief that Sol and Christ were one and the same. Recent archaeology in the necropolis discovered beneath the Vatican in Rome uncovered the earliest known Christian mosaic, dated between 200 and 240 C.E. The mosaic depicts Jesus as the sun god driving the sun chariot drawn by four white horses. (It is now known as the Christus-Helios mosaic.) Behind his head shines the sun. The only factor that identifies the driver of the sun chariot as Jesus, and not Apollo or Helius, are seven rays that radiate out between his head and the sun.

We know that the Roman sun-cults otherwise influenced Christian thought and liturgy. The church fathers frequently condemn Christian veneration of the sun. In early Christian art and literature, the sun is often used as a symbol to represent Christ. The orientation of early Christian churches was changed. Instead of facing Jerusalem like synagogues, churches were oriented to the East. The 'dies natales Solis Invicti' (the birthday of the Invincible Sun) was chosen as the Christian Christmas (Samuele Bacchiocchi, *How It Came About: From Saturday to Sunday*, excerpted in *Biblical Archaeology Review* 4, no. 3 [September/October 1978]: 39).

Blending the cult of the Invincible Sun with the religion of Jesus Christ effected three important results. The Sabbath was transferred from Saturday to Sunday; December 25th became the date of the Nativity; and the halo (the sun's orb) became a prominent symbol in Christian art. In fact, we still dress Jesus as the driver of the sun chariot in our Christian art, the sun shining behind his head. Never do we see Jesus portrayed as the first-century Jewish rabbi that he actually was. Never is he seen wearing the tallit, the outer garment with the four tassels. Never is his face framed with the tzitzit ha-rosh, the side curls, and full beard that distinguished the observant religious man.

The worship of Sol Invictus as the primary protector of the emperors greatly affected the structure of the gentile church as well. Since the time of Augustus, each emperor had been the Pontifex Maximus, the High Priest of Rome, as well as imperator. Apollo had been the titular deity of Augustus Caesar, and Sol Invictus was the titular deity of Constantine. As a consequence, the Christian emperors remained the Pontifex Maximus for as long as they remained in Rome and Italy. (It was after the emperors abandoned Rome and moved to the eastern empire that the bishop of Rome assumed the title and office of Pontifex Maximus.) That meant that the "folksy" and "homey" Passover table fellowship of the family of God that existed in the Jewish church could not survive in the gentile church once it became the official religion of the Roman Empire. The Roman church was the emperor's church. It must conform to the august dignity of the August Caesar. An excellent example of this can still be found in Ravenna, Italy. The Christian emperor Justinian built a royal chapel at Ravenna, which was the Byzantine capital of the west from the sixth to the eighth century. To this day it survives in all its splendor as the Church of San Vitale. Two magnificent, mosaic murals display just how much the Christian emperors changed the simple Eucharist of the Apostles into a ritual suitable for the presence of a Pontifex Maximus. In one mural, Emperor Justinian holds the large, leavened loaf of bread that will become the Eucharist. He is crowned, "haloed," bejeweled, and robed in purple. Next to him stands the bishop, Maximianus, holding a large, golden, jeweled cross. Maximianus, without a halo, wears an alb, stole, and golden chasuble. The emperor and his chaplin are assisted by five priests. Two of them also wear albs and show that their hair has been cut into the clerical tonsure. One of them holds a gold-covered and bejeweled book of the Gospel, while the other holds a censer for burning incense. The three others wear some kind of mantle over their albs that show a wide band of royal purple crossing below their chests. Behind them stand a group of soldiers holding spears, and one of them grips a shield displaying the royal seal of the Chi Rho.

Across from the mural of Justinian is the mural of Empress Theodora. She is presenting a large, jewel-encrusted, gold chalice for the Eucharist. She is heavily bejeweled with pearls and other gems. The empress wears royal purple robes, as well, and behind her head shines a large halo. She is assisted by a number of richly adorned ladies-in-waiting and two priests dressed in the mantles banded in royal purple. The priest next to the empress wears a mantle of white, while next to him stands the other, whose mantle is golden. The priest with the golden mantle holds back a curtain so that a white marble baptismal font can be seen.

If the Christian emperors of Rome had only added pomp and ceremony to the Eucharist, the damage might not have been so great. As the head of the Christian church, the emperors did not exemplify Christian service (Mt 20:25-28) or Christian humility (Jn 13:12-17). No one could accuse the Roman emperors of humility. Instead, they took the classless community of the Church of the Apostles (Gal 3:28) and turned it into a heirarchical society with the emperor, as Pontifex Maximus, on top. Bishops were no longer patriarchal heads of extended family communities; they were now official members of the government and rulers over dioceses.

The average Christian, the layman and lay woman, was more and more excluded from the central life of the church. Seduced by the cult of Sol Invictus, the ordinary Christian gradually gave in to other pagan cults as well. The cult of Isis, "The Mother of God (Horus)," was mixed with the veneration of the mother of Jesus. The goddess Victoria (Nike), a woman with wings, became the Christian angel, and the ever popular Cupid, son of Venus and Mars, became the Christian cherub. Once the titular gods had been abolished, patron saints had to be substituted. The church was no longer the joyous community of the living saints (Acts 2:42-47; 4:32-36); rather, it was a suffering society in debt to the dead who were officially canonized just as the emperors had been formally declared gods.

The greatest calamity to befall the gentile church, however, was the abandonment of the New Covenant. The Romans had no understanding of what a divine Covenant was. The Greco-Roman society was devoid of real compassion and love. Rather, it understood and admired passion, infatuation, lust, cupidity, and the complete exploitation of sex. The Roman world was built upon slavery and militarism, neither of which have any room for charity, forgiveness, nor the selfless serving of others. People who enjoy watching others slashed, smashed, pierced, torn, gnawed, or burned to death in their theaters, hippodromes, and coliseums had no place for the gentle virtues of love and caring in their lives. Gladitorial combats lasted long into the Christian era of Rome.

In the Bible, the Hebrew word for covenant, "b'rit," was translated into the Greek of the Septuagint as "diatheke." Unfortunately, the ordinary Greek meaning of "diatheke" is "last will and testament." Even so, the Greek-speaking Jews understood that whenever the word "diatheke" appeared in the Bible or religious writings, it meant "covenant." As long as the Christian church remained predominantly Jewish, all Christians understood that "diatheke" meant "covenant." But as the church became gentile and anti-Jewish, that meaning was lost. When the Bible was translated into Latin, the word used to translate "diatheke" was "testamentum" or "testament." From that grievous translation evolved the tradition of calling the Hebrew Scriptures "The Old Testament" and the Greek Scriptures "The New Testament." The translation became really disastrous when the words of consecration said over the chalice were translated into Latin. The words of Jesus at the Last Supper (Mt 26:27,28) became "For this is the chalice of my blood, *of the new and everlasting testament* (novi et aeteni testamenti)." Cut off from Judaism, the official church abandoned the New Covenant and completely forgot the meaning of a covenant relationship with God. No longer was the church the community of all of those gathered in the table fellowship of the Lord's Supper. Forgotten, as well, was the concept of the Lord's Supper as the zikkaron/anamnesis of the Last Supper. The Latin liturgy, followed by the English, stated, "Haec quotiescuque feceritis in mei Memoriam facietis," or, "As often as you shall do these things, you shall do them in memory of me" (Rev. F.X. Lasance, the consecration of the wine, "The New Roman Missal" [New York: Benziger Brothers, Inc., 1937], 783).

So now, the New Covenant of Christ and his new commandment of agape-love was replaced by the mandate of Emperor Constantine: to establish the primacy of Rome over Jerusalem. To end the controversy over whether the Pascha of Christ should be observed on the 14th-15th of Nisan, "the day on which the Jews had been commanded to sacrifice the lamb" (Eusebius, *History of the Church*, 230), or the following Sunday, it was determined that the Christian Pascha (Easter) would be held on the first Sunday following the full moon that fell on or just after the spring (vernal) equinox according to the Roman solar calendar. Emperor Constantine's letter to the bishops at the Council of Nicaea (325 C.E.) stated,

> We ought not therefore to have anything in common with the Jews, for the Savior has shown us another way [the Imperial Sun Cult]....In unanimously adopting this mode [Easter Sunday] we desire, dearest brethren, to separate ourselves from *the detestable company of the Jews*" (Bacchiocchi, *How It Came About: From Saturday to Sunday*, excerpted in *Biblical Archaeology Review* 4, no. 3 [September/October 1978], emphasis mine).

It became official policy to hate Jews and to reject Israel, the firstborn of the Lord (Ex 4:22).

The legacy of the Caesars, the first Pontifici Maximi, has been the breaking apart of the brother-sister fellowship of the body of Christ. Men turned their backs on ministry as service to others and instead sought power, prestige, and wealth (see

Lk 22:24-27). In the cacophony of claims and counterclaims as to who possessed the authentic authority, hate replaced love. Christians no longer greeted each other with a sincere, "holy kiss" (1 Cor 16:20), and they either ignored each other or confronted one another with suspicion, ridicule, and open hostility. This, in spite of the fact that it is written in the Bible we all share,

> If anyone says, 'I love God,' but hates his brother, *he is a liar;* for whoever does not love a brother whom he has seen cannot love God whom he has not seen. *This is the commandment we have from him; whoever loves God must also love his brother* (1 Jn 4:20-21 NAB, emphasis mine).

On the other hand, there have always been the few truly authentic disciples, such as Mother Teresa and the Salvation Army, who have seen the face of Jesus in the humbled, the homeless, the hungry, and the hurting (Mt 25:35-40). They know that God is where love (agape) is because "God is Love" (*o Theos agape esti,* 1 Jn 4:16). It is the Lord Jesus himself who said,

> "I give you a *newcommandment:* love one another [*agapate allelous*]. As I have loved you, so you also should love one another. *This is how all will know that you are my disciples, if you have love for one another*" (Jn 13:34-35 NAB, emphasis mine).

## NOTES

1. Bar mitzvah (son of the commandment) celebrated the boy's attainment of manhood and his assuming responsibility for the observance of all of the mosaic law.

2. "Tana" (an authority quoted in the Mishnah) means "teacher"; from the Aramaic *t'na,* meaning "to repeat, teach or study, to report a tradition." (Alcalay, *The Complete Hebrew-English Dictionary,* col. 2809.

3. The tana'im as a class were vital to the writing of the Mishnah, the oldest part of the Talmud. After the destruction of the Temple and the Jewish state, the rabbis gathered the surviving tana'im to recite all that they remembered. The rabbis then wrote the memories down in order to preserve them for posterity.

4. Christians, from the Greek *christos*, meaning "anointed," were known first as "Nazarines" (Ha-Notzrim), because they were disciples of Rabbi Jesus of Nazareth, Rav Y'shu' a Ha-Notzri.

5. Kittel, *Theological Dictionary of the New Testament* 3:804-809, s.v. "koinonia," "the fellowship which arises in the Lord's Supper."

6. Varda Sussman, "Lighting the Way Through History," *Biblical Archeology Review* 11, no. 2 (March/April 1985): 42-56.

7. In Hebrew, Saturday is the only day with a name: *shabbat* (sabbath). The other days of the week were simply *yom rishon* (first day), *yom sheni* (second day), *yom shlishi* (third day), *yom rivi'i* (fourth day), *yom chameshi* (fifth day), *yom shishi* (sixth day).

8. "Genesis," *The Anchor Bible* 8:5n.

9. Birnbaum, *Ha-Siddur Ha-Shalom*, 552.

10. Ibid.

11. Ibid.

12. "Pascha" was the original word for Easter, which remains "Pascha" in Greek, *Paques* in French, *Pasqua* in Italian, and *Pascua* in Spanish. The name "Easter" did not come into being until the conversion of the Saxons to Christianity. The Anglo-Saxon goddess of Spring was Oerstra and from her we get the English "Easter" and the German "Ostern" — and also her prolific companion, a hare or rabbit.

13. The Gospel account mentions a well, which could mean either a cistern used to collect rainwater or a well over an underground stream.

14. In Israel and in many other Middle Eastern countries, it is still the custom to salt bread at the beginning of a meal. In countries with a hot summer climate, extra salt in the diet is important.

15. Silverman, "Shulcan Orekh," *Passover Haggadah*, 35.11.

16. Silverman, *Passover Haggadah*, 37.

# APPENDIX

## Pronunciation

Transliteration, the writing of Hebrew words using the letters of the English alphabet, still seems to be in a period of transition. Many scholars prefer to treat Hebrew, especially biblical Hebrew, as a dead language. Simplicity appears to be paramount. I call their school the "A bet is a bet is a bet" mode. It is always easier to give the Hebrew letter "bet" the English equivalent of "b," but that leads to confusion. If your Bible is like mine, you will find examples of this school in Exodus 13:4; 23:15; 34:18; and Deuteronomy 16:1, each mentioning "the month of Abib." Why can't these scholars once again treat Hebrew as a living language, stop being so mysterious, and write the word as it is pronounced, which is "Aviv?" Perhaps the reader might recognize that it is the same word they already know in "Tel Aviv" and that "Aviv" simply means "spring!"

The Hebrew language today is alive and very well. It is the spoken language of the Nation of Israel and of many Jews throughout the world, especially here in the United States. The desire to speak and understand Hebrew is growing rapidly beyond the Jewish community; many Christians want to be conversant with the language of the Bible. Speaking Hebrew is much more than learning another tongue; it is immersing oneself in another culture, the Jewish culture, the culture of the Bible. Learning what the words of the Bible mean in the original is restrictive and one dimensional. Readers must understand the culture of the Bible as well as the language because culture gives fuller meaning, depth, and nuances to those words, bringing them to life. Fortunately, learning Hebrew today is much easier than it was a few years ago. There are records, tapes, videos, and even Scrabble in Hebrew available. There are also sing-along records and books of children's song, folk songs, and the traditional songs of the Sabbath and Feast Days. And for those who are really lucky, you can spend time in Israel at an Ulpan, a Hebrew language school, and really go "native!" To be honest, it's the American way. Picking up hitch-hikers during the summer months can be an education. Many times, when you try to use what little Hebrew you know to communicate, you're advised, "It's okay, we're from the States!"

Although I have a long way to go before I can carry on an intelligent conversation in Hebrew, I have transliterated the Hebrew words as I learned them in Israel. Three Israelis, originally from Morocco, were working for me, and they used to help me with pronunciation. I owe a great debt to them for their help. Where noted, however, I do make recognition of two Hebrew letters that were pronounced differently in Biblical times. In modern Hebrew, the sixth letter of the Hebrew "alefbet" is pronounced "vav," but in Biblical Hebrew, it was "waw." Ordinarily, that difference would be purely academic, except for the fact that we are all now familiar with the proper name of God, which is "YHWH." If I modernized the name by changing the Biblical "w" to a modern "v," I bet I would be in big trouble. On the other hand, I write the king's name "David" and not a more proper "Dawid." The last letter of the Hebrew alphabet was pronounced "taw," but is now pronounced as "tov," which means "good." But there are a number of Biblical references to "taw" that have to be recognized as having become a part of our culture, such as in the "Taw Cross," or T-shaped cross.

## Transliteration of Hebrew Sounds

### Alphabet

*(The Hebrew letter is given, then the numerical value according the Hebrew system of gematriya, then the pronunciation key. For more on gematriya, see chapter one, page 23 and chapter four, page 116.)*

**Aleph** (1) silent, signifies presence of vowel. Sometimes used as a glottal stop. Sometimes written as ' between two vowels to separate them, as in "Yisra'el."

**Bet** (2) "b" when accented, as in "bet"; "v" when unaccented, as in "vet."

**Gimel** (3) "g" as in "gate."

**Dalet** (4) "d" as in "date."

**Hay** (5) "h" as in "head" (silent at the end of some words, such as the feminine ending "ah").

**Vav (waw)** (6) "v" as in "very." However, "vav" is frequently used as the vehicle for carrying the vowel sounds of "o" and "oo."

**Zayin** (7) "z" as in "zero."

**Chet** (8) pronounced as a hard "h," such as the Russian and Polish pronunciation of "house" or the Spanish pronunciation of "jota." It can also be pronounced as the German "ch" in "ach" or Scottish "loch."

**Tet** (9) "t" as in "teach."

**Yod** (10) "y" as in "yes"; also "y" as pronounced in "key" and "sky."

**Kaf** (20) "k" if accented, as in "keep"; "kh" if unaccented, as pronounced in German "ch" in "ach" or Scottish "loch."

**Lamed** (30) "l" as in "lake."

**Mem** (40) "m" as in "messiah."

**Nun** (50) "n" as in "noon."

**Samech** (60) "s" as in "sister."

**'Ayin** (70) forces the vowel it governs to be pronounced deep in the throat. Many, however, treat the 'ayin as the aleph. The 'ayin is written as '.

**Pey** (80) "p" if accented, as in "pet"; "f" if unaccented, as in "fife."

**Tzadey** (90) "ts" as in "tsetse."

**Qof** (100) "k," but pronounced in the back of the throat as though a "g." Written as a "q" without "u."

**Resh** (200) "r." Semitic "r" is pronounced like Spanish "r" but softer. However, the French-, German-, and American-pronounced "r" is heard commonly north of Be'er Sheva.

**Shin** (300) "sh" as in "shoe"; "s" when so marked, as pronounced in "Yisrael."

**Tov** (400) "t" as in "Torah." In biblical Hebrew, pronounced "th" at the end of a word, as pronounced in "beth (house)."

*Vowels*

(*The vowels in modern Hebrew are much simpler than those in biblical Hebrew.*)

**A, a:** "a" as pronounced in "father"; sometimes as pronounced in "awe."

**E, e:** "e" as pronounced in "get."

**I, i:** "ee" as pronounced in "machine."

**O, o:** "o" as pronounced in "go."

**U, u:** "oo" as pronounced in "dune"; sometimes as pronounced in "pull."

: between two consonants, "e" as pronounced in "the." Written as ' as in "Y'shu'a (Jesus)."

**Ay, ay:** "i" as pronounced in "bite."

**Ey, ey:** "a" as pronounced in "bay."

# GLOSSARY

Arm: Aramaic
Eng: English
Grk: Greek
Heb: Hebrew
Lat: Latin

**Abba** (Heb;Aram) papa, daddy. ("Av" means "father.")

**Adam** (Heb) mankind, humanity, man, human being, person, someone. (Colloquial: the first man.)

**Adonai** (Heb) the Lord, God. A spoken substitute for "YHWH" when written.

**Adoni** (Heb) sir, my lord (when addressing another).

**Afikoman** (Heb) piece of paschal lamb or unleavened bread eaten at the conclusion of the Passover Supper.

**Agape** (Grk) the love of the New Covenant of Christ. The true love of God that is expressed by an active loving, caring for, and sharing with others (1 Jn 4:20,21).

**Anamnesis** (Grk) reactualization. An action whereby the events of the past are brought into the present. The bringing into the present all of the actions of the Lord Jesus at the Last Supper, Crucifixion, and Resurrection by the later community of disciples. The Eucharist.

**Avotenu** (Heb) our ancestors, forefathers, and foremothers.

**Bar** (Heb) son, son of.

**Bar Mitzvah** (Heb) literally, Son of the Commandment. A Jewish boy of thirteen, the age at which he assumes his religious obligations; under obligation to observe the Mosaic Law.

**Barakh** (Heb) to bless, praise, thank; from the verb *barach*, "to kneel, to bend the knee."

**Barekh** (Heb) grace, thanksgiving, blessing said after the Passover seder supper.

**Bat** (Heb) daughter, daughter of, girl. (Used for female as "ben" for male.)

**Bat Chavah** (Heb) daughter of Eve, woman, female individual, female person, mortal.

**Bayt** (Heb) house, home, family, household, tribe, temple, school.

**Ben** (Arm)(Heb/Arm) son, son of, boy, male child; native, member of, individual of, worthy of.

**Ben Adam** (Heb/Arm) son of Adam, Son of Man, human being, man, mortal.

**Ben David** (Heb/Arm) son of David, Messiah.

**Beyt (Bet/Beth)** (Heb) house of, home of, family of, place of, source of, household of, temple of, school of.

**Beyt Avot** (Heb) parental household, family.

**Beth (Beyt) Hillel** (Heb) School of Hillel. The academy of the great Rabbi Hillel that preserved his teachings and sayings. Rabbi Hillel strongly influenced Pharisaic Judaism. Hillel was well known for his compassion and humanitarianism.

**Beth (Beyt) Shammai** (Heb) School of Shammai. The acadamy that preserved the teachings and sayings of the eminent Rabbi Shammai. Rabbi Shammai was known for his rigid interpretation of the Mosaic Law and for his proliferation of religious regulations intended to protect the commandments of the Torah.

**Beyt Y'shu'a** (Heb/Arm) School of Jesus. The 120 disciples that traveled with Rabbi Jesus, under the administration of the Twelve Apostles or Elders, to whom the Lord Jesus imparted his teachings. The Lord Jesus also formed his Beyt (School) into a Passover chavurah in preparation for his final imparting of his abiding physical presence in the Eucharist and commissioning them as the fellowship community of the New Covenant at the Last Supper.

**Birkat HaMazon** (Heb) blessings, grace said in thanksgiving for the food (mazon).

**B'rakhah** (Heb) blessing, benediction.

**B'rakhot** (Heb) blessings (i.e., the Eighteen Blessings said at the daily service, but not on the Sabbath).

**Chag** (Heb) feast, pilgrimage feast, especially associated with the three pilgrimage feasts: Sukkot (Tabernacles), Shavuot (Pentecost), and Pesach, Chag HaPesach (Passover).

**Chaggigah** (Heb) festival offering. The extra sacrifices brought to the Temple on the major feasts, such as Passover.

**Chametz** (Heb) leaven, leavened; also, any food or vessel not kosher for Passover.

**Charis** (Grk) to find favor, to be loved. Used to translate Hebrew "chesed," God's love for Israel within the covenant relationship. In New Testament, used to describe God's love for us in the New Covenant.

**Charoset** (Heb) clay. Fruit condiment traditional for Passover. Made of chopped fruit, apples, nuts, raisins, honey, wine, and spices.

**Chavurah** (Heb) company, society, association, especially of those gathered in a fellowship society for the sacrifice and eating of the paschal lamb.

**Chesed** (Heb) God's love for his people within the relationship of the Sinai Covenant. Usually written, "chesed w'emet," which means "everlasting love."

**El** (Heb) God; power; a strong, mighty one; a hero. Hebrew generic term for God, god. Seldom used alone in the singular for the God of Israel. More commonly used to identify alien gods.

**El 'Elyon** (Heb) The Most High God.

**El 'Olam** (Heb) Infinite, Eternal God.

**El Shaddai** (Heb) Almighty God.

**Elohim** (Heb) God. Masculine plural of El. Commonly used for the God of Israel.

**Elohenu** (Heb) Our God. Adonai Elohenu, "The Lord Our God."

**Emet** (Heb) truth. As it is written with the first, middle, and last letters of the Hebrew alphabet, it also means "everlasting," "first, last, and always."

**Eucharist** (Eng) the Sacrament of the Lord's Supper, Holy Communion; the consecrated elements of the Lord's Supper.

**Eucharistia** (Grk) gratefulness, thanksgiving, especially, thanksgiving or Grace after a meal.

**Gemara** (Heb) literally, "completion." The second and supplementary part of the Talmud, providing a commentary on the Mishnah.

**HaMotzi** (Heb) the blessing, breaking, and sharing of bread at all Sabbath, Havdalah, and festival meals.

**Haftorah** (Heb) chapters of the Prophets read after the portion read from the Torah, but only on Sabbath and holidays.

**Haggadah** (Heb) telling, tale, narrative. The book containing the narrative of the events of the Exodus read during the Passover supper or seder. Also, Haggadah shel Pesach, Haggadah for use at Passover.

**Haggid** (Heb) to tell, to narrate.

**Hallel** (Heb) Psalms 113 to 118 and 136. Called the Great Psalms of Praise. Recited or sung on all major feasts.

**Halleluyah** (Heb) literally, to sing the Great Psalms of Praise to the Lord (YHWH), "Praise you the Lord."

**Havdalah** (Heb) literally, separation, division. The Havdalah ceremony takes place Saturday evening after the conclusion of the Sabbath. It separates and divides the Sabbath from the work week, and it sybolizes the separation of the sacred from the mundane. The original ceremony is attributed to the men of the great assembly in the forth and fifth century B.C.E. It is mentioned in the Talmud (BT Pesachim 102b). It was adopted by the first generation of Christians as the weekly koinonia agape-eucharist supper (Lord's Supper) as it began the Lord's Day.

**Hoshi'a Na** (Heb) Hosanna. "Salvation Now," "Save us O Lord."

**Kaddesh** (Heb) at Passover, "Sanctify the Name of God." Blessing said over the wine.

**Kaddish** (Heb) prayer recited in mourning for the dead.

**Karpas** (Heb) greenstuff. The traditional hors d'oeuvres of the Passover supper.

**Kiddush** (Heb) "sanctifying the wine and sanctifying festival" prayer said at the beginning of every Sabbath, and feast day supper, especially Passover.

**Kiddush HaShem** (Heb) "Sanctify the Name." Ritual suicide when faced with no longer being able to practice the Jewish faith.

**Kipah** (Heb) cap, skullcap. Yarmulke. At time of Second Temple, a head covering worn to secure the tallit (outer garment) when worn over the head.

**K'tuvim** (Heb) the Writings. From "k'tav" (writing, handwriting) and "katav" (scribe, writer); the Hagiography, the third of the three divisions of the Hebrew Scriptures.

**Kohen** (Heb) literally, priest. The top loaf of matzot used in the ritual of the Passover seder.

**Kohen HaGadol** (Heb) literally, the great pries;. the high priest of the Temple.

**Koinonia** (Grk) from "koinon," "to share with someone in something." In the New Testament, "the fellowship of those sharing in the Lord's Supper." Based upon the Hebrew concept of "chavurah." Paul calls the Jewish chavurah "the fellowship of those sharing in the altar" (1 Cor 10:18, translation mine). The Christian chavurah is the "koinonia tou somatos kai aimatos Christos," "the fellowship community of those sharing in the body and blood of Christ" (1 Cor 10:16,17).

**Korekh** (Heb) binding, binding together. Place in the seder where items are bound together in the "Hillel Sandwich."

**Kos** (Heb) cup, glass, vessel, goblet.

**Kos Shel B'rakhah** (Heb) toast cup, grace cup. The cup over which Grace is said after meals. Hence, Eucharistic Cup or "cup of blessing" (1 Cor 10:16 NAB).

**Kos Shel Eliyahu** (Heb) Cup of Elijah, put on the seder table for the Prophet Elijah, who, by Jewish tradition, is believed to visit the home and taste the wine at Passover.

**Levy** (Heb) literally, Levite. The middle of the three loaves of matzot used in the ritual of the Passover seder.

**Maggid** (Heb) literally, narrator, herald, preacher. The section of the Haggadah where the events of the Exodus are narrated (recited, read).

**Manna** (Heb) literally, portion, ration, share. The "bread from heaven" that fed the Israelites in the wilderness.

**Mar** (Heb/Arm) mister, sir (from "lord").

**Mara'** (Arm) lord, master, rabbi.

**Maran** (Arm) our Lord, our master, our teacher, our rabbi.

**Maranatha** (Arm) Our Lord, Come! (Come Lord Jesus!)

**Maror** (Heb) bitter herbs eaten at Passover, horseradish.

**Masoretic Text** (Heb) the codified and accurate transmission of the standard Hebrew biblical text. It was the work of the Masoretes, the keepers of a cumulative body of biblical textual tradition (Masorah). By the eighth century C.E., they had developed a standard Hebrew text and provided the script with fixed vowel signs and accents.

**Matzah, Matzot** (Heb) unleavened bread. Made quickly of pure flour and pure water to prevent the chance of any leavening or contamination by impurities.

**Matzah Cover** (Eng) special decorated cloth covering for the three matzot used in the ritual of the seder. Matzah covers contain three pockets for the three Matzot: one for Kohen (priest), one for Levy (Levite), and one for Yisrael (the people of God).

**Mazal** (Heb) luck, fortune, fate, destiny.

**Mezuzah** (Heb) literally, doorpost, doorjamb. Parchment scroll containing Deuteronomy 6:4-9 and 11:13-21, etc., attached to doorpost in a wooden or metal case.

**Midrash** (Heb) literally, study, commentary, sermon. Homiletic interpretation of biblical passages.

**Mikveh, Mikva'ot** (Heb) ritual bath into which a person immerses to remove "uncleanliness" and attain ritual purity. Was obligatory preparation for participation in Temple sacrifices. Today, many Orthodox bathe in preparation for Sabbath and other observances.

**Minyan** (Heb) literally, number, quorum. The minimum number, ten, of adult male Jews required for congregational prayers.

**Mishnah** (Heb) literally, study, opinion. The written collection of the oral laws completed by Rabbi Judah HaNasi, which forms the basis of the Talmud.

**Mitzvah** (Heb) commandment, command, precept, law. (Colloquial: a meritorious deed, a good deed, a religious duty, an obligation.)

**Nasi** (Arm) prince, chief, chieftain, president. (Talmud: head of the rabbinical Sanhedrin.)

**Navi** (Heb) prophet, seer, spokesman.

**Navi'im** (Heb) the Prophets, the second section of the Hebrew Bible.

**Pascha** (Arm/Grk) originally meaning was "Passover." After Council of Nicaea, the meaning was confined to the Feast of Easter. Source of paschal lamb, paschal mysteries, paschal feast, and paschal candle.

**Paterfamilias** (Lat) head of the family. Father of the family. Head of household.

**Pesach** (Heb) Passover. The seven day Feast of Passover. The Passover lamb. The Passover sacrifice. The second Passover sacrifice of the priests and Levites. The Passover supper. From "pasach" (to skip, pass over) and "pisach" (to leap, jump, skip over, hop).

**Rachatz** (Heb) to wash, rinse, wash away. The second washing of the hands at the seder before the blessing of the Matzah.

**Ruach** (Heb) wind, breeze, air; soul, life, breath of life, spirit, mind, ghost.

**Ruach Elohim** (Heb) the Spirit of God; divine inspiration; divine wisdom.

**Ruach HaKodesh** (Heb) Spirit of the Holy One, the Shekhinah, the Holy Spirit.

**Seder** (Heb) literally, order, arrangement, succession, sequence. The seder. The Passover supper, because it is arranged in a sequence of events.

**Seder Plate** (Eng) large plate or platter set on the seder table upon which is arranged a number of symbolic items; a lamb bone, roast egg, horseradish, parsley, charoset, and salt water.

**Seder Table** (Eng) festival table especially set for the celebration of the Passover seder. The table will be set with at least two candles, the seder plate, the Cup of Elijah, matzah and a matzah cover, kiddish cup, and if possible a pitcher, towel, and basin for washing the hands.

**Septuagint** (Grk) the first official translation of the Hebrew Scriptures into Greek. It was done by some seventy rabbis (hence the name) in Alexandria in Egypt under the patronage of Ptolemy II, king of Egypt, between the third and second century B.C. E.

**Shalom** (Heb) peace, quiet, tranquility, well-being, welfare, health, contentment, success. Common form of greeting and salutation in Hebrew. From "shelem" (whole, entire, intact, complete, perfect, total).

**Shekhinah** (Heb) the Divine Presence, Godhead.

**Shem** (Heb) name. (HaShem: the Name, the Holy Name, the Name of God)

**Shulchan 'Orekh** (Heb) literally, set table. The section of the seder when the Passover supper is eaten.

**Tallit** (Heb) fringed and tasseled outer garment worn by all religious Jews at the time of the Temple in keeping with the commandment in Numbers 15:37-41. When a man removed his tallit, he was considered "naked." Also "tallis," modern Jewish prayer shawl.

**Talmid** (Heb) disciple, student, scholar, pupil; a disciple who is also a colleague.

**Talmud** (Heb) literally, study, learning, instruction. The commentaries on the Mishnah. Also, the Mishnah, Gemara, and the Commentaries. The Jerusalem (Palestinian) Talmud was completed in 375 C.E. and is known as the "Talmud Yerushalmi." The Babylonian Talmud was completed in about 500 C.E. It is known as the "Talmud Bavli."

**Tana (Tanna)** (Arm) literally, teacher. An authority on the oral law quoted in the Mishnah. From the Aramaic "t'na" (to repeat, teach, report a tradition, study). Plural, tana'im.

**Tanakh** (Heb) the Bible, the Hebrew Scriptures, the Holy Scriptures. An acrostic of the initials of the names of the three sections of the Hebrew Scriptures, Torah (The Law, Pentateuch), Navi'im (The Prophets), and K'tuvim (The Writings).

**T'fellin** (Heb) Phylacteries. Small boxes containing handwritten scrolls of biblical passages worn on the head and hand in fulfillment of the Commandments in Exodus 13:9 and 16 and Deuteronomy 6:8 and 11:18, to wear a sign of God's law upon the hand and between the eyes. The t'fellin shel yad, the hand phylactery, is worn on the left hand and strapped to the left arm. The t'fellin shel rosh, the head phylactery, is worn on the forehead and strapped to the head.

**Torah** (Heb) the Law of Moses, the Pentateuch; law, doctrine, dogma; instruction, teaching; custom, manner; system, definition, designation.

**Tzitzit** (Heb) tassel, fringe; forelock. The four tassels attached to the corners of the outer garment (tallit) and the prayer shawl (tallis) in fulfillment of the commandment in Numbers 15:37-41.

**Tzitzit HaRosh** (Heb) the forelock, or side curls worn by religious Jews in fulfillment of the commandment in Leviticus 19:27 not to cut the hair at the temples. A sign of sincere religious observance.

**Urchatz** (Heb) literally, hand washing. First washing of the hands at the seder.

**YHWH** (Heb) the Divine Name, "Yahweh." "The enigmatic formula in Ex 3:14 which in biblical Hebrew means 'I AM who I AM,' if transposed into the form in third person required by the causative YAHWEH, can only become YAH-WEH ASHER YIWEH (later YIHYEH), 'He Causes to be what Come into Existence'" (Brown et al., *Jerome Biblical Commentary* 3:12, 59). Sometimes known as "Jehovah" resulting from an error in reading of the Masoretic Text by a sixteeth-century German scholar who did not realize that the vowel marks supplied were for "Adonai" (The Lord), which must be read instead of vocalizing YHWH.

**Z'ro'a** (Heb) literally, shank bone, forearm, leg joint. The lamb bone or shank bone set on the seder plate as a reminder of the paschal lamb.

**Zikkaron** (Heb) literally, commemoration, celebration, remembrance, memorial (Ex 12:14). Technically, the bringing of past events into the present so as to participate in them. To quote from the Talmud, "In every generation a man is bound to regard himself as though he personally had gone forth from Egypt, because it is said, 'And thou shalt tell thy son in that day, saying: *It is because of that which the Lord did for me when I came forth out of Egypt'* (Ex 13:8). Therefore, it is our duty to thank, praise, laud, glorify, exalt, honour, bless, extol, and adore Him who wrought all these miracles for our Fathers *and ourselves; he brought us forth from bondage into freedom, from sorrow into joy, from mourning into festivity, from darkness into great light, and from servitude into redemption.* Therefore, let us say before Him, Hallelujah!" (BT Pesachim 116b, emphasis mine).

## Primary Sources for Glossary Terms

Alcalay, Reuben. *The Complete Hebrew-English Dictionary.* Ramat-Gan-Jerusalem, Israel: Massada Publishing Co., 1963. Three volumes; numbered by columns.

Brown, Raymond E., S.S.; Fitzmeyer, Joseph A., S.J.; Murphy, Roland E., O.Carm.; editors. *The Jerome Biblical Commentary.* Englewood Cliffs, NJ: Prentice-Hall, Inc., 1968.

Kittel, Gerhard. *Theological Dictionary Of The New Testament* trans. Geoffrey W. Bromiley. Grand Rapids, MI: William B. Eerdmans Publishing Company, 1965. Ten volumes.

Kolatch, Alfred J. *The Jewish Book Of Why* and *The Second Jewish Book Of Why.* Middle Village, NY: Jonathan David Publishers, Inc., 1981. Two volumes.

# SELECTED BIBLIOGRAPHY

## Haggadahs (Haggadot)

Berkowitz, Rabbi Martin. *Haggadah For The American Family*. Florida: Sacred Press, Inc., 1966.

Central Conference of American Rabbis, The. Revised. *The Union Haggadah: Home Service For The Passover*. New York: 1923.

Gilbert, Rabbi Arthur. *The Passover Seder: Pathways Through The Haggadah*. New York: Ktav Publishing House, 1965.

Glatzer, Nahum N., editor. *The Passover Haggadah*. Based on the commentaries of E. D. Goldschmidt. New York: Schocken Books, Inc., 1969.

Kaplan, Mordecai M., editor. *The New Haggadah For The Pesach Seder*. New York: Behrman House, Inc., 1941.

Raphael, Chaim. *Passover Haggadah* and *A Feast of History*. New York: Gallery Books, W.H. Smith Publishers Inc., 1972.

Silverman, Rabbi Morris. *Passover Haggadah*. Hartford, CT: Prayer Book Press, 1959.

# Special Haggadot

Soltes, Avraham. *Haggadah For Young Children*. New York: Shengold Publisher, Inc., 1966.

Waskow, Arthur I. *The Freedom Seder: A New Haggadah For Passover*. Washington, DC: The Micah Press; New York, Chicago, San Francisco: Holt, Rinehart & Winston, 1969.

## Sources for Records, Tapes, and Music For Passover

Nefesh Ami. *Soul Of My People*. Hicksville, New York. (Catalogue available).

"A Treasury Of Jewish Music." Catalogue. Cedarhurst, NY: Tara Publications.

*Seder Melodies* and *Seder Melodies Cassette*. Cedarhurst, NY: Tara Publications, 1977.

## Source of Supplies of Passover Items and Paraphernalia

The Source For Everything Jewish
Hamakor Judaica, Inc.
6112 North Lincoln Avenue
P.O. Box 59453
Chicago , IL 60559
1-800-621-8272
(Catalogue available)

# Christian Haggadot

Grailville. *The Paschal Meal*. St. Meinrad, IN: Abbey Press, 1956.

Hynes, Arleen. *The Passover Meal: A Ritual For Christian Homes*. New York: Paulist Press, 1972.

Lipson, Eric Peter. *Passover Haggadah: A Messianic Celebration*. San Francisco, CA: Jews For Jesus Publishing, 1986.

Mackintosh, Sam. *Passover Seder For Christian Families*. San Jose, CA: Resource Publications, Inc., 1986.

# Background Information on Passover

Bokser, Baruch M. *The Origins Of The Seder*. Berkeley & Los Angeles, CA: University Of California Press, 1984.

Feeley-Harnik, Gillian. *The Lord's Table: Eucharist And Passover In Early Christianity*. Philadelphia, PA: University of Pennsylvania Press, 1981.

Fredman, Ruth Gruber. *The Passover Seder: Afikoman In Exile*. Philadelphia, PA: University Of Pennsylvania Press, 1981.

Raphael, Chaim. *A Feast Of History: The Drama Of Passover Through The Ages*. New York: Gallery Books, W.H. Smith Publishers, Inc., 1972.

*Babylonian Talmud, Tractate Pesachim*. London: The Soncino Press, Ltd., 1967.

# Historical Background

Cornfeld, Gaalya, general editor. Mazar, Benjamin, and Maier, Paul L., consulting editors. *Josephus: The Jewish War*. Grand Rapids, MI: Zondervan Publishing House, 1982.

de Vaux, Roland. *Ancient Israel*. 2 vols., *Social Institutions and Religious Institutions*. Scarbourough, Ontario, Canada: McGraw-Hill Ryerson, Ltd., 1965.

Eban, Abba. *Heritage: Civilization And The Jews*. New York: Summit Books, 1984.

Eusebius. *The History Of The Church*. trans.Williamson. New York: Dorset Press, 1965.

Harris, Lis. *Holy Days: The World Of a Hasidic Family.* New York: Summit Books, Simon & Schuster, Inc., 1985.

Jeremias, Joachim. *The Eucharistic Words Of Jesus.* Philadelphia, PA: Fortress Press, 1966.

Werner, Eric. *The Sacred Bridge: Liturgical Parallels in Synagogue and Early Church.* New York: Schocken Books, 1970.

# Biblical References

Albright, W. F., and C. F. Mann. "Matthew." *The Anchor Bible* 26. Garden City, NY: Doubleday & Company, Inc., 1971.

Brown, Raymond E., S. S. "The Gospel According to John (1-12)." *The Anchor Bible* 29. Garden City, NY: Doubleday & Company, Inc. 1966.

_____. "The Gospel According to John (13-21)." *The Anchor Bible* 29a. Garden City, NY: Doubleday & Company, 1970.

Brown, Raymond E., S. S.; Fitzmyer, Joseph A., S. J.; Murphy, Roland E., O. Carm. *The Jerome Biblical Commentary.* Englewood Cliffs, NJ: Prentice-Hall, Inc., 1968.

Fitzmyer, Joseph A., S. J. "The Gospel According to Luke (1-9)." *The Anchor Bible* 28. Garden City, NY: Doubleday & Company, 1981.

_____. "The Gospel According to Luke (10-24)." *The Anchor Bible* 28a. Garden City, NY: Doubleday & Company, 1985.

*Interlinear Bible.* Hebrew/Greek/English. Lafayette, IN: Associated Publishers And Authors, Inc., 1976.

Mann, C. S. "Mark." *The Anchor Bible* 27. Garden City, NY: Doubleday & Company, 1986.

*New American Bible with Revised New Testament*. Nashville: Thomas Nelson Publisher, 1987.

Orr, William F., and James Arthur Walther. "1 Corinthians." *The Anchor Bible* 32. Garden City, NY: Doubleday & Company, 1976.

# Archaeological Reference And Evidence

Avigad, Nahman. *Discovering Jerusalem*. Nashville, TN: Thomas Nelson Publisher, 1980.

Ben-Dov, Meir. *In The Shadow Of The Temple: The Discovery Of Ancient Jerusalem*. San Francisco, CA: Harper And Row Publishers, Inc., 1982.

Mackowski, Richard M., S. J. *Jerusalem: City Of Jesus*. Grand Rapids, MI: William B. Eerdmans Publishing Company, 1980.

# Periodicals

*Biblical Archaeology Review*, 3000 Connecticut Ave., N.W., Ste. 300, Washington D.C. 20008.

*Catholic Biblical Association of America*, The Catholic University of America, Washington, D.C. 20064.

*Biblical Archeologist*, 1053 LS&A Building, University of Michigan, Ann Arbor, MI 48109.

# Supplementary and Background Information

Alcalay, Reuben. *The Complete Hebrew-English Dictionary*. Ramat-Gan-Jerusalem, Israel: Massada Publishing Co., 1963. Three volumes; numbered by columns.

Birnbaum, Philip. *Ha-Siddur Ha-Shalom: Daily Prayer Book.* New York: Hebrew Publishing Company, 1949.

Brown, Driver, and Briggs. *Hebrew and English Lexicon of the Old Testament.* Oxford, England: Clarendon Press, 1968.

Daniel-Rops, Henri. *Daily Life in the Time of Jesus.* New York: Hawthorn Books, Inc., 1962.

Kelly, J. N. D. *Early Christian Doctrines.* New York: Harper & Row Publishers, 1958.

Kittel, Gerhard. *Theological Dictionary of the New Testament..* trans. Geoffrey W. Bromiley. Grand Rapids, MI: Wm. B. Eerdmans Publishing Company. Ten volumes. Volume 1, 1969; Volume 10, 1967.

Reader's Digest. *Jesus And His Times.* Pleasantville, NY & Montreal: The Reader's Digest Association, Inc., 1987.

Teringo, J. Robert. *The Land & People Jesus Knew.* Minneapolis, MN: Bethany House Publishers, 1987.